"The Ni

Who Wrote "The Night Before Christmas"?

Analyzing the Clement Clarke Moore vs. Henry Livingston Question

MacDonald P. Jackson

McFarland & Company, Inc., Publishers

Jefferson, North Carolina

Library of Congress Cataloguing-in-Publication Data
British Library cataloguing data are available

ISBN (print) 978-1-4766-6443-9
ISBN (ebook) 978-1-4766-2425-9

Front cover illustration from *The Night Before Christmas or*
A Visit of St. Nicholas (New York: McLoughlin Bros., 1896,
in Van Deusen–Kosinski Collection)

Printed in the United States of America

McFarland & Company, Inc., Publishers
Box 611, Jefferson, North Carolina 28640
www.mcfarlandpub.com

Acknowledgments

When in 2011 I became interested in debates about the authorship of "The Night Before Christmas" I could read texts of Clement Clarke Moore's *Poems* (1844) through the electronic database *Literature Online* (http://literature.proquest.com) and the book itself through the Internet Archive: Digital Library (https://archive.org), while poems by Henry Livingston were available on Mary Van Deusen's website devoted to him (www.henrylivingston.com). In December of that year I emailed Mary to ask a few questions. Before long she established a "Research Site" that provided me with ever-increasing information. Through her technological skills, and those of her superbly expert husband Paul Kosinski, I gained access not only to searchable texts and the contents of the "Thomas Collection" of materials relevant to claims made by Livingston's descendants that their ancestor composed "The Night Before Christmas," but also to comprehensive word lists and word frequencies for both Moore and Livingston. Mary's assiduous research and Paul's wizardry as computer programmer have been essential to the investigation reported on here.

The help of linguist Lyn Bates was indispensable in developing tests based on phonemes. I am extremely grateful to Mary, Paul, and Lyn for the extraordinary amount of work they have put into this project, not knowing what the results of the authorship tests I applied would be or how I would interpret all the data they supplied.

And of course anybody attempting to determine the authorship of "The Night Before Christmas" owes an enormous debt to Stephen Livingston Thomas, custodian of the Thomas Collection, and to his father and grandfather who amassed so much valuable material. I am grateful to Stephen and to Mary for allowing me unrestricted use of it.

I should also like to thank Seth Kaller, who generously and helpfully answered the queries I addressed to him early in my investigations, when neither he nor I could foresee the outcome; Paul Vincent for his meticulous editorial work on my manuscript; Brian Boyd for reading it and suggesting improvements; Rob Lovett for designing graphs; Daphne Lawless for compiling the index; and Nicole Jackson for constant support.

Contents

Acknowledgments   v

Preface   1

1. Introduction to the Problem   5
2. Moore and Livingston: External and Internal Evidence   9
3. Reindeer Names, Exclamations and Other Clues   15
4. The Question of Sources   27
5. The Evidence of Meter   31
6. Statistical Interlude   34
7. Attributive Adjectives   38
8. Rhyme Links with Moore and Livingston   41
9. Shared Three-Word Sequences and Parallels   44
10. Phoneme Pairs   49
11. Categories of Phoneme Pairs   54
12. Individual Phoneme Pairs More Favored by Moore
    or Livingston   60
13. Definite and Indefinite Articles   64
14. Very High-Frequency Words   69
15. Favorite Expressions and Quirks of Style   73
16. Common Words That Discriminate   78
17. Words of Medium-High Frequency   85
18. Checking the Tests: Moore's Manuscript Poems   90
19. The Moore Creation Myth   102

20. The Livingston Version   108
21. Further Considerations: Claims and Connections   116
22. "Old Santeclaus" and Moore   121
23. Summary and Conclusions   126

Appendix I: Henry Livingston: Selected Poems and Prose   137
Appendix II: Lists of the Poems of Livingston and Moore   164
Appendix III: Printer's Copy for "Visit" in Moore's Poems (1844) 173
Notes   175
Bibliography   187
Index   191

Preface

"The Night Before Christmas" or "A Visit from St. Nicholas" may be the best-known poem of the English-speaking world—apart, perhaps, from the odd nursery rhyme. A classic of popular culture, it is an all-time favorite among children. The modern Western Santa Claus could hardly have existed without its vivid portrayal of Saint Nicholas as a jolly, rosy-cheeked, white-bearded, round-bellied bearer of gifts that he transports by an airborne reindeer-drawn sleigh, carries in a sack slung over his shoulder, and delivers by way of the chimney on Christmas Eve. The poem has been endlessly reprinted and illustrated. It has spawned by-products on film, television, and radio. It has featured in comics. There have been musical and theatrical versions, and thousands of translations, adaptations, and parodies. "Poetry makes nothing happen," declared W. H. Auden, but these unpretentious verses did make something happen.[1] After they had been published, Christmas celebrations would never be the same.

But who was the author of "The Night Before Christmas," which made its first public appearance anonymously in a New York newspaper called the *Troy Sentinel* on 23 December 1823? Traditionally, it has been credited to Clement Clarke Moore, who included it in his *Poems* (1844). But counterclaims have been made on behalf of Henry Livingston, who died in 1828. His descendants maintain that he had composed it and read it to his family around 1808. My aim in this short monograph is to establish the truth of the matter, or, at the very least, to determine where the probabilities lie. Either Moore or Livingston gave pleasure to millions through writing the famous verses. This is no small achievement. We should give credit where credit is due. But to whom?

Moore (1779–1863) and Livingston (1748–1828) each produced a substantial body of verse.[2] The poems that Moore thought worthy of preservation, at least up till 1844, were included in his collection of that date. To John Duer's translation of *The Third Satire of Juvenal* (1806), to which Moore contributed an introductory essay on the defects of contemporary poetry, were added "miscellaneous poems, original and translated," including several by Moore over the pseudonym "L," but these were all reprinted in *Poems.* Also, among Moore's unpublished papers there is an autograph notebook of verse written during the period 1843–52, long after "The Night Before Christmas" had appeared in print. An eminent classical scholar, Moore compiled *A Compendious Lexicon of the Hebrew Language* (1809), published *George Castriot, Surnamed Scandenberg, King of Albania* (1850), an adaptation of Zachary Jones's 1596 English translation from the French of Jacques de Lavardin, and was also the author of political pamphlets.

Livingston's verse, in contrast to Moore's, was never gathered into a printed book. He contributed poems anonymously or under pseudonyms to newspapers and magazines, as did other minor writers of his time, or addressed them to his children, nephews, nieces, other relatives, and friends. But the survival of bound manuscript leaves in which many of his poems are written out in his own handwriting allows a solid corpus of authentic works to be formed. A core poetic canon has been established and publicly available for several years. Livingston also published short essays and other prose pieces on a variety of topics.

This means that we have two bodies of verse to compare in our efforts to discover to which "The Night Before Christmas" rightly belongs. In the pages that follow, more autobiographical details of Moore and Livingston may be found. The external evidence of authorship is, of course, considered. Arguments put forward by parties to the controversy are assessed and in some instances refuted or strengthened. Some previously overlooked material is brought to light. Literary critical claims are made. But the main effort here is directed at discovering quantifiable features of the two men's poetic styles that serve to differentiate them, so that poems known to be by Moore or by Livingston fall into their correct authorial categories.

Attribution problems of the "Author A" versus "Author B" kind are potentially much more readily soluble than problems in which an anonymous work could be by any one of dozens of possible writers. We need not undertake the enormously difficult task of finding features that are, either singly or in combination, unique to either Moore's or Livingston's style, and so identify the poet against all-comers. We need look only for features that are significantly more common in one candidate's style than in the other's. The relevant task is simply to discover characteristics that discriminate between the two. No one discriminator is likely to achieve perfect separation between all Moore's poems and all Livingston's, but from the combined evidence of several independent discriminators, strong probabilities in favor of one or other poet's authorship of "The Night Before Christmas" should emerge. The one essential requirement is that items for testing not be "cherry-picked" in order to produce a particular outcome, but be selected according to predetermined principles, so that the two authorial candidates are treated exactly alike.

Computers and electronic databases greatly facilitate the necessary analyses. An excellent survey of modern computer-aided approaches to the attribution of anonymous or disputed texts has been published by Patrick Juola.[3] Hundreds of different kinds of stylistic features have served for the basis of one or more of the investigations he describes, and statistical methods of varying degrees of sophistication and complexity have been employed. The present study has used only simple and straightforward tests of significance, familiar to all students of statistics and probability theory. These are mostly tests designed first to answer the question "Could the two sets of figures for some particular feature in poems or blocks of poetic text by Moore and by Livingston have been drawn from a single population, or are they so different as to indicate two distinct populations?" Given a statistically significant difference, the question then becomes "To which group does 'The Night Before Christmas' more probably belong, and how much more probably?" Statistical tests used are explained in Chapter 6, "Statistical Interlude," shortly before they are employed.

Apart from Moore's short Christmas poem "From Saint Nicholas" of about 1822, and two other loose manuscript pieces, also short, for "Little Clem" and "Fanny," his unpublished work is here reserved till late in this book for the purposes of checking the reliability of our authorship tests.

My interest in the authorship of "A Night Before Christmas" was first aroused by a chapter on the subject in Donald Foster's book *Author Unknown* (2000).[4] Like many people, I had been impressed by Foster's successful unmasking of the anonymous author of the political roman à clef entitled *Primary Colors* (1996) as journalist Joe Klein and by the methods used to identify him. On the other hand, as a Shakespearean scholar who had expended a good deal of time and energy on determining the limits of the Shakespeare canon, I had been unconvinced by Foster's attribution of "A Funeral Elegy" to Shakespeare, and had explained why in a review.[5] This long poem had been published in 1609 with a title-page ascription to "W.S." Foster's research persuaded three experienced editors to include the "Elegy" in Shakespeare's *Collected Works*, but he and they were wrong, as Foster himself had the good grace to concede, when eventually faced with strong evidence that the title-page initials were misleading and that the true author was John Ford, best-known for his tragedy '*Tis Pity She's a Whore*.[6] But Foster's *Author Unknown* chapter arguing that Livingston wrote "The Night Before Christmas" seemed, on a first reading, compelling. A point about two of the reindeer names, in particular, struck me as a palpable hit. My checking, via the electronic database *Literature Online*, of its significance uncovered material for a brief note.[7] But skeptical rejoinders to Foster's case by Joe Nickell, Seth Kaller, Stephen Nissenbaum, and others soon alerted me to the complexities of the authorship problem.[8] Foster's opponents appeared also to have landed a palpable hit: the poem drew on materials that had not been published when Livingston was said by his descendants to have composed it. Or did it? One question led to another. This small monograph is the result.

I have used the titles "The Night Before Christmas" and "A Visit from St. Nicholas" interchangeably, usually preferring to abbreviate the latter as "Visit," especially where it has been necessary to name the poem several times within a short space. The original *Troy Sentinel* text is transcribed at the beginning of Chapter 1.

After my final chapter I have included a small sample of Livingston's verse and prose, so that readers may gain a sense of the kind of creative mind he possessed.

References to websites include the http:// prefix, but for direct access this should in some cases be omitted. Mary Van Deusen's Henry Livingston site is found at www.henrylivingston.com.

1

Introduction to the Problem

For the Sentinel

ACCOUNT OF A VISIT FROM ST. NICHOLAS.

'Twas the night before Christmas, when all thro' the house,
Not a creature was stirring, not even a mouse;
The stockings were hung by the chimney with care,
In hopes that St. Nicholas soon would be there;
The children were nestled all snug in their beds,
While visions of sugar plums danc'd in their heads,
And Mama in her 'kerchief, and I in my cap,
Had just settled our brains for a long winter's nap—
When out on the lawn there arose such a clatter,
I sprang from the bed to see what was the matter.
Away to the window I flew like a flash,
Tore open the shutters, and threw up the sash.
The moon on the breast of the new fallen snow,
Gave the lustre of mid-day to objects below;
When, what to my wondering eyes should appear,
But a miniature sleigh, and eight tiny rein-deer,
With a little old driver, so lively and quick,
I knew in a moment it must be St. Nick.
More rapid than eagles his coursers they came,
And he whistled, and shouted, and call'd them by name:
"Now! Dasher, now! Dancer, now! Prancer, and Vixen,
"On! Comet, on! Cupid, on! Dunder and Blixem;
"To the top of the porch! to the top of the wall!
"Now dash away! dash away! dash away all!"

As dry leaves before the wild hurricane fly,
When they meet with an obstacle, mount to the sky;
So up to the house-top the coursers they flew,
With the sleigh full of Toys—and St. Nicholas too:
And then in a twinkling, I heard on the roof
The prancing and pawing of each little hoof.
As I drew in my head, and was turning around,
Down the chimney St. Nicholas came with a bound:
He was dress'd all in fur, from his head to his foot,
And his clothes were all tarnish'd with ashes and soot;
A bundle of toys was flung on his back,
And he look'd like a peddler just opening his pack:
His eyes—how they twinkled! his dimples how merry,
His cheeks were like roses, his nose like a cherry;
His droll little mouth was drawn up like a bow,
And the beard of his chin was as white as the snow;
The stump of a pipe he held tight in his teeth,
And the smoke it encircled his head like a wreath.
He had a broad face, and a little round belly
That shook when he laugh'd, like a bowl full of jelly:
He was chubby and plump, a right jolly old elf,
And I laugh'd when I saw him in spite of myself;
A wink of his eye and a twist of his head
Soon gave me to know I had nothing to dread.
He spoke not a word, but went straight to his work,
And fill'd all the stockings; then turn'd with a jirk,
And laying his finger aside of his nose
And giving a nod, up the chimney he rose.
He sprung to his sleigh, to his team gave a whistle,
And away they all flew, like the down of a thistle:
But I heard him exclaim, ere he drove out of sight—
Happy Christmas to all, and to all a good night.[1]

"The Night Before Christmas" created the modern image of Santa Claus in "arguably the best-known verses ever written by an American."[2] In a country far from the poem's origins, the *New Zealand Herald* of 19 December 2011 printed a photograph of the American first lady, Michelle Obama, seated beside Santa and reading the words aloud at the Children's National Medical Center in Washington, D.C. No doubt this photo circled the globe. On 2 December that year, joined by Kermit the Frog, she had read

it at the National Tree Light-
ing Ceremony, as she had
done in previous years, and
would do again: you can hear
her on YouTube. In Auck-
land, New Zealand, a subur-
ban shopping center featured
the complete text of "The
Night Before Christmas," distributed line by line to suc-
cessive shop-front windows.
This is true celebrity. Author,
author! But to whom are the
accolades really due?

There survives no pre-
publication manuscript of the
poem, whether authorial or
scribal. It first appeared in
print, under the title "Account
of a Visit from St. Nicholas,"
in the *Troy Sentinel*, 23 December 1823. The author was
not named. But in *The New-
York Book of Poetry* (1837)

**Figure 1. Clement Clarke Moore, aged about
60. Courtesy Cornell University Library,
Making of America Digital Collection.**

Charles Fenno Hoffman attributed the poem to the New York professor
of Greek and Oriental literature Clement Clarke Moore (1779–1863), who
later included it in a collection of his *Poems* (1844). Descendants of Henry
Livingston (1748–1828) of Poughkeepsie, however, maintain that their
ancestor composed the rollicking anapests that have achieved such prodi-
gious popularity and that he read them to his children around 1808. There
are undoubted inaccuracies and discrepancies in the Livingston family
accounts, but the more plausible derive, in several separate lines of descent,
from three of Livingston's sons, the wife and former childhood neighbor
and playmate of the elder of those, and two daughters.[3] In *Author Unknown*,
Donald Foster made out an impressive case for Livingston's authorship of
the Christmas poem, using "psychological profiling," together with the kind
of stylistic analysis that had enabled him to identify journalist Joe Klein
as the author of the anonymously published satirical novel *Primary Colors*
(1996). Fifty-six lines of verse afforded him a relatively small amount of
material, however, and his chapter on "Visit" has since been attacked by

Figure 2. Henry Livingston, Jr., date unknown. A portrait thought to have been made by one of his children. Courtesy Van Deusen–Kosinski Collection.

scholars who endorse Moore's claims. Can further progress be made toward determining the probable authorship of this iconic text?

The following chapters employ both traditional approaches to the determination of authorship and the newly developed attribution methods of computational stylistics. The verse of Moore and of Livingston is characterized in literary critical terms and some of the key arguments and counterarguments that have been put forward by contending parties are evaluated, before computer-assisted counts of features more favored by one or other of the poets are introduced. These data include rates of use of high-frequency words, which are part of the armory of most contemporary attributionists, but which have not hitherto been investigated in connection with the controversy over who wrote "The Night Before Christmas." An innovation is the statistical analysis of phonemes, the constituents of language as sound: for this set of tests the poetry of the rival candidates is first transcribed into the phonetic system known as Arpabet, described in Chapter 10. The efficacy of the several means of distinguishing between Moore and Livingston is then checked on a dozen of Moore's poems that were never published but exist in manuscript. After the deployment of all this "internal evidence," which demarcates the poetic styles of Moore and Livingston, we return to the stories from the contending camps about the origin of "The Night Before Christmas," subjecting them to detailed scrutiny, along with discussion of related considerations. The closing chapter summarizes the findings of the investigation and the conclusion to which they lead.

2

Moore and Livingston:
External and Internal Evidence

Ostensibly, the external evidence is unequivocal in supporting Moore's claims. Not only was the poem attributed to Moore by Charles Fenno Hoffman in 1837 and wittingly included by Moore among his *Poems* in 1844, but as early as 1829 Orville Holley, editor of the *Troy Sentinel*, had reprinted "Visit" and recorded his newly acquired understanding that the author belonged "by birth and residence" to the city of New York and was "a gentleman of more merit as a scholar and writer than many of more noisy pretensions."[1] Wherever Holley's information came from, it fits the New York scholar Moore rather than the Poughkeepsie landowner, army major, surveyor, and justice of the peace, Livingston, who had died the previous year. Moreover, Hoffman's ascription of 1837 was evidently believed by illustrator Robert Walter Weir and poet-anthologist William Cullen Bryant, both said to have been friends of Moore's.[2] Also a believer was Moore's daughter Mary Moore Ogden, who in 1855 reproduced the poem in calligraphy within floral borders and accompanied by a picture of the Moore residence.[3] By this time the aged Moore himself was placidly making and signing autograph copies of his *Poems* text of "Visit," four having survived from the period 1853–62.[4]

The opposing camp's explanation of all this evidence is that a visitor to "Locust Grove," the Livingston homestead in Dutchess County, New York, had taken a copy of "The Night Before Christmas" and left it at Moore's house, from which a text found its way to the *Troy Sentinel*. Hence the poem became associated with Moore. Those who accept that Moore was the writer also invoke at least one intermediary who was responsible for the initial, unauthorized publication. Moore himself is not known to have claimed credit for the poem before 1844, when he published his *Poems*

9

in "compliance," he averred in the preface, with his children's "wishes," and felt the need to apologize for including "mere trifles" such as "relate solely to our own domestic circle," though, on his own estimation, "Visit" and "The Pig and the Rooster" would be the only pieces falling within this category. Livingston's supporters assume that once a false rumor had connected the poem to Moore and his name had been attached to it in print without any challenge arising, Moore simply took the line of least resistance and let the mistake prevail. If he had read "Visit" to his children in 1822, they might naturally have supposed it was his own, though the proud calligrapher Mary had been only three at the time, and no testimony is recorded from Margaret, then seven, or Charity, then six but who died at the age of fourteen, let alone Benjamin or Clement, who were four and two.[5] In short, it is argued, a small piece of misinformation, which Moore failed to correct, grew into an untruth of which it would have taken considerable moral courage to disabuse all those who believed it.

By 1837, when Hoffman attributed "Visit" to Moore, Henry Livingston, who had died in 1828, could not protest. Even had he been alive and the poem's author, it is doubtful whether a mistaken attribution would have bothered him. He consistently had his verse published, in the *Poughkeepsie Journal*, the *New-York Weekly Museum*, and other such media, either anonymously or under a pseudonym such as the letter "R" (possibly standing for "Reader"). Long after 1837, "Visit" continued to be recycled, with no name attached, in newspapers, magazines, and almanacs. It is not surprising that it was not until about 1860 that the poet Livingston's granddaughter Jane, then married to Lester Hubbard, brought to her mother's attention the fact that "Visit" was being attributed to Moore and received the emphatic response, "Some one has made a mistake—Clement Moore did not write the 'Night Before Christmas.' Your grandfather Henry Livingston wrote it."[6] This mother, Eliza (née Brewer), had as a child been a neighbor and playmate of the Livingston children, and she married Henry Livingston's eldest son by his second marriage (to Jane Patterson), Charles. But the earliest written record of the Livingston claims is by another Eliza, the fifth child of Henry Livingston's second marriage (who became wife to a Thompson and later a Lancing). In a letter of 4 March 1879 she wrote of the family's "astonishment" when they saw the poem credited to Moore and asserted that many years after her father's death her brother Sidney had found the original in the poet's own handwriting, along with "his many fugitive pieces which he had preserved."[7] Other accounts that were passed down to descendants of Sidney and of another Livingston–Patterson daughter, Susan, and that appealed also to the memories of their brother Edwin, tell essentially the same story, of Henry Livingston having composed the poem and read it to his children around 1808, and of Charles reading it many times, as his father's, to his own children. The autograph of "Visit" is said to have ended up with Edwin and perished when the Wisconsin home of his sister Susan, with whom he was, or had been, living, burned down.[8]

It is easy enough for Moore's supporters to ridicule such narratives. But the myths surrounding Moore's alleged composition of "Visit" cannot be taken on trust either. Moore resided at "Chelsea House," a few miles north of New York City. Inspired by seeing a "portly, rubicund Dutchman" while on an errand (in some versions dashing over the snow in a sleigh equipped with jingling bells) to buy a Christmas turkey, he is alleged to have enjoyed sudden inspiration on the way home, retired to his study, and jotted down the resultant composition. A Livingston autograph manuscript consumed by fire should provoke no more skepticism than this flowery tale.[9] Written testimony to there having been a conflagration in Susan's home in Wisconsin in 1869 was afforded in a letter by her daughter Jeannie Livingston Gurney, who would have been nineteen at that time.[10] No specific explanation has been advanced for the nonexistence of any original draft by Moore. Yet the documentary evidence, taken at face value, does favor Moore's authorship.

However, no reader of poetry with any sense of literary style and value could compare Moore's body of verse with Livingston's without recognizing that "The Night Before Christmas" is a conspicuous misfit within Moore's canon but would be comfortably at home within Livingston's. In his *Poems* (1844) Moore is a moralist, a pedagogue, and a satirist. He is prim, judgmental, and, to be frank, dull. He is a competent rhymester, but nobody today could read his verse with much profit or pleasure. There is no trace of the verve, imagination, humor, whimsy, and sheer joyous inventiveness that one encounters in Livingston's poems and in "The Night Before Christmas." Livingston is an entertainer, a celebrator, and a warm-hearted chronicler of life's delights and sorrows. He left behind a manuscript music book of more than two hundred pages in which he had collected popular songs and hymns, to which his own verse is akin.[11] His is a folk art that often achieves something durable. His poems can be moving—not only his epitaphs, but even so improbable a narrative piece as "The Vine and the Oak," an allegory, with classical origins, that might be described as a botanical love story with a happy ending.[12] His shorter pieces have a natural grace. Moore's poems are apt to meander and stall, clogged down by earnest cogitation. Livingston's are shaped with the same skill that rivets the child listener's attention through beginning, middle, and end of "Visit."

Livingston's love of anapestic tetrameters, as employed in "Visit," aligns him with the poets and songwriters of such anthologies as *The Goldfinch, or New Modern Songster* (Glasgow, 1777, 1782, 1785) in which the meter is extremely common.[13] In support of Moore's claims to "Visit," it has been pointed out that not only did he include the anapestic moral fable "The Pig and the Rooster" in his *Poems*, but that among his unpublished manuscripts in the Museum of the City of New York is a short anapestic piece entitled "From Saint Nicholas" and addressed to his eldest daughter.[14] Moore's note to the former of these explained that it had been written as a "piece of fun" when boys at a grammar school attended by one of his sons were set as an essay topic the question "Which are to be preferred, the pleasures of a pig or a chicken?" A lazy mud-bathing pig and a strutting young rooster—figures of grubby sloth and preening vanity—after quarrelling fiercely over their characters and lifestyles, ask a wise old owl to adjudicate. "Each to his own and live and let live" is the gist of the verdict: "'Tis the life of a cockerel to strut and look big, / And to wallow in mire, is the bliss of a pig." The overt moral, preaching tolerance, is at variance with the contemptuous tone. In his preface to *Poems* Moore justifies his mixing lighter with serious verses with the maxim that "a good honest hearty laugh … is healthful both to body and mind." Such heavy-handed sententiousness does not betoken a keen sense of humor, and "The Pig and the Rooster," with its squabbling fop and glutton, barely raises so much as a smirk. The Saint Nicholas poem reads as follows:

> What! My sweet little Sis, in bed all alone;
> No light in your room! And your nursy too gone!
> And you, like a good child, are quietly lying,
> While some naughty ones would be fretting or crying?
> Well, for this you must have something pretty, my dear;
> And, I hope, will deserve a reward too next year.
> But, speaking of crying, I'm sorry to say,
> Your screeches and screams, so loud ev'ry day,
> Were near driving me and my goodies away.
> Good children I always give good things in plenty;
> How sad to have left your stocking quite empty:
> But you are beginning so nicely to spell,
> And, in going to bed, behave always so well,
> That, although I too oft see the tear in your eye,

I cannot resolve to pass you quite by.
I hope, when I come here again the next year,
I shall not see even the sign of a tear.
And then, if you get back your sweet pleasant looks,
And do as you're bid, I will leave you some books,
Some toys, or perhaps what you still may like better,
And then too may write you a prettier letter.
At present, my dear, I must bid you good bye;
Now do as you're bid; and, remember, don't cry.

This is a sour piece pretending to be sweet. In defending Moore's authorship of "Visit," Joe Nickell denied to journalist Burkhard Bilger that it was "mean-spirited": "Look, he's taken the time to compose this little moral lesson, to write out a fair copy. This is a loving thing." In other words, as Bilger quipped, Moore "may have dashed a little girl's dreams, but he was careful to explain why. He was a spoilsport with only the best intentions."[15] And if his daughter stopped being such a noisy crybaby, she could expect to be rewarded next year. Moore's mouthpiece is still the stern Saint Nicholas, conferring or withholding his favors like an Old Testament Jehovah.

"From Saint Nicholas" is undated. If, as Nickell deduced from the probable age of "Sis" (Moore's daughter Charity), who was "beginning so nicely to spell," it is closely contemporary with "The Night Before Christmas," the contrast between Moore's Saint Nicholas and the "right jolly old elf" of the longer poem is so glaring that "From Saint Nicholas" does as much to undermine as to buttress the Moore party's case. Livingston does not teach children "moral lessons." He blesses them:

To My Little Niece Anne Duyckinck, Aged 9 Years.

To his charming black-ey'd niece
Uncle Harry wisheth peace!
Wishes roses ever strow'd
O'er her sublunary road!

No rude winds around her howl
O'er her head no tempests scowl;
No red lightnings flash around
No loud thunders rock the ground!

Bright has been her morning sun
Brighter still be that to come!
All a blue serene above,
Within, all innocence and love.[16]

Livingston's earliest extant poem, hastily scribbled while he was serving with the revolutionary army in 1775, is a loving benediction upon his infant daughter.[17] "To My Little Niece Sally Livingston on the Death of a Little Serenading Wren She Admired" is touching because the poet so evidently shares the child's sense of loss. The Roman poet Catullus famously lamented the death of Lesbia's sparrow, but Lesbia was an adult.[18] Livingston's poem blends affection for his young niece with affection for the tiny dead creature. His "Letter Sent to Master Timmy Dwight, 7 Years Old" wishes that the boy never lose his ball down a well nor his kite in an elm tree; that his marble hit the mark aimed at; that when he plays hide-and-seek he will triumphantly overhear his playmates exclaim, "Timmy never can be found"; and that his luncheon should be larger than Ben's, with extra helpings of puddings and jelly. Livingston knows what matters to Timmy and delights in entering into his seven-year-old world.

No doubt, Clement Clarke Moore loved his wife and children, gained the affection of his friends, and was philanthropic with his inherited wealth. But Foster's verbal portraits of the contrasting personalities of Moore and Livingston *as they appear in their poetry* must correspond to the reactions of all critics who have read the verse of both poets. And it is Livingston whom one can more readily imagine writing "The Night Before Christmas" so attuned to the child psyche. It sets a scene, arousing expectation, and then bounces along, generating excitement with its burst of repetitions as St. Nick calls to his reindeer—repetition being a device Livingston favors. It is crammed with pictorial detail. The dominant qualities that create its magic, "the childhood level of miniature, the motion of flying, the adjectives of joy, and the speed of action, are characteristic of Major Henry's verse, and woefully lacking in Moore's."[19] St. Nick says nothing, but does a lot, and his sole object is to make children happy: there is no hint that gifts may be conditional upon good behavior.

3

Reindeer Names, Exclamations and Other Clues

Literary-critical considerations can take us so far. But objective and quantitative measures may take us further. Some of Donald Foster's key arguments have not been rebutted, for instance, (a) that Livingston always referred to "Mamma/Mama," as in "Visit," whereas Moore used the appellation "Mother"; and (b) that in 1822 to wish anybody a "Happy Christmas," as in the last line of "Visit," instead of a "Merry Christmas" was exceptional, but in Livingston's earliest surviving piece of writing, dated 30 December 1773, he wishes a "happy Christmas to my dear Sally Welles," whom he later married.[1]

The significance of (a) is less easily assessed than that of (b).[2] As Foster observes, the first instance of "happy Christmas" recorded by *Literature Online* (*LION*) is in Richard Cobbold's poem "Christmas Day, 1826," three years after "Account of a Visit from St. Nicholas" had appeared in the *Troy Sentinel* and long after Livingston's use of the phrase in 1773. *LION*'s second use is in Edward Bulmer Lytton's novel *Eugene Aram* (1832). But neither Cobbold nor Bulmer Lytton offers an exact parallel to the wish "Happy Christmas": Cobbold writes, "I've wished you all a happy Christmas Day!" and Bulmer Lytton, "Ah! it will be such a happy Christmas, Ellinor." Up to 1835 *LION* yields twenty-eight instances of "Merry Christmas" or "merry Christmas." It was the customary salutation.[3]

One especially awkward detail for Moore's champions deserves closer scrutiny than it has yet received. Crucial in Foster's case are the names of the last two of St. Nick's eight reindeer. In the *Sentinel* they are "Dunder and Blixem," the two that end the previous line being "Prancer, and Vixen." Henry Livingston's mother was Dutch, as were his maternal grandparents and his paternal grandmother. So too was the Christmas poem's Saint

Nicholas, who has named two reindeer in accordance with his origins. *Donder en Bliksem* is Dutch for thunder and lightning, and, in various phonetic spellings or corrupt forms, an oath repeatedly attributed to Dutchmen in English and American texts printed within Livingston's lifetime, always with "x" rather than "ks." It would often have been heard in Dutchess County. *LION* finds (up to the year 1850) "Dunder and Blixem/Blixum," with or without the capitals, in works by Alexander Coventry (1786); Washington Irving (1809), twice; James Kirke Paulding (1819); Timothy Flint (1826); Charles Augustus Davis (1834); Charles Fenno Hoffman (1840), twice, with "und" rather than "and"; and Donald Grant Mitchell (1850). Variants are "Donder and blixim" by Miles Peter Andrews (1781), "Donder Blood and Blixten" by John Collins (1804); "dunder and blixums" by Washington Irving (1809); "dunner and blixum" by Samuel B. H. Judah (1827); "Donder ant blixen" by Joseph Holt Ingraham (1839); "Donder und blixem" by Charles Fenno Hoffman (1840), twice, in the same novel, *Greyslaer*, that has "Dunder"; and "Donder and Blixum" by James Kirke Paulding (1847). The Davis book of 1834 also has "DONDER EN BLIXEM" within a passage of Dutch. James Fenimore Cooper has "Blixum and philosophy!"; Paulding (1836) recognizes "blixem," "blixum," and "blixen" as "little better than swearing"; and Ingraham (1846) has "tunder and blixens."

"Dunder/Donder and Blixem/Blixum" were clearly the prevailing forms, so it is natural to suppose that the *Sentinel* in 1823 preserved the original authorial spellings. "The Night Before Christmas" was endlessly reprinted over the ensuing years, and unauthoritative changes crept into the text. "Blixem" first became "Blixen," to provide a perfect rhyme with "Vixen," in David McClure's *United States National Almanac* (1825). Hoffman's *New-York Book of Poetry* (1837) perpetuated this change and also altered "Dunder" to "Donder." But the major new variant came in Clement Clarke Moore's *Poems* (1844).

Moore had been reluctant publicly to claim credit for what he dismissed as an embarrassing trifle. Before including "The Night Before Christmas" among his *Poems*, he wrote on 23 February 1844 to Norman Tuttle, who had owned the *Troy Sentinel* when the poem was first published there, enquiring how a text had first reached the newspaper. Tuttle replied on 26 February that the manuscript had been passed, as author unknown, to the editor, Orville Holley, by the wife of a Troy merchant called Daniel Sackett.[4] Daniel and Sarah Sackett lived within a ten-minute walk of the *Sentinel* office, which was next door to Sackett's store.[5] How Sarah may have acquired a copy of the poem is a topic for later discussion.[6] Tuttle sent Moore a recent reprint of a *Sentinel* broadsheet that had first been published in 1830, and this served, through an intermediary transcript, as copy-text for *Poems*.[7] Moore made four small substantive changes, including replacing "Dunder and Blixem," as they still were in the broadsheet, by "Donder and Blitzen." Thus one of a Dutch Saint Nicholas's Dutch-named pair of reindeer became German. "Donder" had been introduced in 1837 by Hoffman, who had first attached Moore's name to the poem. But it was Moore who first renamed "Blixem" as "Blitzen." Since the German for thunder and lightning is *Donner und Blitz* or *Donner und Blitzen*, some subsequent versions have coupled Moore's "Blitzen" with "Donner," instead of "Donder." The "correction" from "Blixem" to "Blitzen" is made in a hand-written annotation to the copy of the *Sentinel* broadsheet preserved among Moore's papers,[8] and in his four known autograph copies from the text in *Poems* Moore perpetuated the renaming: "Donder and Blitzen."

Foster comments sardonically that "Clement Clarke Moore did not know the original names of his own Dutch reindeer!" Moore's "corrupt 'Blitzen' is," he writes, "one more indication that he stole 'Christmas'— Santa Claus, sleigh, reindeer, and all—from a … Dutchman named Henry Livingston."[9]

But this is by no means an end of the matter. We need to keep thinking. If Moore was the author of "The Night Before Christmas," in changing "Blixem" to "Blitzen" he was either (a) correcting an error, "Blitzen" having always been his name for the last reindeer, or (b) replacing his original "Blixem" with a name that he now preferred. We must consider each of these alternative possibilities in turn.

Seth Kaller, aiming to rebut Foster's arguments, favors the first explanation. Foster, he says, "overlooks the Knickerbocker pseudo-Dutch heritage movement, which could easily have induced an editor such as Holley to change German to Dutch or to 'correct' a variant spelling."[10] This is improbable. It is true that Washington Irving and the Knickerbocker Group were associated with the New-York Historical Society, to which Moore also belonged.[11] Several of the above-listed writers besides Irving were associated with the group or contributed to the *Knickerbocker* magazine (1833–65): Cooper, Hoffman, Paulding. Loathing "democrats and capitalists who were taking over their city and their nation," they adopted Saint Nicholas as their patron saint in their efforts to forge "a pseudo-Dutch identity for New York."[12] The domestication of Christmas as a "family values" affair rather than occasion for riotous street festivities was part of their agenda. Holley is not known to have had either connections to the highly conservative Knickerbocker Group or close Dutch relations.

More importantly, the original *Sentinel* printing of the poem shows signs of an *absence* of editing. The spelling "jirk" for "jerk" (in line 50) was still used in the nineteenth century, but it was extremely rare. *LION* finds 244 examples of "jerk" during the period 1820–50 but only three of "jirk," yet the *Sentinel* of 23 December 1823 allowed the variant spelling. It also accepted the eccentric placement of exclamation marks in "Now! Dasher, now! Dancer, now! Prancer, and Vixen, / On! Comet, on! Cupid, on! Dunder and Blixem." It was not until the *Sentinel* broadsheet of 1830 that the exclamation marks and commas were transposed, to read "Now, Dasher!" and so on. The original printing's comma after "Prancer" was anomalous too.

It is, in any case, somewhat contradictory of Moore's champions to (a) on the one hand, first stress the influence of Irving and his confrères on the poem's imagery as a contribution to a reinvigoration of a Dutch heritage, and then suppose that Moore, despite his membership of the New-York Historical Society, of which Saint Nicholas was the patron saint, in 1822 gave the second of these reindeer a German name; and then (b) on the other hand, appeal to the same social context as a reason why an editor not known to have been subject to these influences should have made such a noteworthy alteration to the text.

As already noted, no prepublication manuscript, whether penned by Moore, Livingston, or another, has survived, and both the Moore and the Livingston legends about how the poem reached the *Sentinel* in 1823 invoke at least one person who made (or was given) a copy.[13] But only an exceptionally high-handed copyist would have changed the names "Donder and Blitzen" to "Dunder and Blixem."

What, then, can be said in favor of the alternative explanation—that Moore's 1844 "Blitzen" was a revision? Ted Mann suggested that perhaps Moore was influenced by Washington Irving's story "Dolph Heylinger" in *Bracebridge Hall* (1822), where a German doctor exclaims, "Donner und Blitzen."[14] But Saint Nicholas was not German, and if Moore had known enough Dutch to call his reindeer "Dunder and Blixem" when he composed the poem, it would be surprising were he to give "Blixem" a German name when revising. However, a *LION* search for forms of "Donner and Blitzen" up to the year 1850 turns up some interesting results. "Donner and blitzen" occurs six times and "blitzen and donner" once in Sir Walter Scott's *Guy Mannering* (1815), where it is put into the mouth of the Dutch smuggler Dirk Halteraick, whose dialect is often more German than Dutch. On a dozen other occasions Halteraick employs an exclamatory "donner," either alone or coupled with "hagel" or "wetter" (*Hagel* being German for "hail" and *Hagelwetter* "hailstorm"). Scott, evidently knowing no Dutch, was content to make Halteraick "speak foreign." In *Quentin Durward* (1823) he did better: of a German soldier, he writes, "'Donner and blitz!' was his first salutation in a sort of German-French, which we can only imperfectly imitate." The same character also says "donner and hagel."

In the next three *LION* works after *Guy Mannering* in which "blitzen" occurs, the speaker is German: "Dunder and blitzen" and "Donder and blitzen" in a play by John Howard Payne (1822); "Donner and Blitzen" by Washington Irving (1822); and "Donner and blitzen" by James Fenimore Cooper (1823). But eight years later the waters become muddied. "Blitzen," standing alone, is assigned to a Dutchman by James Kirke Paulding (1831), and "Donder and blitzen" to another Dutch smuggler in a play by the Englishman George Almar (1836); "Donder and blitzen" is twice uttered, along with plain "Blitzen," in a play by the Irishman Samuel Lover (1838) and "Tonder and blitzen" once by a German in a play by the Englishman Charles James Matthews (1838), while Edgar Alan Poe has "Donner und blitzen" and "Donder und Blitzen" in separate stories (1840); then "donner and blitzen" is Dutch for Lydia Maria Francis Child (1843) and five times (with "Donner" capitalized) for Peter Hamilton Myers (1848), with two more instances in another work (1849). In fact, in Myers's *The First of the Knickerbockers: A Tale of 1673* (1848) not only do the five exclamations appear, but also Governor Stuyvesant's servant Hans says, "Hark!" and is asked what he hears: "It's Donner and Blitzen!" said the lad; "I know their gallop." Their riders are Jed and Rudolph with news that the Dutch have recaptured New York.

Table 3.1 makes the pattern of usage clearer. When "The Night Before Christmas" was first published in 1823, only Scotsman Sir Walter Scott, among writers covered by *LION*, had applied "blitzen" to a Dutch character, and by 1823 he knew he had been wrong. Irving, who had twice used "Dunder and Blixem" as a Dutch expletive in 1809, traveled in Germany in 1821 and attributed "Donner and Blitzen" correctly to a German in 1822, and Payne, who collaborated with Irving at about this time, followed suit, while participating in what became a common confusion between "Donner" and "Donder" (once "Dunder" for Payne).[15] Cooper got the German right in 1823. It was not till 1831 that Paulding, who elsewhere had used, or was to use, variants of the correct Dutch, associated the isolated word "Blitzen" with a Dutch person. The English playwright Almar gave "Donder and blitzen" to a Dutch character in 1836, but in America "Donner and blitzen," the exact German, was presented as a Dutch oath only by Child in 1843 and Myers in 1848 and 1849. Both Child and Myers were associated with the Knickerbocker Group, and in 1843 an anonymous story in the *Knickerbocker*

TABLE 3.1: *Literature Online* record
of uses of "blitzen," 1820–1850

Date	Form of exclamation	Speaker	Author	Origin	
1822	Dunder and blitzen	German	Payne	USA	K
	Donder and blitzen	German	Payne	USA	K
	Donner and Blitzen	German	Irving	USA	K
1823	Donner and blitzen	German	Cooper	USA	K
1831	Blitzen	Dutch	Paulding	USA	K
1836	Donder and blitzen	Dutch	Almar	UK	
1838	Donder and blitzen (twice)	German	Lover	Irish	
	Blitzen	German	Lover	Irish	
1838	Donder and blitzen	German	Matthews	UK	
1840	Donder und blitzen	German	Poe	USA	
	Donder und blitzen	German	Poe	USA	
1843	donner and blitzen	Dutch	Child	USA	K
1848	Donner and blitzen (5 times)	Dutch	Myers	USA	K
1949	Donner and blitzen (twice)	Dutch	Myers	USA	K

NOTE: "K" denotes an author with known connections to the Knickerbocker Group. The table excludes the instances by Scott mentioned in the text.

magazine has a stereotypical pipe-smoking Dutchman with "a fair round paunch" exclaim "Dunder and blitzen!"

The only precedent for offering Moore's exact "Donder and Blitzen" as Dutch is Almar's of 1836. It is impossible to say whether the names of Myers's horses were indebted to the Christmas poem's reindeer, or the similarity is pure coincidence. "Thunder" and "Lightning" are likely enough names for an equine pair.[16] The overall patterns of usage seem to confirm that Moore is most unlikely to have written "Donder and Blitzen" in 1822, when he is said to have composed the poem, but a shift toward mistaken applications of "Donner/Donder/Dunder and Blitzen" might conceivably have induced him to revise the names in 1844. Yet it would remain odd that a poet who gave Saint Nicholas's reindeer appropriate Dutch names in 1822 (when Moore is alleged to have composed "Visit") should in 1844 have deliberately made one name inappropriately German or shared a later misapprehension that "Blitzen" was Dutch.

There is one further reason for disbelieving that Moore ever wrote the "Dunder and Blixem" of the Troy Sentinel's text of 1823. In the poem, "Blixem" rhymes with "Vixen." This kind of "m"–"n" nasal rhyming is liberally scattered through the verse of Henry Livingston: "men"–"fame," "flown"–"room," "reign"–"name," "design"–"sublime," "shine"–"gleam," "fane"–"name," "beam"– "seen," "seen"–"stream," "same"–"again," "time"–"thine," "doom"–"soon," "gone"–"tomb," "shines"–"sublime," "gleam"–"seen," "pine"–"climb," "divine"–"sublime," "fun"–"room," "combine"–"time," "whim"–"keen," "flame"–"maintain," "gloom"–"tune," "come"–"sun," "remain"–"fame," "again"–"name," "scenes"–"dreams," "glean"–"beam," "glean'd"–"seem'd," "time"–"Old Lang Syne," "welcome"–"welkin," and so on.[17] In his *Poems* (1844) Moore uses hundreds of these words and final sounds as rhyme words, but *always* to form perfect rhymes: "beams"–"seems," "scene"–"serene," "known"–"tone," "climb"–"time," "dreams"–"screams," "time"–"sublime," "shame"–"blame," "shine"–"combine," and so on.[17] If in 1822 he rhymed "Vixen" with "Blixem," it was, with a single exception, the only time he composed a nasal "m"–"n" near-rhyme, despite composing twice as many rhyming lines as Livingston. The exception occurs in "From Saint Nicholas," where "empty" rhymes with "plenty." So in that little poem Moore proved that his aversion to the use of an "m"–"n" rhyme was not absolute, but statistically he is very much less likely to have invented "Vixen"–"Blixem" than Livingston, to whom employing such near-rhymes was second nature.

If Moore in 1844 was working from the printed *Sentinel* broadside text of a poem by Livingston, there is no problem. Ignorant of the import of the Dutch and having noticed one or more of the recent instances of "blitzen," Moore opted to call the reindeer "Blitzen," which, though still not a perfect rhyme, at least eliminated the "m"–"n" approximation.[18]

Moore's other two major substantive emendations to the broadside copy could be (a) genuine corrections, restoring readings of the lost manuscript original (whether Moore's or Livingston's); or (b) post–1823 readings that he considered improvements (whether to his own original work or Livingston's). The *Sentinel* text of 1823, followed, in this instance, by the broadsheet, read:

> As dry leaves before the wild hurricane fly,
> When they meet with an obstacle, mount to the sky;
> So up to the house-top the coursers they flew (lines 25–27).

Moore added "that" after "leaves." Strictly speaking, the *Sentinel* text requires the reader to either understand an implicit relative after "leaves" or an implicit "and" linking the first and second of these lines, though in fact we barely notice the slight syntactical looseness. Metrically, we must either (a) regard "As DRY" as an initial iamb, so that "DRY leaves" has the main stress on the adjective, or (b) take "As dry LEAVES" as an anapestic foot followed by an iambic second foot, "beFORE." Either is possible. Anapestic rhythms can certainly enforce stressing that would be unusual in speech. Thirty-three of the other fifty-five lines of "Visit" begin with an iamb, whereas there are no other examples of an iambic second foot, but an iambic first foot here would make "leaves" the sole metrically unstressed noun in the whole poem. Both poets include an occasional noun in a metrically unstressed position in anapests undoubtedly theirs, and one can read the three lines without being conscious of any oddity. But the insertion of "that" does tighten the syntax and regularize the meter: "As dry LEAVES that beFORE." Aspects of the two poets' versification are examined in Chapter 5.

Moore's other emendation was to the line "A bundle of toys was flung on his back," also retained in the broadsheet, though with "Toys" capitalized. Here, as nowhere else in the poem, the third foot ("was flung") is iambic, and "was flung on his back" is somewhat abnormal usage for a state rather than an action: "was *slung* on his back" would be more idiomatic.[19] Moore regularized meter and grammar by changing "was flung" to "he had flung."

As it happens, the correction to "he had flung" had already been made in *The New-York Book of Poetry*, which had also changed "As dry leaves" to "As leaves that," omitting "dry." There can be no certainty about the variant readings, but it seems unlikely that the fastidious Moore would ever have composed the offending lines as they appeared in the *Sentinel* in 1823. Either they were corrupt in the *Sentinel* or Livingston, whose muse was less finicky, had left them in that form. Both Livingston and Moore elsewhere employ in anapestic poems occasional lines in which the third foot is iambic,[20] though there are none in Moore's long "The Pig and the Rooster."[21] Metrically the two altered lines would not have been beyond Moore in 1822, but it is hard to imagine him ever, even in original composition, being satisfied with the grammar of either passage.

The phrase "was flung on," meaning "had been flung on" is similar to "The stockings were hung by the chimney" in the poem's third line, where the stockings had already been hung by the chimney; but in their case use of "were hung" is idiomatic and normal. Outside "The Night Before Christmas" *LION* yields four instances of "was flung on," always to denote action, as in "she was flung on shore again" or "a gun … was flung on the floor." Keying in the archaic spelling "flonge" does, however, turn up a parallel to the usage in "Visit." In John Herman Merivale's "The Abbot of Dol" (*Poems Original and Translated*, 1844), the narrator, entering a chapel, "Beheld the figure of a kneeling knight" and noted that a "bauldricke was across its shoulders flonge." Here the poet, deliberately spicing his text with orthographical archaisms, is describing an existing state. The expression "was flung on" evidently did not bother readers until *The New-York Book of Poetry* altered it in 1837, and it so happens that "flung" is a word that Livingston used three times in his poems, twice in "was flung," though always in connection with an action.[22] The word does not appear elsewhere in Moore's *Poems.*

 The curious placing of exclamation marks in the original 1823 printing of "Visit" has already been mentioned. But it deserves further comment. Calling his reindeer by name, St. Nick cries:

> Now! Dasher, now! Dancer, now! Prancer, and Vixen,
> On! Comet, on! Cupid, on! Dunder and Blixem.

The idiosyncrasy is not in the profusion of exclamation marks but in their placement. Once the lines had been repunctuated in the 1830 *Sentinel* broadsheet reprint as "Now, *Dasher!* now, *Dancer!* now, *Prancer!* now, *Vixen!* / On, *Comet!* on, *Cupid!* on *Dunder* and *Blixem!*" reprints regularly put the exclamation marks in the first line after the names, and in his *Poems* of 1844 Moore also followed the broadsheet in shifting the exclamation marks in the second line. Subsequent editors have all accepted these changes as more in accord with the natural rhythmic flow of the lines. But, while the new punctuation better reflects the way the couplet should be recited, the 1823 version is perfectly consistent with Livingston's idiosyncratic preferences.

 In autograph copies of his poems Livingston often places an exclamation mark after an exclamatory or emphatic *word* that introduces a larger exclamatory unit of sense. He writes, for example, "And Love how infinite! to men"; "The passions! that deform the soul"; "But all! one radiant scene afford"; "But Man! a nobler theme inspires"; "Yet would I praise—forever praise! / The sov'reign of the skies!"; "All beauteous to behold! serene she glides"; "And is your boasted leader gone? / His pow'r! the power but to die? / His kingdom! but a narrow tomb?"; "When all the nations shall obey / Messiah! the anointed King!"; "That period when Phoebus to meet keener fires / Down! down to his Thetis in glory retires"; "Beyond where billows roll or tempests vex / Is gone! the best, and loveliest of his sex"; and

> Tho thousand and ten thousand trivial things
> Which Luxury and her sister Folly brings,
> Be wanting there—yet there! yet there I'll find
> That richest furniture! a quiet mind.

In the last four passages (from "Messiah!" onward) commas would be normal, rather than exclamation marks. In all the others the sense runs straight on past the exclamation mark without pause, and no punctuation is required. The exclamation marks serve a purely rhetorical function.

 Foster noted that, as in "Visit," Livingston's "offbeat exclamation marks" may interrupt the anapestic meter: "And happy,—thrice happy! too happy! the swain / Who can replace the pin or bandana again."[23] In prose written toward the end of his life, "he still registers the old exuberance," addressing letters to his "Dear, Dearest! Son!" and "Dear! very dear Grandson!"[24]

Joe Nickell claims that Moore shares what Foster called Livingston's "odd practice of peppering his verse with offbeat exclamation marks" and cites "That once, ah! let not truth offend" and "Home! home! whose very name has magic power." "There is," Nickell writes, even an instance in Moore's "From Saint Nicholas."[25] The only exclamation marks in that little piece come at the beginning: "What! My sweet little Sis, in bed all alone; / No light in your room! And your nursy too gone!" But all these examples conform to quite normal nineteenth-century usage. The marking of an "ah!" or an "oh!" or an "alas!" is standard and the other exclamations have a degree of separation from what follows. More comparable to the Livingston examples is the first line of Moore's "Translation of Metastasio's Ode to Nice": "Thanks! Ellen, to thy treacherous wile!" But there are no further such examples in Moore's *Poems*, and even this—marking an opening exclamation—is less gratuitous than some of Livingston's, such as that in "But all! one radiant scene afford." So the placing of exclamation marks in the couplet of "Visit" listing the reindeer names is more in accord with Livingston's practices than with Moore's. If Moore had deliberately punctuated the lines in the odd way in which the earliest printing, in the *Troy Sentinel* in 1823, presented them, in 1844 he meekly accepted the altered placing of the exclamation marks that he found in the copy of the *Sentinel* broadsheet sent him by Norman Tuttle. If, on the other hand, the punctuation of the calls to the reindeer in 1823 was due to a copyist or typesetter who misrepresented Moore's own manuscript, it is odd that the textual corruption should have made the poem more Livingston-like.

So, in its variations from the version in Moore's *Poems*, the *Troy Sentinel* text of "Visit" seems more Livingston-like than Moore-like. "Dunder and Blixem" is very definitely and strikingly so, especially since the two lines of reindeer names are punctuated in a manner more suggestive of Livingston's practices than Moore's. The phrase "was flung on" is more in Livingston's vein than Moore's. The absence of the relative pronoun from "as dry leaves before" may well have been due to a printer's or copyist's accidental omission, and Moore (like Hoffman) could readily have repaired it without having been the author. But the syntactical looseness of the *Sentinel* version would not have been beyond Livingston. A couplet in his

"War Rebus" is comparable: "What the peasant enjoys when his labor is o'er / And the seaboy embraces the hurricane's roar." The syntax is elliptical, since the meaning of the second line is "And what the seaboy enjoys when he embraces the hurricane's roar" or conceivably "And what the seaboy who embraces the hurricane's roar also enjoys." We can be sure of this, because Livingston is drawing on the famous speech in Shakespeare's *Henry IV, Part 2*, in which the King laments that his "poorest subjects," and even the wet seaboy aloft in a storm, can slumber peacefully while he, on his "kingly couch," cannot, concluding: "Uneasy lies the head that wears a crown" (3.1.1–31). This speech was alluded to and paraphrased by several subsequent writers, including Nathaniel Lee, Thomas Warton and, notably, Charlotte Turner Smith, who in her sonnet "To Sleep" (in *Elegiac Sonnets*, 1797–1800) has "On his hard bed the peasant throws him down; / And the poor sea boy in the rudest hour, / Enjoys thee more than he who wears a crown." The answer to the clue of Livingston's rebus is "rest" (a restful sleep), which both peasant and the seaboy, in contrasting circumstances, can attain.[26]

There is one other revealing variant, occurring twice, between the 1823 *Troy Sentinel* printing and the text of "Visit" in Moore's *Poems*. In the *Sentinel* the speaker "sprung from his bed" in line 10 and St. Nick "sprung to his sleigh" in line 53.[27] In each case, Moore has the correct "sprang," having been anticipated by the *Poughkeepsie Journal* as early as 1828 and also by the 1830 broadsheet.[28] Elsewhere in *Poems* Moore carefully preserves the distinction between past tense (or preterit) and past participle in his use of the verbs "to spring" and "to sing": past tense "sprang" and "sang" each occur three times: there are no instances of "sprung," but one instance of "sung" as past participle ("had … sung"). Livingston arguably would not have cared about the distinction. He had written, "Thus Stephen sung beneath the shade" in "Past is the Hour,"[29] where "sang" would have been grammatically correct, and the same mistake occurs in "On a Robin's Being Taken in a Young Lady's Bed-Chamber," which is probably Livingston's, while "begun" occurs instead of the correct "began" in "An Occasional Thought," also quite likely to be by Livingston. Moore did once use past-tense "sung" for the sake of a rhyme with "tongue" in a short hymn he composed.[30] But in this detail too the original *Sentinel* text is more in line with Livingston's practices than with Moore's.

Even the *Sentinel*'s unusual spelling "jirk" for "jerk" seems more likely to have originated with Livingston than with Moore. Livingston's verse, including that in his own handwriting, is sprinkled with spellings that were rare in the period within which his poems were composed: "harmonius," "gladsom," "beveridge," "blase," "gase," "lullabye," "hankerchief," "sweld," "couzin," "decres'd," "sherriff," "oblidged," "stragling," "obeisence." Such rarities are in addition to spellings that were common in Livingston's day but are nonstandard now, such as "chearful," "compleat," "tygers," "controul," "marr," and "stop'd." Moore's spelling was everywhere less eccentric. So altogether five independent textual variables suggest that behind "Account of a Visit from St. Nicholas" lay a script by Henry Livingston.

4

The Question of Sources

One piece of evidence has been held to be incompatible with Livingston's having composed "The Night Before Christmas" as early as 1808. Washington Irving's *History of New-York from the Beginning of the World to the End of the Dutch Dynasty by Dietrich Knickerbocker*, first published in 1809, was reprinted in 1812 with additions to the text. Seth Kaller says, "It is this latter edition that is acknowledged by Christmas scholars as an obvious source of the poem's inspiration." He quotes:

> the good St. Nicholas came riding over the tops of the trees, in that self same waggon wherein he brings his yearly presents to children…. And when St. Nicholas had smoked his pipe, he twisted it in his hatband, and laying his finger beside his nose, gave the astonished Van Kortland a very significant look; then mounting his waggon, he returned over the tree tops and disappeared.

Kaller comments: "St. Nicholas's gesture of 'laying his finger beside his nose,' one of the 1821 additions, was taken up by Moore in his *Visit*. This is an important piece of evidence supporting 1822 as the date that the poem was written, not earlier, as the Livingston claim alleges."[1] Kaller's "1821" is a mistake, which he makes twice. The words quoted are all in the 1812 edition.[2] So if the passage influenced the poem, it could have done so any time after 1812, though not in 1808.

In "The Night Before Christmas," St. Nick, after filling all the stockings hung up in anticipation, "turn'd with a jirk [*sic*], / And laying his finger aside of his nose / And giving a nod, up the chimney he rose." But is the poem's indebtedness to Irving's *History* so certain? Kaller's ellipses bring some ingredients of the poem into close conjunction: Saint Nicholas riding in the sky, known to give presents to children, smoking a pipe, and making the conspiratorial gesture of laying his finger beside his nose before leaving. But these elements are part of a dream by the sleeping Oloffe Van Kortland.

He recognizes Saint Nicholas by "his broad hat, his long pipe and the resemblance he bore to the figure on the bow of the Goede Vrouw"—the first emigrant ship from Amsterdam with a figurehead that Irving has described earlier, with the addition of "a huge pair of Flemish hose."[3] Van Kortland dreams that the saint sits down and lights his pipe and the smoke spreads like a cloud over the whole area. Through this haze the dreamer catches a visionary glimpse of a city "where in dim obscurity he saw shadowed palaces and domes and lofty spires, all which lasted but a moment and then faded away." It is a prophetic vision of New Amsterdam–New York. Irving's broad-hatted Saint Nicholas, equipped with a long pipe is far from the poem's plump, rosy-cheeked, jolly elfin figure, who smokes the "stump of a pipe," carries a sack full of toys, and has a team of eight tiny reindeer drawing his miniature airborne sleigh. Of course, elsewhere in his *History* Irving states that "in the sylvan days of New-Amsterdam" Saint Nicholas would come "riding jollily among the tree tops or over the roofs of the houses, now and then drawing forth magnificent presents from his breeches pockets and dropping them down the chimnies of his favourites," whereas "now one night in the year … he rattles down the chimnies of the descendants of the patriarchs, confining his presents merely to the children."[4] And Irving's words are held, in any case, to be merely one of the stimuli to Moore's creative imagination.

The visits of Irving's Saint Nicholas are associated with St. Nicholas's Day (6 December) and the New Year, not Christmas Eve. But the clinching detail establishing Irving's influence in 1812 on "The Night Before Christmas" is supposed to be the shared gesture of laying a finger to the side of one's nose. Irving had portrayed it before. He represented the sage Wouter Van Twiller (not Saint Nicholas) as "laying his finger beside his nose" in the 1809 edition of his *History*.[5] But this gesture enjoining secrecy, implying collusion, or indicating shrewd cogitation (and comparable to "a nod and a wink") is very often described in drama and prose from the mid-eighteenth century onward. *Literature Online* (*LION*) finds it as early as in Tobias Smollett's *Peregrine Pickle* (1751) and, even more significantly, Lawrence Sterne's *Tristram Shandy* (1760), where Tristram's father is pointedly "nodding his head and laying his finger upon the side of his nose" as he stops his pipe toward the end of volume V, chapter 31. This even provides a parallel to St. Nick's "nod" in "The Night Before Christmas." The potential significance of this antecedent stems from the fact that Sterne is the only novelist, apart from Sir Walter Scott, whom Livingston praises in his verse. In his "Alcmena Rebus," conjecturally dated 1787, one clue is "The author of Shandy, all laughter and glee / Whose pencil from gall was forever kept free." Livingston obviously delighted in *Tristram Shandy* and would have found there a memorable precedent for St. Nick's "laying his finger aside of his nose."[6]

In a letter to William S. Thomas, dated 12 October 1921, William P. Tryon pointed out a mention of the same gesture in the satirical magazine *Salmagundi*, which Irving wrote in collaboration with his brother William and James Kirke Paulding during the period 24 January 1807 to 15 January 1808:

> In the "Salamagundi" papers, issue of Feb 4, 1807, we find that "Fengus ... conveys most portentous information, by laying his finger beside his nose." In the issue of March 20, 1807, under caption "Theatrics," we read: "Except, replied I, one of those slaps on the breast, which I have sometimes admired in some of our fat heroes and heroines, which make their whole body shake and quiver like a pyramid of jelly." In an issue of April 18, 1807, we have a reference, final article, to "Miss Dashaway."[7]

In fact the conveyor of "portentous information" goes by the name, not of Fengus, but of Ichabod Fungus. Tryon's insinuation was that Irving had somehow already encountered Livingston's poem—with its finger-tapping gesture, the phrase "shook ... like a bowl full of jelly," and repeated "dash away"—and been influenced by it. Alternatively, Livingston could conceivably have been a reader of *Salmagundi*, and have unconsciously amalgamated a few echoes from it.[8]

Be that as it may, neither St. Nick's "laying his finger aside of his nose" nor the other ingredients of "The Night Before Christmas" need have derived from Irving's *History*. Livingston, as Donald Foster has shown, could readily have created the poem—"with its mishmash of fairy lore, religious tradition, and Norse mythology"—out of the Dutch traditions inherited from his mother and grandparents; his reading in "books that provide accounts of Scandinavian elves, of Lapland reindeers, and of the Norse god Thor" with his goat-drawn chariot; his fascination with "Heaven's brilliant coachman" Phoebus Apollo's fiery "coursers" and chariot; his familiarity with the pipe-smoking Dutchmen of the Hudson Valley and with his own horses and sleigh; his empathy with everyone and everything around him; and, above all, his convivial temperament and lively fancy.[9] This was a poet who, as Foster notes, could—remembering both *A Midsummer Night's Dream* and Mercutio's Queen Mab speech in *Romeo and Juliet*—picture the "sprite" Oberon, King of the Fairies, in a nutshell carriage drawn by a team of katydids, while exulting in his real new white-stockinged colt who, like the Dauphin's horse in *Henry V*, "moves as if he danced on air."[10] That phrase, incidentally, suggests why Livingston would have named one of St. Nick's airborne "coursers" "Dancer."

Foster is absolutely right to stress Livingston's delight in airborne creatures and to observe that in this poet's imagination the sky "is a busy place,"[11] to which children, souls, storms, sparks, and even a lambkin and a dinosaur "upward fly," like the Christmas poem's dry leaves and reindeer. At death "the freed spirit wings its way" to its eternal home. In the sublunary world, a living vine is "lifted … to the skies." The poet notices a butterfly that "wings it along," a beetle that hums by at twilight, and the "insect that flits o'er the lawn." The "tempest-tost bee" hies to its hive. A fly and gnats come to his attention. Cupids flutter round, graces flutter about. Both are pictured as "playing round" the "nymph" Arabella. Graces also "hover," Seraphs "carol above," "Venus's doves flutter," and Cupids "clap their wings." Livingston is exceptionally aware of birds, mentioning skylarks, linnets, thrushes, nightingales, sparrows, robins, swallows, turtle doves, wrens, owls, crows, and whip-poor-wills. A talented draughtsman, he put flocks of them into his sketches of landscapes and seascapes, besides drawing a perching eagle and pigeon. His imagination dwells on little things. A kitten bounds, a grasshopper chirps. Cupid is "Venus's arch little hoodwinked boy." The fairy king Oberon appears five times in Livingston's verse. In one of his whimsical prose pieces, "Description of the Baby House of Miss Biddy Puerilla," a miniature estate, complete with river "enriched with delightful tadpoles," is to be landscaped and palaces are to be built for the accommodation of Biddy's dolls. A mole has already begun the earthworks. In another flight of fancy, "Astronomical Intelligence," a Russian professor, who has constructed a huge telescope, using slabs of ice from the Volga as lenses, observes life on Venus, where a secretary takes the minutes of a meeting "with a quill from the wing of a sparrow." Livingston's free-ranging imagination has all the equipment with which to invent a miniature sleigh drawn by eight tiny reindeer and driven by "a little old driver, so lively and quick" as to be recognized at once as the "jolly old elf" Saint Nicholas. Livingston's Oberon, like his St. Nick, is not only little, but "old" and "brisk."[12]

It is the elfin stature and the tininess of his reindeer and sleigh that distinguishes the Saint Nicholas of "The Night Before Christmas" from all those manifestations of him in writings, in verse and prose, that have been supposed to have influenced the poem.[13] And this detail of the portrayal of St. Nick is precisely what we might have expected from Livingston, who knew that no child would stop to wonder how the challenge of delivering life-size toys could so magically be met. Later depictions, more down-to-earth, "re-inflated" Santa to a human scale.[14]

5

The Evidence of Meter

In English prosody, an "anapestic tetrameter" line of verse, consisting of four anapestic "feet," runs ti-ti-TUM ti-ti-TUM ti-ti-TUM ti-ti-TUM, where the capitalized syllable carries the stress. Livingston used anapestic tetrameters throughout his career and was expert at handling them. Although in any kind of triple meter the pattern is so assertive as to override natural speech when necessary, Livingston is adept at working the natural stressing of phrases into the meter and ensuring that the ictus or stress falls on important words, mainly nouns and verbs. Sometimes fitting clues into a rebus necessitated a little distortion. But Livingston demonstrates the skill that is evident in "The Night Before Christmas." Small words such as "all" are placed in stressed or unstressed positions in accord with their function in a phrase: "when ALL thro' the HOUSE" and "Happy CHRISTmas to ALL, and to ALL a good NIGHT," but "NESTled all SNUG in their BEDS" and "He was DRESS'D all in FUR." Livingston's "Letter to Brother Beekman" is typical in its pace and energy, as well as in the vividness of its detail:

To my dear brother Beekman I sit down to write,
Ten minutes past eight and a very cold night.
Not far from me sits with a vallancy cap on
Our very good cousin, Elizabeth Tappen,
A tighter young seamstress you'd ne'er wish to see
And she (blessings on her) is sewing for me.
New shirts and new cravats this morning cut out
Are tumbled in heaps and lie huddled about.
My wardrobe (a wonder) will soon be enriched
With ruffles new hemmed and wristbands new stitched...[1]

Moore's two anapestic pieces stumble by comparison. The awkward placing of "too" in "From Saint Nicholas" is typical: "No light in your room! And your nursy too gone!" and "And, I hope, will deserve a reward too next year." But perhaps the simplest index to Livingston's greater facility is the two poets' use of two-syllable words in metrically unstressed positions. All disyllabic words carry a primary stress on either the first or second syllable. So allowing one to cover the two metrically unstressed positions of an anapestic foot involves down-playing an actual stress. The phrasing can make this perfectly natural, as when in "Visit" we have "With a LITTle old DRIVer" but "His DROLL little MOUTH." But for purposes of computation we must ignore such niceties and simply count proportions of metrically unstressed disyllables per line. The results are shown in Table 5.1.

The figures associate "The Night Before Christmas" with Livingston, not with Moore. Moore's writing of "From Saint Nicholas" and his alleged writing of "The Night Before Christmas" were virtually contemporaneous, and "The Pig and the Rooster" cannot have been composed earlier than 1830, if we are to believe Moore's account of its inception.[2] Yet the ease with which anapests are handled in "The Night Before Christmas" and in Livingston's verses in that meter are lacking in Moore's two pieces. If Moore wrote "The Night Before Christmas" he displayed in it a facility that deserted him in his efforts in the same meter both at about the same time and a decade later.

As a coda to this chapter we can address Joe Nickell's contention that "like 'A Visit,' Moore's 'The Pig and the Rooster' is a *children's* ballad which has magical elements" and his challenge to "Livingstonites" to exhibit something similar from Livingston's pen.[3] The obvious point to be made in reply is that Moore's sneering poem has never, and never could have, delighted the world's children, as has "Visit," and is "magical" only in the sense that a pig, a rooster, and an owl exchange words. This places it in the tradition of Aesopian fable, and in fact Livingston's "The Crane and Fox" and "The Frog King" (which should really be entitled "The Frogs Who Desired a King" or "King Log," "The Frog King" or "The Frog Prince" being the title of a folktale collected by the Brothers Grimm) are both retellings of animal fables by Aesop, while "A Fable" versifies Aesop's "The Bat, the Birds, and the Beasts": it is a veritable menagerie and aviary of contending creatures, and sentence is pronounced by "Judge advocate Crow," just as Moore's owl is the arbitrator in "The Pig and the Rooster."[4]

So Livingston was proficient at verse narrative. But "Visit" is sui

TABLE 5.1: Metrically unstressed disyllables in anapestic tetrameter poems

Title	metrically unstressed disyllables	lines	rate per 100 lines
Livingston poems			
Nine Sisters Rebus	4	20	20.0
Deity Rebus	2	20	10.0
Apollo Rebus	4	22	18.2
The Dance (Nancy Crooke)	4	18	22.2
Hero Rebus	6	38	15.8
Letter to Brother Beekman	7	47	14.9
War Rebus	6	38	15.8
Sages Rebus	4	32	12.5
Acknowledgment	2	26	7.7
Hogs (Tenant of Mrs. Van Kleeck)	4	26	15.4
Marriage Tax	3	25	12.0
Careless Philosopher	1	14	7.1
Belle (Lap-dog)	5	16	31.3
Alcmena Rebus	6	30	20.0
To Miss ("Hail …")	2	12	16.7
Epithalamium	0	14	0.0
Monarchs Rebus	3	18	16.7
Carrier Address 1803	14	84	16.7
Carrier Address 1819	3	22	13.6
Total	66	523	12.6
Moore poems			
Pig and Rooster	22	86	25.6
From Saint Nicholas	6	23	26.1
Total	28	109	25.7
The Night Before Christmas	8	56	14.3

generis, and the crucial question is whether objective measures of style assign it to Livingston or to Moore. In its metrical qualities, it is more akin to Livingston's anapestic pieces than to Moore's.[5] We shall shortly see how it fares on other stylistic and linguistic tests.

6

Statistical Interlude

"Lies, damned lies, and statistics." Literary people are apt to suppose that statistics can be manipulated to concoct specious proofs of "anything." But the claim that a particular poem, play, or novel is "more like" the work of A than B is essentially a claim about frequency—that A employs a certain kind of linguistic unit (sentence, phrase, word, phoneme) more (or less) often than B, relative to the sizes of their respective corpora. And to make the claim good, counting is imperative, and the assessment of the resultant tallies by statistical tests of significance highly desirable, so that we can gauge whether a difference between A and B is likely to be due to mere chance. The point has now been reached where it seems advisable to explain the basic statistical concepts that are introduced in the chapters that follow, though readers with more than the most elementary knowledge of statistics will scarcely need the explanation, while others may prefer to skip the lesson.[1]

A group of figures has a mean, the arithmetical "average" of common parlance. The mean is, of course, the sum of all the figures divided by their number. Thus (a) 11, 6, 9, 7, and 12 add up to 45, and their mean is 9. The total for (b) 4, 16, 15, 1, and 9 is also 45, and the mean is again 9. But the first five figures range from 7 to 12, the second from 1 to 16. The second set of figures or values is more widely dispersed around the mean. The statistical measure of dispersal around the mean is the standard deviation, which is calculated by squaring each value's difference from the mean, adding all the squared differences, dividing the total by the number of values, and then finding the square root of the figure that results. Any scientific calculator can easily perform these operations. In group (a) the differences from the mean of 9 are, in turn, 2, 3, 0, 2, and 3; their squares (2 multiplied by 2, 3 by 3, and so on) are 4, 9, 0, 4, and 9, giving a total of 26. Dividing 26 by 5 gives 5.2, and the square root of 5.2 is (to three decimal points) 2.280. The standard deviation for group (b) is much higher, namely 5.899 reflecting the wider spread of the values.

Suppose we have a much larger set of values—for example, measurements in centimeters of the heights of one hundred eight-year-old boys of the same ethnicity and socioeconomic background. Most of the measurements will be fairly close to the mean for the group, with the numbers becoming fewer as the distance above or below the mean increases. If the numbers of measurements falling within specified distances from the mean are graphed—numbers on the vertical axis, heights on the horizontal— they will tend to form a bell-shaped curve. They will approximate a "normal distribution." Some 95 percent of values in a perfect normal distribution fall within two standard deviations either side of the mean. Values are likely to be distributed normally, if the mean and the median roughly coincide. The median is the middle value when all values are ranked from the largest to the smallest (or vice versa). In both groups (a) and (b) described above it is 9, the same as the mean. The median for the hundred measurements of height would be half way between the measurement for the fiftieth and fifty-first tallest boys.

The probability that a value will be found within a particular normal distribution depends on its distance, in terms of standard deviations, from the mean. When a set of values does not necessarily comprise the complete population, it is prudent to use the "inferential standard deviation," which is calculated by dividing the sum of the squared differences from the mean by the number of values less one, rather than by the full number. Obviously the larger the number of values, the smaller the effect of this adjustment.

Two large samples of values drawn from the same population will tend to form a single bell-shaped curve. If two samples belong to different populations they will have different means and distributions, forming two curves that may barely overlap. If the one hundred boys whose heights had been measured at age eight were to be measured again at aged twenty, a graph of the numbers who were of specified heights would create an entirely separate bell-shaped curve. The standard statistical test to determine whether two sets of values belong to a single population is the *t*-test. The formula for calculating *t* can be found in any textbook on statistics. But there are now websites where the two sets of values can be entered, one by one, in separate columns, and the calculation performed in less than a second.[2] The probability, given the size of *t*, that the two sets of values belong to a single population is also given. The larger the result of *t*, the more distinct the groups, though probabilities also take account of the "degrees of freedom"—the combined number of values in the two columns minus two.

Most of the tables in this book present figures for various words or phonemes (defined later) in Livingston's and Moore's acknowledged poems—expressed as rates of use per 550 or 1,000 words or percentages in relation to other words or phonemes. The statistical significance of any difference between the groups of figures for Livingston and Moore is determined by *t*-tests. If the test establishes with a high degree of probability that they belong to two separate populations, we can then measure into which one "The Night Before Christmas" more probably falls and how much more probably.

I have also employed the chi-square test (always of the simple two-column, two-row type) in order (a) to select high-frequency items as potential discriminators and (b) to evaluate differences between "The Night Before Christmas" and the poems by Moore claimed by his supporters to be most akin to it. Chi-square compares actual frequencies with frequencies "expected" according to chance.

For example, Moore seems to be fonder of "that" than Livingston. This impression can be checked in the following way. In his corpus as a whole Moore uses "that" 253 times and some other word 20,340 times, while Livingston uses "that" 83 times and some other word 12,872 times. We can arrange these figures in what is called a "2 × 2 contingency table":

	Instances of "that"	Instances of other words	Row total
Moore	253	20,340	20,593
Livingston	83	12,982	13,065
Column total	336	33,322	**Grand total** 33,658

The two row totals and the two column totals both add up to the same grand total, which is of all Moore's words and all Livingston's. Expected frequencies are calculated by multiplying the row total by the column total and dividing by the grand total. Thus 20,593 × 336 = 6,919,248; divide this by 33,658 = 205.575. This is the figure "expected" in the upper left quadrant on the assumption that Moore and Livingston use "that" at the same rates. The actual figure is 253. Chi-square is reckoned by squaring each of the four differences between actual and expected frequencies, dividing each by the expected frequency, and adding the four results. Again, there are reliable websites that can perform the operation in a flash, giving the chi-square value and the probability that it is due to chance. The larger the value of chi-square, the less likely that Moore's and

Livingston's different proportions of "that" to total words have arisen at random. Interpreting a chi-square value also involves knowing the degrees of freedom (d.f.): in a "2 × 2 contingency" case such as this, there is 1 d.f. And in such two-row, two-column cases it is customary to use a modification of the chi-square test called Yates's chi-square, in which 0.5 is deducted from each difference between the actual and expected figure before this difference is squared. When the figures are very large, as in the present example, the distinction between Yates's chi-square (which works out at 27.872) and ordinary chi-square (28.469) is immaterial. If the figures for "that" had been assigned to Moore and Livingston on a purely random basis, the chances of obtaining such a chi-square are fewer than one in thirty million.[3]

7

Attributive Adjectives

One feature that contributes to the celerity with which "The Night Before Christmas" moves is its parsimonious way with attributive adjectives, or adjective-plus-noun combinations, such as "a miniature sleigh" and "a little old driver." Lines are not congested with unnecessary modifiers. Does Livingston differ from Moore in this regard? "Visit" contains 542 words. Table 7.1 presents the results for the number of adjective–noun combinations per 550 words in blocks of verse by each poet. Counts were not of the numbers of adjectives but of the numbers of nouns preceded by modifiers, including nouns used adjectivally, such as "Saviour's name" and "pigmy face"; "all," "each," "every," "many," "more," "no," "own," "some," "such" (sometimes with an indefinite article intervening before the noun) and numbers used adjectivally were included, but titles such as "Master," "Miss," "Aunt," and "Uncle" were not. Personal and demonstrative pronouns followed by a noun did not qualify, unless between pronoun and noun there was an adjectival form that did qualify. Whether compound formations were counted as adjectives plus nouns or regarded as nouns depended, not on how they were erratically printed in the texts by Moore or Livingston, but on whether they could be found in hyphenated or single-word form in the *Oxford English Dictionary*. For instance, in the *Troy Sentinel* printing of "Visit" the combination "sugar plums" is set as two words, but "sugar-plums" is given a separate dictionary entry, so was classed as a noun. In "Visit" the items included in the counts were as follows: "broad face," "droll little mouth," "dry leaves," "each little hoof," "eight tiny rein-deer," "good night," "Happy Christmas," "little old driver," "little round belly," "long winter's nap," "miniature sleigh," "new fallen snow," "right jolly old elf," "such a clatter," "wild hurricane," and "wondering eyes." Counts were made for every poem of at least 500 words, and successively printed or displayed shorter poems were amalgamated until together they yielded a total of 500 or more words. Moore's very long "A Trip to Saratoga" was divided into its six cantos.[1]

TABLE 7.1: Nouns modified by attributive adjectives per 550 words			
Verse blocks by Livingston		**Verse blocks by Moore**	
Size of text in words	**Rate**	**Size of text in words**	**Rate**
735	33.7	1042	52.8
677	55.2	850	47.9
530	48.8	1724	48.2
830	43.7	1421	44.5
501	54.9	880	48.1
533	61.9	892	48.7
534	35.0	570	63.7
642	47.1	590	54.1
687	34.4	545	46.4
735	42.7	541	50.8
599	30.3	1135	61.1
594	24.1	588	78.6
659	51.7	584	44.3
503	38.3	782	39.4
612	31.5	1069	45.3
540	51.9	1130	60.8
603	27.4	615	71.5
819	43.0	574	62.3
513	41.8	744	59.1
593	36.2	815	66.1
560	33.4	500	75.9
		805	58.1
		610	51.4
		673	73.6
		914	61.4
Means of blocks:	41.286		56.564

"The Night Before Christmas" ("Visit"): Size of text: 542 words; Rate: 16.236

A *t*-test shows that there is a less than one in 75,000 chance that the two authorial sets of proportions were drawn randomly from a single population (p = 4.91; 44 d.f.; p = 0.000013). In other words, Moore and Livingston are significantly different in their rates of usage, and clearly Livingston uses fewer adjective-plus-noun combinations than Moore. Only one block by Moore has a lower rate than Livingston's mean, and only one block by Livingston has a higher rate than Moore's mean. In "The Night

Before Christmas" they occur at a rate even lower than one might expect from Livingston. But of the two candidates, Livingston's authorship of the poem is, in terms of these data, far more probable than Moore's. Livingston's blocks have an inferential standard deviation of 10.179, so that the rate for "Visit" is 2.464 standard deviations from Livingston's mean, which might be expected of one in seventy-three similar-sized blocks of his verse—and we know that many of his poems have not survived. Moore's blocks have an inferential standard deviation of 10.794, so that the rate for "Visit" is 3.736 standard deviations from Moore's mean, which might be expected of one in 5,376 similar-sized blocks of his verse. Notably, the block of text by Livingston with the lowest rate of use of adjective-plus-noun combinations (24.1) comprises two anapestic pieces, the "War" and "Sages" rebuses. No block of text by Moore comes remotely near "Visit" in infrequency of usage. His 785-word "The Pig and the Rooster," cited by Moore's supporters as proving his ability to write a narrative poem in anapests, has a rate of use of 39.4 adjective-plus-noun combinations per 550 words, while the rate for the short "From Saint Nicholas" is 36.0.

8

Rhyme Links with Moore and Livingston

In studies of early modern drama, rhymes have proved efficacious as indicators of authorship and may have something of value to contribute to the problem under consideration here.[1] Six of the rhymes in "The Night Before Christmas" are used in Livingston's acknowledged poems: "around"–"bound" (twice), "care"–"there" (twice), "clatter"–"matter" (twice), "elf"–"self," "jelly"–"belly," and "sight"–"night." "Self" in the "elf"–"self" rhyme includes "myself" in "Visit" and "himself" in a Livingston rebus. Seven of the rhymes in "The Night Before Christmas" are also to be found in Moore's poems: "around"–"bound," "beds"–"heads," "bow"–"snow," "came"–"name," "fly"–"sky," "head"–"dread," and "sight"–"night" (twice).

This evidence may seem to favor neither candidate. "Visit" shares seven rhymes with Moore, six with Livingston. But three of the rhymes are used twice by Livingston, whereas only one is used twice by Moore, and this last is a rhyme that Livingston also uses ("sight"–"night"). On the other hand, one rhyme that Livingston uses twice ("around"–"bound") is also used once by Moore. Taking rhymes that occur twice in either poet's oeuvre as constituting two rhyme links with "Visit," there are nine links to Livingston, eight to Moore. Since, in terms of numbers of rhymed lines, Livingston's poetic corpus is less than two-thirds (0.63) the size of Moore's, Livingston might be held to have a statistical edge over his rival in this regard.

More importantly, three of the Livingston rhymes ("jelly"–"belly," "clatter"–"matter," and "elf"–"self") are less common in poetry up till 1850 than the least common of the Moore rhymes ("bow"–"snow"). None even of these rhymes is, in absolute terms, exceptionally rare within the huge amount of rhymed verse included in the *Literature Online* (*LION*) database.

But the relative infrequency of the rhymes that link "Visit" to Livingston, compared with those that link "Visit" to Moore can be simply demonstrated, though not before a large amount of work has been undertaken. Up until 1850 there is only a single *LION* nondramatic poet who uses all six of the Livingston rhymes somewhere in his verse, and that is the Englishman Richard Harris Barham, alias Thomas Ingoldsby, the prolific author of the ballads collected as *The Ingoldsby Legends* (1840). These had been contributed to *Bentley's Miscellany* and the *Monthly Magazine* from 1837 onward.[2] So no *LION* poet's body of verse published before "The Night Before Christmas" made its first public appearance in the *Troy Sentinel* in 1823 had used all six of the rhymes that the poem shares with Livingston.

In itself, this finding tells us far less than it may appear to do. Had the Herculean task been attempted of checking all of the Christmas poem's rhymes, rather than simply those that it shares with Livingston, in the works of every poet, it is certain that dozens of poets would have been found to use many more than six of the poem's rhymes—if only because hundreds of individual poets composed a great many more rhymed lines than did Livingston. The significance of the finding emerges only when the seven rhymes that "Visit" shares with Moore's verse are checked in the same way as Livingston's six were checked. Six poets used all seven of the Moore rhymes: Samuel Cobb, Hannah Flagg Gould, Alexander Pope, Winthrop Macworth Praed, Samuel Jackson Pratt, and Lydia Howard Sigourney, and the works of all but Gould and Praed were earlier than 1823. So it is clear that the Christmas poem's rhyme links with Livingston involve less widely employed rhymes than its rhyme links with Moore.

Moreover, the above analysis has ignored the rhyme "house"–"mouse," which "Visit" shares with a poem that may be Livingston's, "Affectation," which also uses "elf" as a rhyme word, though paired with "pelf," not "self." It has also ignored two instances of "fly"–"sky" in poems probably Livingston's, "Carrier Address 1816" and "The Filly and Wolf." So the evidence of rhymes connects "Visit" more firmly with Livingston than with Moore.

The pattern of rhyme links reflects the difference between Livingston's and Moore's poetic output, and the traditions within which they worked. Rhymes such as "jelly"–"belly," "clatter"–"matter," and "elf"–"self" appear mainly within ballads, songs, and light and occasional verse, which form the bulk of Livingston's poetry. Moreover, the "clatter"–"matter" rhyme is often specifically "clatter"–"*the* matter," as in "Visit" and "A Tenant of Mrs. Van Kleeck." Moore never uses "the matter" anywhere at all. Moore, though a less gifted poet than Livingston, aspired to join a lyric and satirical mainstream and his rhymes are the more obvious ones that abound in verse of a conventionally serious kind.

One further observation is worth making about the rhyming words in "Visit": 76.8 percent of them are nouns, the parts of speech with which children begin labeling the world around them. No poem by Moore has anything like such a high proportion of nouns at the ends of rhymed lines. For "From Saint Nicholas" the percentage is 47.8; for "The Pig and the Rooster" it is 50. Livingston's "Nine Sisters Rebus" comes close to matching "Visit" with 75 percent, and several more of his poems yield comparable figures: "Procession" 70.6 percent, "Scots Wha Hae" 70 percent, "Montgomery Tappen" 70 percent, "Spadille" 69.2 percent, "Marriage Tax" 68 percent, "Hezekiah" 67.9 percent, and "Sages Rebus" 65.6 percent. So in this respect, too, the rhyming of "Visit" tends to associate it with Livingston's verse rather than with Moore's.

9

Shared Three-Word Sequences and Parallels

Several attribution scholars have proposed that shared "trigrams" can help establish identity of authorship.[1] These are sequences of at least three words. We can check how many of those in "Visit" can be found among Moore's poems, and how many among Livingston's. The poem's subject matter is so original that in fact few trigrams link it to either author. In the following lists simple plurals are not counted as separate from the singular forms, nor is "an" differentiated from "a." Trigrams shared between "Visit" and Livingston's verse are "new fallen snow" ("new fall'n snows"), "meet with an" ("meet with a"), "to the sky" ("to the skies," four times), "the top of," and "out of sight." Trigrams shared between "Visit" and Moore are "to the sky" ("to the skies," three times), "not a word," and "out of sight." Thus both men use the poem's "to the sky," though with the noun in the plural ("skies") and "out of sight." One of Moore's examples of "to the skies" affords a more extended correspondence with "Visit," "mount to the sky" in "Visit" finding a parallel in "mounts ... to the skies" in Moore's "The Organist." So Livingston uses "to the skies" more often than Moore, but Moore provides a four-word correspondence. We must count this as a "hit" for Moore. This would leave Livingston sharing with "Visit" three trigrams that are not used by Moore, and Moore sharing with "Visit" one trigram and one extended trigram not used by Livingston. In view of the greater size of Moore's poetic corpus, this inconclusive result favors Livingston, pointing in the same direction as the evidence from rhymes. It gains a modicum of support from the fact that one further trigram in "Visit," "in a moment," occurs as many as five times among Livingston's handful of published prose pieces. Also, "the top of" is repeated in "Visit," so might be held to create two links with Livingston, rather than just one.

In the case of trigrams, as of rhymes, those linking "Visit" to Livingston are less common in *Literature Online* (*LION*) poetry of 1750–1850 than those linking it to Moore. There are no fewer than 1,579 instances of "to the sky/skies," 342 of "in a moment," 217 of "the top of," 180 of "out of sight," and 172 of "not a word." There are only twenty-eight of "meet with a/an" and thirty of "new fallen/fall'n snow/snows"—both shared between "Visit" and Livingston but not Moore. When preceded by "mount/mounts," "to the sky/skies" is of comparable rarity, occurring thirty times. So Livingston provides two of the less common links, Moore one.

Concentrating on trigrams avoids subjectivity in the citation of "verbal parallels." Joe Nickell provided Seth Kaller with a list of some words and phrases that occur within Moore's poems and "Visit."[2] But the only impressive one, the exact "And Mama in her 'kerchief, and I in my cap" was in the table by a mistake that has now been corrected: the counterpart in Moore's "A Trip to Saratoga" is "kerchief, cap, or book," which does indeed collocate "kerchief" and "cap" but has no further similarities to the line in "Visit." Since "A Trip to Saratoga" cannot have been written before 1833, the year of the first train run to Saratoga, Moore could, in any case, have been influenced by "Visit" without being its author. Most of Nickell's other parallels consist of single words, and a similar table of inconsequential links with Livingston could easily be compiled.

Nickell notes that, as scholars have pointed out, "Not a creature was stirring, not even a mouse" recalls the opening scene of *Hamlet*, where Barnardo asks "Have you had quiet guard?" and his fellow soldier Francisco replies, "Not a mouse stirring," and that the author of "Visit" seems to have read William King's "The Toast: An Heroick Poem" (1747). He supposes that "the theologian and scholar" Moore is more likely to have been indebted to such sources than Livingston.[3]

Clearly, Nickell did not know that Livingston was extraordinarily well read. He shows familiarity not only with Roman and Greek mythology, literature, and history, and with the biblical Old Testament, but also with Alexander Pope's *Dunciad* and Edward Young's *Night Thoughts*. He praises the Scots poets James Thompson, Robert Burns, and Allan Ramsay, and the poet and novelist Sir Walter Scott. In his "Monarchs Rebus" he calls Shakespeare "The pride of the world, and delight of the stage," and he specifically mentions elsewhere *Othello* and *The Taming of the Shrew*.[4] He obviously loved *A Midsummer Night's Dream* and knew *Romeo and Juliet*, and, as we have seen in Chapter 3, a clue in one of his rebuses derives, whether directly or indirectly, from *2 Henry IV*. He uses several phrases that resemble "not even a mouse" in seeming to glance at Shakespeare: "tempest-tost" recalls the Witches' spell in *Macbeth*, for instance, and, most notably, Timmy's "cormorantal belly" in "Master Timmy" has only a single parallel in the whole of *LION*, and that is "cormorant belly" in the opening scene of Shakespeare's *Coriolanus*. Livingston was a reader of Ovid, Horace, and Catullus, and he knew the name of Don Quixote's palfrey. He was interested in every branch of human knowledge and was au fait with recent American and European history and with current events. He compiled an amusing mock war diary of Alexander the Great and reported on discoveries at archaeological sites and on scientific inventions. He was, in fact, a true polymath. As for the specific indebtedness to William King's "The Toast," Nickell appears to have forgotten that Donald Foster cited this poem—one of "the most popular anapestic works of the eighteenth century" and one that "remained popular well into the nineteenth century"—as seminal to the poetic tradition in which Livingston wrote but which Moore pronounced frivolous.[5]

   None of the parallels that Nickell itemizes between "Visit" and Moore's works are as complex as the following links with Livingston. In "Visit,"

> The moon on the breast of the new fallen snow
> Gave the lustre of mid-day to objects below.

Here the moon can turn night into day. A similar idea is expressed in Livingston's rebuses: "That goddess refulgent whose glance pours the day / Where midnight and error and ignorance lay," with "refulgent" matching "lustre" ("War Rebus"); or "That goddess refulgent whose ray through the gloom / Of error's dark midnight can light up a noon," where we even have "noon" matching "mid-day" ("Sages Rebus"); or "The goddess refulgent whose far-beaming rays / Can pour upon error meridian blaze," where "meridian" means "of mid-day" ("Apollo Rebus"). In each case the overall solution to the rebus is a name requiring that the quoted couplet yield an answer beginning with "T."[6] So the goddess must be Theia or Thea, glossed in the index to Edith Hamilton's *Mythology* as "(shining), name sometimes given to the moon."[7] The moon's shedding of bright light that turns night to noonday is a recurrent notion in Livingston's verse that links it to the lines in "Visit." There is nothing comparable in Moore's *Poems*. The two "Visit" lines are also Livingstonian in the three-word sequence "new fallen snow," as we have seen, since "new fall'n snows" appears in "On My Sister Joanna's Entrance to Her Thirty-Third Year." And "the breast of the ... snow" is a kind of reversal of Livingston's image, in "As on a Summer's Fervid Day," of "her snow-white breast," since each phrase links "snow" and "breast." Later in "Visit" St. Nick's beard is "white as the snow." Livingston writes of "snow-white sails" in "To the Memory of Sarah Livingston" and Moore of "snow-white teeth" in "A Trip to Saratoga." The compound "snow-white" and the simile "as white as snow" are, of course, commonplace, but the imagery in "Visit" that has moonlight transforming night to noon, incorporates in the scene "the new fallen snow," and links it to the word "breast" furnishes a multifaceted parallel to Livingston alone.

St. Nick is described in "Visit":

He had a broad face, and a little round belly
That shook when he laugh'd, like a bowl full of jelly:
He was chubby and plump, a right jolly old elf,
And I laugh'd when I saw him in spite of myself.

Here are juxtaposed two relatively uncommon rhymes that can both be found in Livingston's verse: "belly"–"jelly" occurs in "Master Timmy" and "elf"–"himself" in "A Rebus (on the Name Nancy Crooke)," where Narcissus is called "a forlorn witless elf." Moore never, in his published *Poems*, uses the words "belly," "jelly," or "elf." St. Nick, in contrast to Narcissus, is "a right jolly old elf." Besides the appearance in both poems of "elf" as a rhyme word, the phrase "a right jolly old elf" contains in "right jolly" an idiom employed by Livingston but not by Moore: "right willing" occurs in "A Valentine." Moreover, the adjective "jolly" occurs four times in Livingston's verse but nowhere in Moore's *Poems*. Here again, it is the concentration of Livingstonisms that seems significant.

Even the poem's closing line—"Happy Christmas to all, and to all a good night"—brings together several Livingston markers. There is the highly significant "Happy Christmas," as distinct from "Merry Christmas," a rarity already remarked on. There is the chiasmic structure used by Livingston elsewhere: "abba," with "a good night" balancing "Happy Christmas" and "to all" repeated in between; compare "The forests and copses ... / The copses and forests" in "Invitation to the Country," or "I rise when I please, when I please I lie down" in "Careless Philosopher's Soliloquy," or "Live with my swain, and with my swain will die" in "Frontier Settlement," where, as in "Visit," it is the final line.[8] And there is the ending on a wish, as in the "Carrier Address 1819": "So bowing I wish you a Happy New Year." In "Carrier Address 1787" the wish of a "Happy Year" is explicitly to "all." "Carrier Address 1803" ends "To all what they wish if they wish nothing wrong"; again there is chiasmic balance, with "they wish" either side of "if," and "what" (the content of their wish) set against "nothing wrong" (the content of their wish). Livingston was adept at these topical addresses, which he composed as spokesman for a newspaper delivery boy, soliciting a tip, giving a summary of the past year's events, and welcoming the New Year. His task was "To present you, my patrons, a Happy New Year": "But now comes blithe Christmas, while just in his rear / Advances our saint, jolly, laughing, New Year" ("Carrier Address 1803"). "The Night Before Christmas" simply extends this tradition. If Moore never used the word "jolly" in his verse, he never alluded to "Christmas" either, but here in his "Carrier Address" Livingston has "blithe Christmas" precede the "jolly" New Year, a festive "saint," like his "jolly" St. Nick.

10

Phoneme Pairs

Livingston's verses trip off the tongue, whereas Moore's often trip up the tongue. Livingston evidently tends to combine phonemes in more mellifluous ways than Moore. In an attempt to quantify this difference, the Livingston and Moore corpora were converted to Arpabet, the phonetic transcription code developed by the Advanced Research Projects Agency as part of their Speech Understanding Project.[1] It is designed for General American English, and is used in Carnegie Mellon University's *CMU Pronouncing Dictionary* available online. A *Wikipedia* entry gives a full description, with the corresponding symbols in the International Phonetic Alphabet.[2] A phoneme is defined as a unit of significant sound in a specific language, in this case American English, and Arpabet has symbols for every one of the thirty-nine different phonemes. Thus in Arpabet the word "stockings" consists of the seven phonemes S-T-AA-K-IH-NG-Z. The number of letters in a word as printed may coincide with the number of phonemes, as in "cat" (K-A-T), but, because of the vagaries of English spelling, they may not, as in "eight" (EY-T).

Computer analysis of the texts created totals for the use of each of the thirty-nine phonemes of the basic Arpabet system used in *The CMU Pronouncing Dictionary*—totals for single poems and for the Livingston and Moore corpora. As Brian Boyd has remarked in a splendidly illuminating book centered on *Shakespeare's Sonnets*, in poetic patterning "the onsets and endings of words are particularly salient."[3] So the computer was also programmed to make counts of "phoneme pairs" consisting of the last phoneme of one word within a verse line and the first phoneme of the next word. For this purpose each verse line was treated as a separate unit, so that a line's final phoneme could not create a "phoneme pair" with the initial phoneme of the following line. The indefinite article "a" (transcribed AH) formed phoneme pairs with both the preceding and the following phoneme within a line. So "not even a mouse" (N-AA-T IY-V- IH-N AH M-AW-S) yielded T/IY, N/AH, and AH/M. Tallies—for individual phonemes and for phoneme pairs—were organized both in alphabetical order of the phonemes and in order of frequency of phonemes.

From this mass of data, one finding immediately stood out. Among Livingston's forty most frequently used phoneme pairs were nine in which the first element was AH and six in which it was T, whereas among Moore's forty most frequently used phoneme pairs were four in which the first element was AH and eleven in which it was T. The ratio of phoneme pairs with AH beginnings to phoneme pairs with T beginnings thus seemed a likely discriminator between the two poets, and proved to be so.

For each poem the number of AH pairs was calculated as a percentage of AH pairs plus T pairs. The results are recorded in Table 10.1. Poems with totals of AH plus T of less than twenty have been ignored because the fewer the instances, the greater the effect of pure randomness. Such poems tend to be very short. For instance, Livingston's epitaph on the child Catherine Breese Livingston, with six relevant phonemes, has only four lines. Among Livingston poems that do qualify for inclusion, the short "Catherine Sleeping," which has the bare minimum of twenty instances of the relevant phonemes, has the lowest percentage of AH.

TABLE 10.1: Phoneme pairs with phonetic AH and phonetic T as first element

Livingston poems

	AH	T	Percentage AH/AH plus T
Acknowledgment	24	22	52.174
Alcmena	35	15	70.000
American Eagle	40	48	45.455
Apollo	30	24	55.555
Bats (Fable)	24	20	54.545
Beekman	24	39	38.095
Belle	14	15	48.276
Carrier 1787	31	13	70.455
Carrier 1803	44	54	44.898
Carrier 1819	56	42	57.143
Careless	10	12	45.455
Catherine Sleeping	7	13	35.000
Country	42	33	56.000
Crane and Fox	37	52	41.573
Dance	39	17	69.643

	AH	T	Percentage AH/AH plus T
Deity	18	12	60.000
Dialogue	10	14	41.667
Easter	22	19	53.659
Fly	18	16	52.941
Frog King	22	10	68.750
Frosts (Habakkuk)	11	9	55.000
Gentleman	26	21	55.319
Gilbert Cortland	11	9	55.000
God is Love	17	15	53.125
Hero	30	26	53.571
Hezekiah	8	12	40.000
Hogs	12	20	37.500
Isaiah	27	20	57.447
Lo from the East	21	14	60.000
Marriage	13	11	54.167
Marriage Tax	19	15	55.882
Midas	18	17	51.429
Monarchs	21	16	56.757
Montgomery	15	11	57.692
Past is the Hour	10	18	35.714
Procession	20	15	57.143
Queen	15	14	51.724
Sages	33	21	61.111
Settlement	13	17	43.333
Sisters	27	16	62.791
Spadille	9	14	39.130
Tappen	13	12	52.000
Vine	33	33	50.000
War	30	27	52.632
Wren	12	8	60.000
Totals	1011	901	52.877
Mean of percentages for individual poems			52.661

Moore poems

	AH	T	Percentage AH/AH plus T
Ball	23	52	30.667
Birthday	10	18	35.714
Cholera	41	52	44.086
Cowper	8	29	21.622
Daughter's Marriage	29	71	29.000
Farewell	21	38	35.593
Fashion	38	47	44.706
Flowers	10	11	47.619

	AH	T	Percentage AH/AH plus T
Fragment Fair	15	28	34.884
From St. Nicholas	7	23	23.333
Gloves	7	12	36.842
Muse	32	35	47.761
Natural Philosophy	42	49	46.154
Nymphs	55	49	52.885
Organist	34	53	35.052
Paganini	12	23	34.286
Petrosa	12	16	42.857
Pig and Rooster	60	74	44.776
Portrait	28	40	41.176
Saratoga 1	67	104	39.181
Saratoga 2	74	74	50.000
Saratoga 3	118	183	39.203
Saratoga 4	119	137	46.848
Saratoga 5	52	78	40.000
Saratoga 6	55	94	36.913
Snow	15	13	53.571
Southey	43	70	38.053
To a Lady	28	55	33.735
To Fanny	12	13	48.000
Valentine	21	25	45.652
Water Drinker	75	100	42.857
Wife	22	36	37.931
Wine Drinker	57	90	38.776
Yellow Fever	61	92	39.870
Totals	1303	1884	40.885
Mean of percentages for individual poems			39.988
Night Before Xmas	63	41	60.577

NOTE: Percentages are for AH phonemes as a percentage of the total for AH and T in poems with at least twenty instances. Pairs consist of the last phoneme of one word and the first phoneme of the next word within individual lines. The final phoneme in a line is thus disregarded.

"The Night Before Christmas" (60.577) falls within Livingston's actual range, for individual poems, of 35.000 to 70.455, but outside Moore's actual range of 21.622 to 53.571. The mean for Livingston's individual poems is 52.661, and for Moore's 39.988. The actual ranges correspond closely to the range of two inferential standard deviations from the mean: Livingston 34.646 to 70.676; Moore 25.042 to 54.934. In a normal distribution 95 percent of observations may be expected to fall within this range. Inferential standard deviations (where the denominator is $n-1$, rather than n) are 9.008

for Livingston and 7.473 for Moore. Percentages for the Moore poems in the table are thus slightly more stable, less dispersed, than those for the Livingston poems. This is at least partly because, Moore's poems are, on average, longer than Livingston's. A t-test reveals that, statistically speaking, the two author's sets of percentages belong to utterly different populations ($t = 6.66, 77$ d.f.; far beyond the $p < 0.0001$ level of significance). The figure of 60.577 for "The Night Before Christmas" is 0.879 Livingston inferential standard deviations from the mean for Livingston's poems and 2.755 Moore inferential standard deviations from the mean for Moore's poems. So, assuming that the two sets of percentages are normally distributed, as they appear to be, about 37 percent of poems by Livingston (more than a third) might be expected to fall at this or a greater distance from Livingston's mean, whereas only about one in a 165 poems by Moore might be expected to fall at such a distance from Moore's mean. So on this evidence "The Night Before Christmas" belongs with Livingston's authenticated poems rather than with Moore's.

Notably, "From Saint Nicholas"—supposed by believers in Moore's authorship of "The Night Before Christmas" (or "Visit") to have been written almost contemporaneously with it—falls close to the lower limit of Moore's observed range. The contrast with "Visit" is stark: 7:23 (and 23.333 percent) compared with 63:41 (and 60.577 percent): Yates's chi-square test for these two pairs of figures yields a result of 11.495, 1 d.f.; $p < 0.001$ or less than one chance in 1,000 that they could be drawn at random from a single population. The contrast with the much longer "The Pig and the Rooster"—a key poem for Moore's supporters, since it is, like "Visit" a narrative poem written in anapestic tetrameters—is less notable but yields a Yates's chi-square value of 5.239, 1 d.f.; $p = 0.022$, a chance probability of one in forty-five.

This preliminary use of phoneme pairs to cast light on authorship has thus been successful in separating most Livingston poems from most Moore poems, but when we begin to wonder about the nature of phonemes AH and T in the defined positions, we realize that there are further issues to be explored. Discussion will, however, be deferred until more complex tests involving phoneme pairs have been described.

11

Categories of
Phoneme Pairs

Italian is considered a "musical" language largely because words end in vowels, and in English the phoneme AH at the end of a word obviously leads more smoothly into a word beginning with a consonant than does the phoneme T. All nine of Livingston's most common phoneme pairs beginning with AH, and all four of Moore's are followed by consonants, as are nine of Moore's T- pairs and five of Livingston's. So the relative proportions of AH- and T- pairs do appear to indicate, among other things, the more fluent movement of Livingston's verse.

This suggested that an investigation into Livingston's and Moore's use of *categories* of phoneme pairs might serve to differentiate the two poets. Phonemes, as potential indexes to the more euphonious quality of Livingston's verse, were grouped into standard Arpabet classes. For consonants these are: affricate, aspirate, liquid, nasal, semivowel, stop, and fricative; and for vowels: monophthong, diphthong, and r-colored. The computer program was able to provide totals of phoneme pairs classified as Stop/Fricative, Monophthong/Stop, and so on—again, in individual poems and in the Livingston and Moore corpora. Totals for Moore and Livingston of each phoneme-category pair with at least fifty examples in the two corpora combined were tested by chi-square to determine whether one or other author's poetic corpus as a whole used them more frequently to a statistically significant degree.[1] Five that were more favored by Moore and seven that were more favored by Livingston satisfied the statistical requirements. Used more frequently by Moore were: Stop/Fricative, Stop/Stop, Stop/Semivowel, Fricative/Semivowel, and Diphthong/Fricative. Used more frequently by Livingston were: Monophthong/Stop, Stop/Monophthong, Nasal/Monophthong, Monophthong/Nasal, R–Colored/Monophthong, Diphthong/Liquid, and Stop/Aspirate. Notably, five of the seven category pairs more favored by Livingston, but none of the five more favored by Moore, have a monophthong vowel as one of the elements.

For all individual poems totals were compiled of the Livingston-favored and Moore-favored category-pairs. Thus for Moore's "From Saint Nicholas" the figures were: Stop/Fricative 7, Stop/Stop 12, Stop/Semivowel 12, Fricative/Semivowel 8, and Diphthong/Fricative 3, giving a total of 42 Moore-favored category pairs; and Monophthong/Stop 14, Stop/Monophthong 9, Nasal/Monophthong 5, Monophthong/Nasal 5, R-colored/Monothong 0, Diphthong/Liquid 4, and Stop/Aspirate 1, giving a total of 38 Livingston-favored category pairs. Livingston-favored category pairs thus constitute 47.5 percent of the combined total for both poets ([38 ÷ 80] × 100 = 47.5 percent). Table 11.1 gives the results of percentages calculated for individual poems by Livingston and Moore. All poems with at least twenty relevant category pairs are included. Only five very short Livingston poems and Moore's extremely short "Sand" are omitted.

TABLE 11.1: Categories of phoneme pairs more favored by Livingston or Moore

Livingston poems

	Moore-favored	Livingston-favored	Percentage L/L+M
Acknowledgment	25	40	61.538
Acrostic	10	16	61.538
Alcmena	28	41	59.420
American Eagle	63	85	57.432
Apollo	30	49	62.025
Arabella	16	9	36.000
Bats (Fable)	32	37	53.623
Beekman	50	70	58.333
Belle	21	25	54.348
Carrier 1787	35	59	62.766
Carrier 1803	97	111	53.365
Carrier 1819	94	87	48.066
Careless	12	23	65.714
Catherine L Breese	12	9	42.857
Catherine Sleeping	23	26	53.061
Country	32	62	65.957
Crane and Fox	75	100	57.143
Dance	27	64	70.330
Death of Sarah	16	15	48.387

	Moore-favored	Livingston-favored	Percentage L/L+M
Deity	23	29	55.769
Dialogue	15	21	58.333
Easter	25	41	62.121
Fly	24	24	50.000
Frog King	32	35	52.239
Frontier Song	13	9	40.909
Frosts (Habakkuk)	14	14	50.000
Gentleman	45	43	48.864
German Spa	16	22	57.895
Gilbert Courtland	16	14	46.667
God is Love	19	41	68.333
Henry Welles L	14	15	51.724
Hero	48	65	57.522
Hezekiah	28	18	39.130
Hogs	38	32	45.714
Isaiah	28	30	51.724
Joanna	14	16	53.333
Job	16	19	54.286
Lo from the East	15	35	70.000
Original Poems	07	13	65.000
Marriage	27	31	53.482
Marriage Tax	27	28	50.909
Midas	30	39	56.522
Monarchs	19	37	66.071
Montgomery	19	19	50.000
Past is the Hour	24	25	51.020
Procession	22	30	57.692
Queen	16	22	57.895
Rispah	17	21	55.263
Sages	34	51	60.000
Scots Wha Hae	16	15	48.387
Settlement	37	26	41.270
Sisters	25	39	60.938
Spadille	20	24	54.543
Tappen	16	17	51.515
Timmy	22	28	56.000
To Miss	08	19	70.370
Valentine	19	12	38.710
Vine	55	76	58.015
War	38	67	63.810
Wren	10	13	56.522
Totals	1649	2103	56.050
Mean of percentages for individual poems			55.175

Moore poems

	Moore-favored	Livingston-favored	Percentage L/L+M
Ball	79	71	47.333
Birthday	30	14	31.818
Cholera	92	69	42.857
Cowper	50	37	42.529
Daughter's Marriage	93	79	45.930
Farewell	60	33	35.484
Fashion	86	50	36.765
Flowers	26	16	38.095
Fragment Fair	58	42	42.000
From St. Nicholas	42	38	47.500
Gloves	18	17	48.571
Muse	57	64	52.893
Natural Philosophy	85	69	44.805
Nymphs	86	79	47.879
Old Dobbin	21	15	41.667
Organist	58	93	61.589
Paganini	42	27	39.130
Petrosa	33	16	32.653
Pig and Rooster	118	142	54.615
Portrait	60	52	46.429
Saratoga 1	163	155	48.742
Saratoga 2	139	124	47.148
Saratoga 3	259	266	50.667
Saratoga 4	221	229	50.889
Saratoga 5	140	131	48.339
Saratoga 6	145	141	49.301
Snow	30	16	34.783
Song	15	8	34.783
Southey	117	98	45.581
To a Lady	93	52	35.862
To Clem	12	16	57.143
To Fanny	23	15	39.474
Valentine	45	31	40.789
Water Drinker	156	158	50.318
Wife	61	52	46.018
Wine Drinker	165	138	45.545
Yellow Fever	169	144	46.006
Totals	3147	2797	47.056
Mean of percentages for individual poems			44.647
Night Before Xmas	65	113	63.483

NOTE: Categories more favored by Livingston are Stop/Monophthong, Monophthong/Stop, Nasal/Monophthong, Monophthong/Nasal, Stop/Aspirate, R-colored/

Monophthong, Diphthong/Liquid; categories more favored by Moore are Stop/Frica-
tive, Stop/Stop, Stop/Semivowel, Fricative/Semivowel, Diphthong/Fricative. Figures
in the final column are for phoneme pairs in the Livingston-favored categories as a
percentage of phoneme pairs in all twelve of these categories, for all poems that have
at least twenty relevant phoneme pairs. For definition of "phoneme pairs" see note to
Table 10.1, and for further explanations, see text.

There is some overlap between Livingston and Moore, but the two
sets of percentages—for Moore poems and for Livingston poems—belong
to utterly different populations, statistically speaking ($t = 6.68$, 95 d.f.; far
beyond the $p < 0.0001$ level of significance).

The mean for Livingston's poems is 55.175 and the standard deviation,
a measure of dispersion around the mean, is 7.936. Livingston's actual range,
for individual poems, is 36.000 to 70.370. This corresponds very closely to
the range formed by calculating two standard deviations either side of the
mean, namely 39.304 to 71.046. About 95 percent of further Livingston
poems should fall within this range. "Visit," with a percentage of
Livingston-favored category pairs of 63.483 does fall easily within both
the actual range and the two-standard-deviation range. It is 1.05 standard
deviations from Livingston's mean, closer than might be expected of some
34 percent of Livingston poems ($p > 0.293$).

The mean for Moore is 44.647 and the standard deviation is 6.857.
Moore's actual range is 31.818 to 61.589. This corresponds very closely to
the range formed by calculating two standard deviations either side of the
mean, namely 30.933 to 58.360. "Visit" is outside both Moore's actual
range and his two-standard-deviation range. It is 2.747 standard deviations
from Moore's mean, a distance at or beyond which we might expect to find
only one in about 165 Moore poems.

So once again "Visit" looks very much more like a Livingston poem
than a Moore poem. In terms of the probabilities of the normal distribution,
it is about fifty times closer to Livingston's mean than to Moore's mean.

Again "From Saint Nicholas," supposed by Moore's supporters to have
been written just before "Visit," is (at 47.500) close to Moore's mean of
44.647 and very different from "Visit" (at 63.483). Yates's chi-square test
(comparing their scores, 42:38 with 65:113) shows that there is a less than
one in forty chance that they belong to the same population (chi-square =
5.169, 1 d.f., $p < 0.025$).

None even of the five short Livingston poems that have insufficient
data to qualify for inclusion in Table 11.1 has a percentage of Livingston-
favored category pairs that falls outside the lower limit of his range. "To
Miss (Roses)" and the four-line "Catherine Breese Livingston," each with

a percentage of 83.333, actually fall outside Livingston's higher limit, and so a huge distance beyond Moore's. And Moore's "Sand," with only six of the relevant pairs, comes out at 50.000 percent, well within his range. Naturally figures for short poems are far less reliable, because far more subject to random fluctuation, than for longer ones. The other three Livingston poems disqualified for having fewer than twenty relevant pairs are "Anne Duyckinck," "Acrostic (Eliza Hughes)," and "Without Distinction." The total for all five disqualified poems together yields a percentage of 63.636, well within Livingston's range but outside Moore's. Given the brevity, relative to "Visit," even of many poems that are tabulated, the degree of discrimination between Moore's and Livingston's is remarkable.

12

Individual Phoneme Pairs More Favored by Moore or Livingston

It seemed worth carrying out one further trial using phoneme pairs—individual pairs this time, rather than categories. All phoneme pairs falling within either Moore's or Livingston's top hundred, in terms of frequency of use, were tested by chi-square to determine whether they were used significantly more often within the overall corpus of one or other poet. This significance testing uncovered, neatly though coincidentally, ten phoneme pairs more favored by Moore and ten more favored by Livingston.[1]

Moore's were:

T/DH T/F T/S Z/W S/W Z/T IY/T D/P S/S Z/CH

Livingston's were:

AH/N AH/F AH/S AH/B AH/K AH/L AH/P N/AH Z/AO Z/IH

Every one of the pairs more favored by Livingston includes a vowel. All but one of Moore's contain consonants only. Again, this difference must contribute to the greater ease and smoothness (cantabile, as one might call it) of Livingston's verse. In this trial there will obviously be some overlap with the previous two, especially the first featuring phoneme pairs beginning with AH (as Livingston markers) and with T (as Moore markers). But there is considerable variety in the nine consonantal pairs that are here found to be used more frequently by Moore than by Livingston—more frequently not, of course, in absolute terms, since Moore's canon is much larger than Livingston's, but as rates of use per total numbers of pairs. Further, the totals per poem are very much smaller for these individual sets of ten phonemes than were the totals for the contrasting large categories. So we would expect greater random fluctuation. How consistently, nevertheless, are the poets' overall preferences, which may well be unconscious, maintained over their many individual poems?

Table 12.1 presents the results for poems by each poet, the final column giving figures for Livingston-favored pairs as a percentage of the combined Livingston-favored and Moore-favored total. Poems with fewer than twelve relevant phoneme pairs are excluded. These short pieces yield too few data for authorial habits to prevail over pure randomness.

TABLE 12.1: Phoneme pairs more favored by Livingston or Moore

Livingston poems

	Moore-favored	Livingston-favored	Percentage L/L+M
Acknowledgment	6	15	71.429
Alcmena	8	23	74.194
American Eagle	18	32	64.000
Apollo	10	19	65.517
Bats (Fable)	10	16	61.538
Beekman	12	19	61.290
Belle	3	9	75.000
Carrier 1787	7	29	80.556
Carrier 1803	20	30	62.264
Carrier 1819	37	24	60.656
Country	12	32	72.727
Crane and Fox	15	25	62.500
Dance	6	32	84.211
Deity	3	12	80.000
Easter	2	17	89.474
Fly	5	8	61.538
Frog King	6	17	73.913
Frosts (Habakkuk)	4	9	69.231
Gentleman	8	17	68.000
God is Love	4	11	73.333
Hero	14	17	54.839
Hogs	6	12	66.667
Isaiah	15	18	54.545
Lo from the East	7	16	69.565
Marriage Tax	11	13	54.167
Midas	11	11	50.000
Monarchs	4	15	78.947
Montgomery	5	9	64.286
Past is the Hour	10	8	44.444

	Moore-favored	Livingston-favored	Percentage L/L+M
Procession	4	13	76.471
Queen	7	9	56.250
Sages	7	24	77.419
Scots Wha Hae	2	11	84.615
Settlement	8	14	63.636
Sisters	8	20	71.429
Spadille	6	10	37.500
Tappen	5	7	58.333
Timmy	6	6	50.000
Vine	7	21	75.000
War	22	11	75.000
Totals	361	661	64.677
Mean of percentages for individual poems			66.654

Moore poems

	Moore-favored	Livingston-favored	Percentage L/L+M
Ball	21	15	41.667
Birthday	7	5	41.667
Cholera	30	29	49.153
Cowper	19	5	20.833
Daughter's Marriage	22	17	43.590
Farewell	23	9	28.125
Fashion	29	20	40.816
Fragment Fair	12	8	40.000
From St. Nicholas	8	6	42.857
Muse	16	18	52.942
Natural Philosophy	36	27	42.857
Nymphs	25	38	60.317
Organist	20	26	56.522
Paganini	14	11	44.000
Petrosa	19	8	26.230
Pig and Rooster	30	41	57.746
Portrait	18	21	53.846
Saratoga 1	53	32	37.647
Saratoga 2	38	39	50.649
Saratoga 3	103	60	36.810
Saratoga 4	91	65	41.667
Saratoga 5	55	31	36.047
Saratoga 6	43	27	38.571
Snow	9	9	50.000
Southey	34	27	44.262
To a Lady	31	10	24.390

	Moore-favored	Livingston-favored	Percentage L/L+M
To Fanny	7	8	53.333
Valentine	9	10	52.632
Water Drinker	41	47	53.409
Wife	18	13	41.925
Wine Drinker	67	36	34.951
Yellow Fever	59	30	33.708
Totals	1007	748	42.621
Mean of percentages for individual poems			42.912
Night Before Xmas	37	20	64.912

NOTE: More favored by Moore are T/DH, T/F, T/S, Z/W, S/W, Z/T, IY/T, D/P, S/S, Z/CH; more favored by Livingston are AH/N, AH/F, AH/S, AH/B, AH/K, AH/L, AH/P, N/AH, Z/AO, Z/IH. Figures in the final column are for Livingston-favored phoneme pairs as a percentage of combined totals of Livingston-favored and Moore-favored phoneme pairs, for all poems that have at least twelve relevant pairs. For definition of "phoneme pairs" see note to Table 10.1, and for further explanations, see text.

Moore's mean for individual poems is 42.912, with an inferential standard deviation of 9.869. His actual range of 20.833 to 60.317 is close to the two-standard-deviation range of 23.174 to 62.649. "Visit" at 64.912 is outside both Moore's actual and statistically derived ranges. Its score is 2.293 standard deviations from Moore's mean, a distance we might expect to be equaled or exceeded by fewer than one in forty poems by Moore ($p < 0.025$).

The mean for Livingston's forty poems is 66.654, with an inferential standard deviation of 11.293. The actual range of 37.500 to 89.474 corresponds almost exactly to the two-standard-deviation range of 44.068 to 89.239 at the upper limit, but the short "Spadille," which has only sixteen relevant phonemes, is responsible for a slightly anomalous actual lower limit: the next lowest actual figure of 44.444 closely matches the theoretical one. "Visit" is not merely well within Livingston's range but closer to his mean than we might expect from all but 13 percent of his poems ($p > 0.87$).

The test results afford a high degree of discrimination between the two poets' works. Only 4 of the 40 Livingston poems score less than 54.000, and only 2 of the 32 Moore poems score more than 54.000. One of the two high-scorers for Moore happens to be "The Pig and the Rooster," though at 57.746 it is still appreciably further from Livingston's mean than "Visit." And of course, it is noticeably un–Livingston-like on other tests, whereas "Visit," has, in test after test, emerged as more akin to Livingston than to Moore.

13

Definite and
Indefinite Articles

Phoneme pairs—comprised of the last phoneme in one word and the first phoneme in the immediately following word, within a line of verse—obviously depend on choices that a poet makes in putting words together. Certain combinations will make for euphony and ease of movement, while others will not. But phoneme pairs may well be determined more by sense than sound. They inevitably reflect a poet's vocabulary and habits of syntax and his usage of those high-frequency words on which sentence structure is built. A little reflection about those phoneme pairs that include AH and are so dominant among pairs more favored by Livingston than by Moore leads to the realization that they must be mainly composed of the definite and indefinite articles, "the" and "a." In the simple version of Arpabet phonetic transcription, the symbol AH covers the neutral vowel rendered as an inverted "e" in the International Phonetic Alphabet. The second phoneme of the definite article (DH-AH) can serve as the first element of a phoneme pair, while the indefinite article (AH) can form a phoneme pair with either the last phoneme of the preceding word or the first phoneme of the succeeding word. The prevalence of AH as the first element of phoneme pairs more favored by Livingston than by Moore may thus alert us to the probability that Livingston uses "the" and perhaps "a" at higher rates than Moore.

So this potential discriminator was investigated, with the combined totals of "the" and "a" in each poem being expressed as percentages of all words. The results are presented in Table 13.1, which excludes poems of fewer than 100 words.

TABLE 13.1: Definite and indefinite articles in Livingston and Moore

Livingston poems

	Total words	"a"	"the"	"a"+"the"	percent "a"+"the"
Catherine	148	0	7	7	4.730
Easter	210	3	18	22	10.476
Job	139	1	10	11	7.914
Country	333	6	36	42	12.613
Sisters	170	2	25	27	15.882
Frosts (Habakkuk)	120	1	8	9	7.500
Isaiah	211	1	23	24	11.374
Lo from the East	168	2	18	20	11.905
Tappan	150	2	9	11	7.333
Sarah	121	0	8	8	6.612
Queen of Love	129	1	14	15	11.628
Deity	172	2	16	18	10.465
Joanna	124	4	6	10	8.065
Sally Livingston	109	4	8	12	11.009
Settlement	209	2	11	13	6.220
Apollo	260	5	24	29	11.154
Timmy	173	1	8	9	5.202
Dance	284	8	30	38	13.380
Valentine	119	1	2	3	2.521
Gentleman	284	1	25	26	9.155
Hero	327	7	23	30	9.174
Beekman	408	13	10	23	5.637
Vine and Oak	428	8	25	33	7.710
Spadille	171	5	4	9	5.263
War	320	5	25	30	9.375
Sages	274	3	29	32	11.679
Carrier 1787	380	11	20	31	8.158
Acknowledge	217	8	16	24	11.060
Hogs	234	1	11	12	5.128
Death of Wolfe	115	3	11	14	12.174
Fly	154	6	10	16	10.390
Careless	126	4	6	10	7.937
Belle	139	5	8	13	9.353
Alcmena	261	2	31	33	12.644
Rispah	159	1	5	6	3.774
To Miss	104	2	11	13	12.500
Procession	203	3	17	20	9.852
Marriage	195	2	11	13	6.667
Monarchs	157	1	20	21	13.376

	Total words	"a"	"the"	"a"+"the"	percent "a"+"the"
Frog King	227	11	11	22	9.692
Bats	237	4	20	24	10.127
Scots Wha Hae	122	1	4	5	4.098
Crane and Fox	460	12	24	36	7.826
Midas	189	7	10	17	8.995
God Is Love	200	1	15	16	8.000
Dialogue	124	1	9	10	8.065
Carrier 1803	735	6	35	41	5.578
Carrier 1819	677	9	42	51	7.533
Gilbert Cortland	107	0	11	11	10.280
Marriage Tax	203	5	14	19	9.360
Hezekiah	161	0	7	7	4.348
German Spa	125	0	5	5	4.000
Past is the Hour	201	1	10	11	5.423
American Eagle	530	18	21	39	7.358
Totals	12303	215	837	1052	8.551
Mean of percentages for individual poems					8.661

Moore poems

	Total words	"a"	"the"	"a"+"the"	percent "a"+"the"
Saratoga 1	1042	16	48	64	6.142
Saratoga 2	850	13	60	73	8.588
Saratoga 3	1724	29	83	112	6.497
Saratoga 4	1421	27	89	116	8.163
Saratoga 5	880	15	37	52	5.909
Saratoga 6	892	14	40	54	6.054
Portrait	361	10	18	28	7.756
Fashion	570	4	34	38	6.667
Muse	454	6	25	31	6.828
Snow	186	2	13	15	8.065
Natural Philosophy	590	17	25	42	7.119
Cowper	271	4	4	8	2.952
Petrosa	200	3	8	11	5.500
Song	119	1	4	5	4.202
Old Dobbin	152	3	4	7	4.605
Ball	545	9	14	23	4.220
Fragment Fair	334	4	11	15	4.491
To a Lady	541	6	22	28	5.176
Wife	460	10	12	22	4.783
Flowers	150	3	7	10	6.667
Yellow Fever	1135	5	55	60	5.286
Nymphs	588	13	42	55	9.354
Birthday	176	1	9	10	5.682

	Total words	"a"	"the"	"a"+"the"	percent "a"+"the"
Paganini	212	2	10	12	5.660
Organist	584	12	19	31	5.308
Pig and Rooster	783	29	31	60	7.663
Valentine	285	4	16	20	7.018
Wine Drinker	1069	16	38	54	5.051
Water Drinker	1131	19	53	72	6.366
Gloves	140	2	4	6	4.286
Farewell	322	7	14	21	6.522
Cholera	615	6	35	41	6.667
Marriage	575	3	25	28	4.870
Southey	746	13	30	43	5.764
From St. Nicholas	214	4	3	7	3.271
To Fanny	136	2	10	12	8.824
To Clem	103	1	8	9	8.738
Totals	20556	335	960	1295	6.300
Mean of percentages for individual poems					6.127
NBC (Visit)	542	28	34	62	11.439

The actual range for Livingston's poems is 2.521 to 15.882. The mean is 8.661 and the inferential standard deviation 2.930, giving a two-standard-deviation range of 2.801 to 14.520. "Visit" is comfortably within Livingston's actual and two-standard-deviation ranges. It is 0.948 standard deviations from Livingston's mean, a distance at or beyond which about a third of Livingston poems might be expected to lie ($p > 0.343$).

The actual range for Moore's poems is 2.952 to 9.354. The mean is 6.127 and the inferential standard deviation 1.570, giving a two-standard-deviation range of 2.987 to 9.268. "Visit" is outside both the actual and two-standard-deviation range. It is 3.383 standard deviations from Moore's mean. Fewer than one in 1,400 Moore poems of the kinds listed above might be expected to have scores this far from the mean ($p < 0.0007$). The rate of use in "Visit" of the definite and indefinite articles is very much more readily reconciled with Livingston's authorship of the poem than with Moore's.

Livingston uses the definite article "the" at a much greater rate than Moore, the indefinite article "a" at only a slightly greater rate. But including "a" in calculations helps stabilize Livingston's percentages, since when in his poems "the" is infrequent, "a" is often frequent (as in "American Eagle") and vice versa (as in the "Alcmena Rebus"). The difference between the two poets in the frequency of their use of articles is a pointer to Livingston's liking for nouns: "the night," "the house," "a creature," "a mouse." He inclines toward the concrete and the particular.

We need only compare totals for "a" plus "the" in Table 13.1 with totals for phoneme pairs beginning with AH in Table 10.1 to see that the articles are in large measure, in fact almost exclusively, responsible for the AH totals. A few items, such as the name "Petrosa" or the word "idea" make an occasional addition to the figure for a particular poem. Since Table 10.1's totals for T, more favored by Moore, also contribute to the final figure of AH as a percentage of the combined total of AH and T, Tables 10.1 and 13.1 are by no means completely interdependent, but nor can they be regarded as giving substantially independent testimony.

The definite and indefinite articles have a much less considerable effect, however, on the results for preferred categories of phoneme pairs in Table 11.1, where the quantity of data is far greater. If we calculate, as Livingston and Moore totals for poems listed in Table 11.1, only the numbers of Livingston-favored and Moore-favored pairs per 1,000 phonemes, we find that the rate for Livingston is 35.828 per 1,000 phonemes and for Moore 43.189 per 1,000 phonemes. The rate for "Visit" is 38.553, closer to Livingston's overall rate than to Moore's. Although there is a good deal of overlap between rates for individual Moore and Livingston poems, the category phoneme pairs used more often by Moore than by Livingston are obviously making a substantial contribution to the results of Table 11.1.

One possible reservation must be considered. Might Livingston use more definite articles than Moore because of the peculiar generic makeup of his poetic corpus? He wrote several rebuses, which tend to require a high proportion of nouns as clues to their solution. The "Deity Rebus," for example, begins "Take the *name* of the *deity lovers* obey / And the golden-tressed *god* whose bright *car* gives the *day*" (my italics). However, many Livingston poems that are not rebuses—"Easter," "Lo from the East," "Isaiah," "Invitation to the Country," "Fly," "Acknowledgement," "Marriage Tax," and "Procession," for example, along with several shorter pieces—also use articles at rates well beyond Moore's norm. These cover a wide range of themes and kinds, and in fact forty-two of the fifty-four diverse Livingston poems in Table 13.1, or 78 percent, attain scores higher than Moore's mean. And of course "The Night Before Christmas" ("Visit") is not a rebus.

14
Very High-Frequency Words

Having been alerted to Livingston's greater use than Moore's of the definite and indefinite articles, we may consider other high-frequency words. It is well known that the rates at which very common words occur can vary among authors and be a useful aid toward identification.[1] "Function words," in particular, may reflect habits in the construction of phrases and sentences. They form a kind of skeleton of grammar and syntax, which is fleshed out by the "content words": nouns, verbs, adjectives, and adverbs.

A *Wikipedia* article entitled "Most common words in English" ranks the top hundred on the basis of an Oxford Online analysis of the Oxford English Corpus of over a billion words.[2] The ten that head the list are "the," "be," "to," "of," "and," "a," "in," "that," "have," and "I." They are lemmas or lexemes, rather than mere graphic units: thus "be" covers "are," "is," "were," and "was." In other listings based on graphic units "is" attains the top ten. The frequency of the pronoun "I" is likely to be sensitive to context. It occurs ten times in "Visit" in which the narrator is recounting a magical happening that he witnessed, but is not needed at all for the "Sages Rebus," for example, and occurs only once in the "Hero Rebus." As lexemes, the verbs "be" and "have" are not "computer-friendly," and their forms depend on such specifics as whom the poet is addressing and whether he is telling of something that happened in the past, is expressing feelings of the moment, or is looking to the future. If, for our purposes in this chapter, we eliminate these three words, there remain the easily countable "the" and "a," which have already been dealt with, and "to," "of," "and," "in," and "that."

Of these five words, only the overall figures for "to" and "that" are significantly different for Livingston and Moore, as tested by chi-square, "that" being used much more frequently by Moore and "to" slightly more frequently.[3] "To" turns out to be useless as a stand-alone discriminator, however. A t-test shows no significant difference between Moore and Livingston in their rates (per 1,000 words) for individual poems and this remains true when analysis is based on blocks of at least 500 words. For poems and combinations of poems $t = 1.88$, 44 d.f., $p = 0.067$, which is greater than even the marginal $p = 0.05$ level of significance. While the rate for "Visit" (29.520) is closer to Moore's mean (27.026) than Livingston's (21.855), about a third of Livingston blocks of 500 or more words would be expected to fall at least as far as "Visit" from Livingston's mean. In both poets the rate of use is extremely variable.

Despite occurring much less often than "to," "that" is somewhat more effective. Again, poems of fewer than 500 words must be amalgamated into blocks of that minimum size. The results are recorded in Table 14.1. A t-test reveals that the two authorial groups of scores ("that" per 1,000 words) have a less than one in 3,000 probability of having derived from a single population ($t = 3.91$, 44 d.f., $p = 0.000315$). Livingston's mean is 6.319, with an inferential standard deviation of 5.479, whereas Moore's mean is 12.210, with a standard deviation of 4.754. With a rate of 1.845, "Visit" is within Livingston's two-standard deviation range (0–17.277) but outside Moore's (2.704–21.717). It is 0.817 standard deviations from Livingston's mean, 2.180 from Moore's. "Visit" thus uses "that" at a rate that places it more comfortably among Livingston's poems than among Moore's.

However, it must be recognized that, although Moore's mean is approximately double Livingston's, it represents, to the nearest whole number, only 6 instances of "that" in a poem of 500 words, which is not a large difference from the single instance in "Visit." And in fact one Moore poem of 545 words (virtually the same number as in "Visit")—namely "Lines Addressed to a Lady as an Apology for not Accepting her Invitation to a Ball"—also contains but a single example of "that." So Moore would clearly have been capable of the scant use of "that" in "Visit." But the score for "Ball" makes it something of an outlier among Moore's poems, and this sparing use of "that" is more characteristic of Livingston. It is of interest, therefore, that one of Moore's changes to the original *Troy Sentinel* text of "The Night Before Christmas" was the addition of a second "that." In this respect, as in others (mentioned in Chapter 3), the *Sentinel* text is more Livingston-like than the text that Moore printed in his *Poems*.

Also worth noting is the anomalously high score (23.569) for one Livingston block. The reason for its being so unusual is obvious when we check which poems constitute this composite block—"War Rebus" and "Sages Rebus." Their first lines indicate the explanation: "Take the name of the

TABLE 14.1: Instances of "that" per 1,000 words

Verse blocks by Livingston		Verse blocks by Moore	
Size of text in words	Rate	Size of text in words	Rate
735	2.721	1042	12.476
677	1.477	850	9.412
530	0.000	1724	12.761
830	8.434	1421	10.556
501	11.976	880	13.636
533	0.000	892	11.211
534	5.618	570	15.789
642	9.346	590	3.390
687	2.911	545	1.835
735	8.163	541	9.242
599	8.347	1135	7.048
594	23.569	588	11.905
659	6.070	584	6.849
503	11.928	782	10.230
612	3.268	1069	15.903
540	3.704	1130	15.044
603	1.658	615	13.008
819	2.442	574	15.679
513	3.899	744	10.753
593	11.804	815	18.405
560	5.357	500	12.000
805	13.665		
610	24.590		
673	17.831		
914	12.035		
Means of blocks:	6.319		12.210

"The Night Before Christmas" ("Visit"): Size of text: 542 words; Rate: 1.845

hero that dreadful in war," "Take the name of that planet which sages declare." A rebus offers a series of clues, the initial letter of each answer forming part of the overall solution, which is a particular name. Specifying the clues often requires the word "that." The "Hero Rebus" begins in the same way: "That hero whose great and magnanimous mind." It achieves a high rate of "that" (15.291), but, comprising only 327 words, forms a composite block with "To my Brother Beekman," which has only a single "that" in 408 words, characteristic of Livingston's rate outside his rebuses.

We are by no means yet finished with high-frequency words, which will prove in Chapters 16 and 17 to be excellent discriminators when taken in bulk rather than singly. The word "to" will then make its small contribution to distinguishing the verse of Moore from that of Livingston. But first we can relax with a less technical account of some expressions and quirks of style relished by one or other of the two poets but not by both.

15

Favorite Expressions and Quirks of Style

Reading Moore's poems one soon becomes aware of his obsessive fondness for the word "some": "some base culprit," "some belle," "some noisy pack," "some dull scholar's book," "some careless genius," "some child." Reliance on this word is symptomatic of his generalizing vagueness. Livingston does not write of "some child" or "some belle" but specifically addresses his "charming black-eyed niece" or "my Daphne—sweetest maid / That e'er sported in the glade." Altogether, Moore has 75 instances of "some," in contrast to Livingston's 3. Also conspicuous is Moore's liking for the collocations "at length" (12 times), "in vain" (16), and "many a" (17), and for the poetical "oft" (30). Livingston never uses "many a," and uses "at length" only three times, "in vain" twice, and "oft" once. Further, a by-product of our analysis of Moore's and Livingston's contrasting rates of use of "that" is the discovery that Moore is alone in employing "that's" (10 times). So Moore's total for all six locutions is 160 and Livingston's 9. We can consider these words and phrases virtual Moore markers. "The Pig and the Rooster" contains two instances of "some," two of "at length," and one of "many a." Moore carries his poetic diction even into this supposed "piece of fun." The brief "From Saint Nicholas," addressed to his little daughter, contains "oft," while his habitual "some" is used in this short poem no fewer than three times. But "The Night Before Christmas" is free from any of the six expressions favored by Moore and almost entirely eschewed by Livingston.

Moore averages one of his favorite locutions to every 129 words. Table 15.1 shows their distribution across his published canon and three short manuscript pieces. It can be seen that the only poems with no instances have 152, 150, 176, 136, and 103 words altogether, all being less than a third the size of "The Night Before Christmas" (542 words), which would be highly anomalous as a 542-word poem by Moore from which his markers are completely absent. Of course, since Livingston uses the Moore markers only nine times, only a tiny minority of his poems (six in fact) contain even a single instance.

TABLE 15.1: Moore markers, with totals per poem in the columns headed "M"					
Moore poems					
	Total words	**M**		**Total words**	**M**
Saratoga 1	1042	9	Wife	460	4
Saratoga 2	850	8	Flowers	150	0
Saratoga 3	1724	14	Yellow Fever	1135	6
Saratoga 4	1421	10	Nymphs	588	5
Saratoga 5	880	9	Birthday	176	0
Saratoga 6	892	3	Paganini	212	2
Portrait	361	7	Organist	584	8
Fashion	570	4	Pig and Rooster	783	5
Muse	454	7	Valentine	285	1
Snow	186	1	Wine Drinker	1069	10
Natural Philosophy	590	1	Water Drinker	1131	5
Sand	43	1	Gloves	140	2
Cowper	271	2	Farewell	322	3
Petrosa	200	1	Cholera	615	4
Song	119	2	Marriage	575	3
Old Dobbin	152	0	Southey	746	4
Ball	545	3	From St. Nicholas	214	4
Fragment Fair	334	8	To Fanny	136	0
To a Lady	541	4	To Clem	103	0
The Night Before Christmas (Visit)				542	0

In Moore's verse, "And" at the beginning of a line is followed by a comma 40 times out of 307 instances. None of Livingston's 241 instances of "And" at the beginning of a line is followed by a comma, and neither are any of the twelve instances in "The Night Before Christmas." One might attribute the difference between the two authors to the pernickety publisher of Moore's *Poems*, but "And" is twice followed by a comma in the handwritten "From Saint Nicholas," and the punctuation clearly reflects, at least in part, Moore's own practices and his more complex syntax. There are three examples of "And"-plus-comma in "The Pig and the Rooster."

What guarantees that syntax is a crucial component in Moore's and Livingston's contrasting usages with respect to "And" is the evidence of two-word collocations beginning verse lines. A search within the poems of each man for all the two-word collocations that begin lines in "The Night Before Christmas" yields highly significant results. Three of these are very common in Livingston's corpus, but almost nonexistent in Moore's. "To the," "With the," and "And the" are used 14, 13, and 28 times by Livingston, whereas Moore avoids "To the" and "With the" completely and uses "And the" only once. So Livingston's total for all three items—each of which occurs in "The Night Before Christmas"—is 55, while Moore's is 1. Livingston not only has a much greater liking for the definite article than Moore, as we have seen in Chapter 13, but uses it in certain positions—after the prepositions "To" and "With" and the conjunction "And" at the beginnings of verse lines—to an extent that sharply distinguishes his poetry from Moore's. And once again "Visit" is Livingston-like, not Moore-like.

There are eight further line-beginning collocations in "Visit" that are rare in either poet's verse, but that one man uses at least once and the other does not. Livingston, alone of the two men, has examples of "Not a," "With a," "He was" (twice), "And his," and "He had," Moore of "And he" (twice) and "When they." This is a 5–2 majority for Livingston, despite his much smaller canon of poems searched: Moore's contains almost 1.6 times as many words. This of course means that altogether 7 of the two-word beginnings to lines in "Visit" are to be found in Livingston's poetry but not in Moore's ("To the" and "With the" being added to the 5), and only 2 in Moore's poetry but not in Livingston's.

However, the evidence described in the last two paragraphs is not quite so spectacular as it at first appears. Collocations comprised of function words such as prepositions, conjunctions, and pronouns fit more easily into the openings of anapestic lines than into the openings of lines that are basically iambic or trochaic, and, as we have noted, Livingston wrote a much greater volume of anapestic verse than Moore. Nevertheless, 17 of the instances of the line-beginning collocations favored by Livingston occur within his iambic or trochaic poems, and while Moore's sole example of the Livingston favorite "And the" is in his anapestic "The Pig and the Rooster," the contrast with the much shorter "The Night Before Christmas," which has 9 instances of the Livingston collocations, is striking.

Both poets use a range of repetitive structures in their verse. Livingston is the more prolific in this regard, but examples are hard to count and categorize in any systematic and consistent way. However, in addition to Livingston's already mentioned liking for chiasmus—the "abba" rhetorical pattern exemplified by the last line of "Visit"—there is one type of repetition that he works into his verse fifteen times and that Moore uses only twice in his much larger corpus. It involves the exact repetition of two or more consecutive words in the midst of parallel phrase constructions: "Ye join'd *in our* circles and mixt *in our* play"; "Joy laughs *in his* breast—health lives *in his* eye"; "Hail! pride *of each* lass and the wish *of each* swain"; "Blithesome *as the* breathing day, / Smiling *as the* smiling May"; "Here I lounge *at my* pleasure, and bask *at my* ease"; "The pride *of the* world and delight *of the* stage"; "The source *of our* wealth and support *of our* trade"; "Is keen *as the* thorn yet as sweet *as the* rose" ("War Rebus"); "As keen *as the* thorn, yet sweet *as the* rose" ("Alcmena Rebus"); "To raise *a false* wen or expand *a false* bump, / Project *a false* hip or protrude *a false* rump" (two examples); "Our carts *and our* waggons ... / Our cows *and our* bullocks ..."; "Our cows *and our* bullocks ... / Our jaumbs [jambs] *and our* paper ..."; "To brush the cobwebs *from the* wall / And sweep the litter *from the* hall." To qualify for this list the parallelism must be within a single line or two consecutive lines, and the repeated words must be enclosed by words that are not identical but of the same parts of speech. Thus in "Ye join'd in our circles and mixt in our play," the repeated "in our" is in each case preceded by a verb and followed by a noun. My rule might reasonably have been relaxed to allow "Fairer *than the* queen of love, / ... / Sweeter *than the* smiling May, / Calmer *than the* close of day," where the first and last of these lines are not consecutive but built into a series in which "smiling May" and "close of day" both consist of nouns preceded by a modifier, though "smiling" is adjectival and "close" is a noun. This would raise Livingston's total to fifteen. Some more extensive repetitions—such as "There *could not be a* simpler thing: / He *could not be a* bird was clear"—lack this exact structural parallelism, as does "'Tis *well that* violence soon spends its power / And *well that* we forget our fear and pain" by Moore, while in lines such as "To the top of the porch! to the top of the wall!" in "Visit" the repetition is exact from the beginning of the phrase and so is of a different kind. Moore uses the type of construction under consideration here only in "My burning thirst *there let me* slake; / My parched lips *there let me* cool" and "'Tis the joy *of a* cockerel to strut and look big, / And to wallow in mire is the bliss *of a* pig," where "the joy of a cockerel" and "the bliss of a pig" are at opposite ends of their respective lines, and so contribute to a chiasmus. "The Night Before Christmas" affords an example: "A wink *of his* eye and a twist *of his* head." If we count only instances within a single line, we get eleven by Livingston, one in "The Night Before Christmas," and none by Moore.

Simple repetitions, as in "Now *dash away! dash away! dash away* all" in "Visit" are also very rare in Moore's verse, but much less so in Livingston's. The criterion here is that two or more consecutive words be repeated within a single line, but without any extra direct (as distinct from chiasmic) parallelism, such as would be created by the repeated words being preceded or followed by words of the same part of speech. Livingston has ten examples, Moore only two. Livingston: "Thro' thick *and thin and thin and thick*"; "To all, what *they wish*, if *they wish* nothing wrong"; "*Still urges* and *still urges* on"; "I rise *when I please, when I please* I lie down"; "For no *lov'ly girl* can a *lov'ly girl* bear"; "To gay *little things*, he can *little things* utter"; "*The sows*, my sweet madam—*the sows*, I repeat"; "Or ever united *a mind* to *a mind*"; "Be wanting there—*yet there! yet there* I'll find"; "Live *with my swain* and *with my swain* will die." Several of these lines also have the chiasmic pattern. The chiasmic last line of "The Night Before Christmas" also qualifies as containing a simple repetition: "Happy Christmas *to all*, and *to all* a good night." Moore offers only "'*Oh dear! oh dear!*' thought she, 'what shall I do?'"; and "'*To arms!* ye ever-ready belles, *to arms!*'"

Less distinctive, but nevertheless used at a rate 2.6 times greater by Livingston than by Moore are single lines within which at least two instances of "and" connect words of the same part of speech, as in "And he whistled, and shouted, and call'd them by name" in "Visit." Such lines are easily identified, and Livingston's verse affords ten, Moore's six.[1]

The figures for repetitions cited above are of minor evidential value, since Livingston's greater use of certain kinds of repetition is, to some extent, associated with his greater use of anapests. But, in combination, the diverse data in this chapter alone constitute strong stylistic evidence for assigning "The Night Before Christmas" to Livingston, rather than to Moore.

16

Common Words
That Discriminate

Despite the context-sensitive character of many pronouns and verbs, they have been used effectively in dozens of authorship studies, along with other high-frequency words. Very common words that, unlike "that," are ineffective as stand-alone discriminators may have value as members of a substantial group of words, each with *some* discriminatory power. So, as an initial trial, from word lists, ordered by frequency, for Moore and for Livingston, there were extracted each poet's top fifty words. For this purpose, "words" were distinct graphic units, and even those capitalized at the beginning of a verse line were distinguished from those in lower case. A similar list was compiled for "The Night Before Christmas," but from it only words that were listed among the top-fifty lists for Moore or Livingston and occurred at least twice were taken. This left twenty-six of the poem's words, all of which turned out to be present in the top-fifty lists for *both* Moore *and* Livingston. These twenty-six words were then listed in rank order of frequency in "The Night Before Christmas," Moore, and Livingston. The words and their rank orders are given in Table 16.1. Where words occur with equal frequency, the tie is broken by calculating an average rank value of the tied words. For example, in "Visit" "in" and "I" are each found ten times, which ranks them eighth-equal, so that they cover ranks eight and nine; the average of eight and nine is 8.5, and "in" and "I" each receive the rank 8.5. Similarly, in "Visit" "with," "they," and "The" are all found five times, which ranks them fourteenth-equal, so that they cover the ranks fourteen, fifteen, and sixteen, which have an average of 15, the rank that each of the three words receives. In "Visit" seven words are tied with two instances. Words occurring only once in the poem were too numerous to be worth including, and the many ties would have weakened the test now to be described, which requires this assigning of average ranks to ties and is, in any case, unreliable when the number of compared rankings exceeds thirty.

	NBC (Visit)	Livingston	Moore
TABLE 16.1: Rankings according to frequency of words that are in the top fifty for Livingston or Moore and occur at least twice in "The Night Before Christmas"			
the	1	1	1
a	2	6	6
his	3	10	13
of	4	3	4
and	5	2	2
to	6	5	3
And	7	4	5
in	8.5	8	7
I	8.5	9	10
all	10	13	11
was	11	18	23
on	12.5	14	18
he	12.5	25	26
with	15	12	9
they	15	22.5	17
The	15	7	8
when	18	22.5	25
my	18	11	16
When	18	20	24
their	23	15.5	14
not	23	24	20
from	23	17	12
With	23	21	19
But	23	15.5	15
as	23	26	21
A	23	19	22

There is a simple statistical test to determine whether the rank order for "Visit" of the twenty-six high-frequency words more closely matches the rank order for Livingston or for Moore. This is Spearman's rank-order correlation. There are now excellent websites that can carry out the necessary calculations from the raw data. The higher the value of the rank-order correlation coefficient (r_s), the closer the correlation. If the two rank orders are exactly the same, $r_s = 1$; if there is no correlation at all, $r_s = 0$.

Obviously the very nature of the English language ensures that there will be considerable correlation. The word "the" tops each list, for "Visit," Moore, and Livingston, and "a," "of," "and," "to," "And," "in," and "I" are also in each list's top ten, though in different orders.

The correlation between "Visit" and Livingston is $r_s = 0.7638$. The correlation between "Visit" and Moore is $r_s = 0.6633$. This means that the pattern of usage in "Visit" is appreciably closer to the pattern for the Livingston corpus than to the pattern for the Moore corpus.[1]

It so happens that this result is entirely independent of the rankings for "that" and "That," which are, of course, much higher in Moore's fifty-word list than in Livingston's. Since "that" occurs only once in "Visit" and "That" not at all, the word, with or without the capital, is excluded from the tested list of twenty-six.

Ranking tests are not very sensitive, however, and more information can be extracted from Moore's and Livingston's two lists of top-fifty words. We can compare the rates for each word in each poet's corpus of verse, and select those for which Livingston's rate is at least 1.2 times greater than Moore's (Livingston-favored words) and those for which Moore's is at least 1.2 times greater than Livingston's (Moore-favored words). This leaves us with eighteen Livingston-favored words, ranging from 1.2 to 2.6 times more frequent in his corpus than in Moore's, and twenty-two Moore-favored words, ranging from 1.2 to 14.5 times more frequent in his corpus than in Livingston's, in proportion to total numbers of words.[2] At the higher end of the Moore-favored words is "some," the next highest being "this," at 3.0. Some of the forty-one words have already been used in other word tests: "the," "The," "that," "That," and "some." These may be discarded, so that the present test will be entirely new and independent of those for which data is provided in Tables 13.1, 14.1, and 15.1.

**TABLE 16.2: High-frequency words more favored
by Moore or Livingston but not included in
Tables 13.1, 14.1, or 15.1**

Livingston poems

	Moore-favored	Livingston-favored	Percentage L/L+M
Acknowledgment	15	16	51.613
Acrostic	4	15	78.947
Alcmena	8	20	71.429
American Eagle	18	59	76.623

	Moore-favored	Livingston-favored	Percentage L/L+M
Anne	2	5	71.429
Apollo	13	14	51.852
Arabella	8	12	60.000
Bats (Fable)	12	18	60.000
Beekman	38	27	41.538
Belle	6	5	45.455
Carrier 1787	20	22	52.381
Carrier 1803	77	32	29.358
Carrier 1819	23	53	69.737
Careless	8	21	72.414
Catherine L Breese	2	4	66.667
Catherine Sleeping	9	14	60.870
Country	14	19	57.576
Crane and Fox	23	31	57.407
Dance	14	17	54.839
Death of Sarah	3	10	76.923
Deity	7	15	68.182
Dialogue	9	13	59.091
Easter	5	6	54.545
Eliza Hughes	1	5	83.333
Fly	6	11	64.706
Frog King	17	12	41.379
Frontier Song	1	8	88.889
Frosts (Habakkuk)	6	4	40.000
Gentleman	10	15	60.000
German Spa	12	13	52.000
Gilbert Courtland	2	7	77.778
God is Love	11	25	69.444
Henry Welles L	4	5	55.556
Hero	18	20	52.632
Hezekiah	5	22	81.481
Hogs	17	28	62.222
Isaiah	5	4	44.444
Joanna	5	15	75.000
Job	3	17	82.353
Lo from the East	4	6	60.000
Marriage	20	13	39.394
Marriage Tax	17	4	19.000
Midas	9	12	57.143
Monarchs	11	8	42.105
Montgomery	6	12	66.667
Original Poems	7	3	30.000
Past is the Hour	13	24	64.865
Procession	14	8	36.364

	Moore-favored	Livingston-favored	Percentage L/L+M
Queen	3	9	75.000
Rispah	9	18	66.667
Sages	11	19	63.333
Scots Wha Hae	2	10	83.333
Settlement	5	20	80.000
Sisters	4	11	73.333
Spadille	12	24	66.667
Tappen	7	8	53.333
Timmy	5	19	79.167
To Miss	9	5	35.714
To Miss Roses	3	9	75.000
Valentine	5	18	78.261
Vine	18	34	65.385
War	11	28	71.795
Wren	5	10	66.667
Totals	668	992	59.759
Mean of percentages for individual poems			61.417

Moore poems

	Moore-favored	Livingston-favored	Percentage L/L+M
Ball	52	47	47.475
Birthday	7	11	61.111
Cholera	47	27	36.486
Cowper	17	12	41.379
Daughter's Marriage	56	28	33.333
Farewell	14	23	62.162
Fashion	44	12	21.429
Flowers	17	10	37.037
Fragment Fair	39	11	22.000
From St. Nicholas	20	19	48.718
Gloves	14	4	22.222
Muse	23	26	53.061
Natural Philosophy	49	24	32.877
Nymphs	28	32	53.333
Old Dobbin	5	13	72.222
Organist	56	35	38.462
Paganini	14	3	17.647
Petrosa	23	8	25.806
Pig and Rooster	61	56	47.863
Portrait	31	12	27.907
Saratoga 1	102	50	32.895
Saratoga 2	50	41	45.055

	Moore-favored	Livingston-favored	Percentage L/L+M
Saratoga 3	153	96	38.554
Saratoga 4	116	63	35.196
Saratoga 5	85	35	29.167
Saratoga 6	105	45	30.000
Snow	18	2	10.000
Song	15	2	11.765
Southey	62	58	48.333
To a Lady	42	37	46.835
To Clem	5	3	37.500
To Fanny	9	4	30.769
Valentine	21	14	40.000
Water Drinker	102	37	26.619
Wife	50	21	29.577
Wine Drinker	85	43	33.594
Yellow Fever	106	18	14.516
Totals	1743	982	36.037
Mean of percentages for individual poems			36.295
Night Before Xmas	34	53	60.920

Table 16.2 presents the results. Three very short poems with almost no relevant data have been excluded: Livingston's "Catherine Breese Livingston" has only two test words and his "Without Distinction" only four, while Moore's "Sand" has only one. A *t*-test reveals that the chance that percentages for Moore and Livingston poems were drawn from a single population is infinitesimally small (t = 8.16, 98 d.f., far beyond even the p <0.000001 level of significance). The percentage for "The Night Before Christmas" places it almost exactly at the mean for Livingston poems and much above the mean for Moore poems. But, with poems of such varied length, both corpora have a large spread of percentages, so that the inferential standard deviation for Moore is 14.106, which means that the percentage for "The Night Before Christmas" falls within both Moore's two-standard-deviation range (8.083–64.507) and his actual range (10.000–72.222). Nevertheless, it is obvious into which poetic corpus "The Night Before Christmas" more comfortably fits. As a Livingston poem it is right in the middle; as a Moore poem it is an outlier.

"Old Dobbin," at the extreme upper end of Moore's range, is itself an oddity. It is written to a formula popular at the time. In two stanzas the poet invokes his muse to sing the praises of his faithful horse, and then follow four stanzas, each composed of a three-line question and an answering refrain, beginning:

Who, in this world of varying ill,
Keeps on his even tenor still,
Nor fails his duty to fulfil?
                    Old Dobbin.

Numerous verses had been published on this same pattern, such as this in the *Weekly Museum* of 16 March 1805:

Who fed me from her gentle breast,
And hush'd me in her arms to rest,
And on my cheek sweet kisses prest
                    My Mother.

By 8 February 1806 a correspondent to the *Boston Magazine* was protesting: "Many elegantly, pathetic poems have lately appeared in the papers, addressed to My father, My mother, My sister, My brother, My uncle, My aunt, My grandmother, &c. &c. In humble imitation, permit me to address My Boot." "My Barber" and "My Bonnet" were among the successors. The form already invited parody.[3]

17

Words of Medium-High Frequency

The success of high-frequency (top 50) words in discriminating between poems by Moore and poems by Livingston is an encouragement to experiment with words of medium-high frequency—the sixty next most highly ranked in either poet's body of verse. From lists of these were extracted the words that were used at rates at least 1.2 times higher by Moore than by Livingston, and vice versa. It turned out that only two were between 1.2 and 1.3 times as frequent, and both of these were very close to a more demanding 1.3 cut-off point. Sixty words were checked, rather than the fifty of the previous test, because, being of lower frequency, items in this category naturally provided fewer data, in terms of total occurrences. However, a higher proportion of these medium-high frequency words qualified as discriminators. There were thirty-four Livingston-favored words, thirty-seven Moore-favored words, with the word "vain" having been eliminated because of my use of "in vain" as a Moore marker. Again, capitalized and uncapitalized words were regarded as different.[1] The results are displayed in Table 17.1.

TABLE 17.1: Medium-high-frequency words more favored by Moore or Livingston			
Livingston poems			
	Moore-favored	**Livingston-favored**	**Percentage L/L+M**
Acknowledgment	7	8	53.333
Acrostic	3	2	40.000
Alcmena	5	11	68.750
American Eagle	15	35	70.000

	Moore-favored	Livingston-favored	Percentage L/L+M
Anne	4	2	33.333
Apollo	6	12	66.667
Arabella	3	5	62.500
Bats (Fable)	7	10	58.824
Beekman	18	19	51.351
Belle	6	7	53.846
Carrier 1787	9	5	35.714
Carrier 1803	20	24	54.545
Carrier 1819	22	34	60.714
Careless	7	3	30.000
Catherine Breese L	1	2	66.667
Catherine L Breese	3	4	57.143
Catherine Sleeping	9	6	40.000
Country	10	10	50.000
Crane and Fox	14	27	65.854
Dance	12	10	45.455
Death of Sarah	6	5	45.455
Deity	2	8	80.000
Dialogue	5	7	58.333
Easter	4	8	66.667
Eliza Hughes	0	3	100.000
Fly	1	5	83.333
Frog King	6	9	60.000
Frontier Song	3	7	70.000
Frosts (Habakkuk)	0	2	100.000
Gentleman	5	12	70.588
German Spa	6	6	50.000
Gilbert Courtland	3	6	66.667
God is Love	3	3	50.000
Henry Welles L	2	9	81.818
Hero	12	19	61.290
Hezekiah	7	5	41.667
Hogs	6	11	64.706
Isaiah	8	5	38.462
Joanna	4	14	77.778
Job	3	5	62.500
Lo from the East	3	4	57.143
Marriage	6	2	25.000
Marriage Tax	3	7	70.000
Midas	3	6	66.667
Monarchs	1	6	85.714
Montgomery	1	6	85.714
Original Poems	0	4	100.000
Past is the Hour	8	7	46.667

	Moore-favored	Livingston-favored	Percentage L/L+M
Procession	7	6	46.154
Queen	1	5	83.333
Rispah	3	10	76.923
Sages	2	17	89.474
Scots Wha Hae	0	3	100.000
Settlement	9	17	65.385
Sisters	2	9	81.818
Spadille·	10	11	52.381
Tappen	4	11	73.333
Timmy	7	15	68.182
To Miss	2	7	77.778
To Miss Roses	2	5	71.429
Valentine	4	3	42.857
Vine	11	18	62.069
War	4	16	80.000
Without Distinction	3	2	40.000
Wren	3	7	70.000
Totals	366	589	61.675
Mean of percentages for individual poems			63.261
Mean of percentages for individual poems with a total of at least 10 words in the second and third columns			60.814

Moore poems

	Moore-favored	Livingston-favored	Percentage L/L+M
Ball	39	10	20.408
Birthday	14	8	36.364
Cholera	30	10	25.000
Cowper	14	16	53.333
Daughter's Marriage	31	11	26.190
Farewell	23	21	47.727
Fashion	41	7	14.583
Flowers	7	1	12.500
Fragment Fair	31	8	20.513
From St. Nicholas	22	10	31.250
Gloves	4	4	50.000
Muse	27	6	18.182
Natural Philosophy	43	15	25.862
Nymphs	15	12	44.444
Old Dobbin	12	4	25.000
Organist	32	21	39.623
Paganini	7	4	36.364
Petrosa	8	8	50.000

	Moore-favored	Livingston-favored	Percentage L/L+M
Pig and Rooster	38	22	36.667
Portrait	22	4	15.385
Sand	3	2	40.000
Saratoga 1	70	12	14.634
Saratoga 2	36	19	34.545
Saratoga 3	115	52	31.138
Saratoga 4	81	33	28.947
Saratoga 5	51	22	30.137
Saratoga 6	61	20	24.691
Snow	13	5	27.778
Song	10	3	23.077
Southey	34	16	32.000
To a Lady	35	25	41.667
To Clem	7	0	00.000
To Fanny	7	3	30.000
Valentine	19	3	13.636
Water Drinker	53	20	27.397
Wife	33	9	21.429
Wine Drinker	68	30	30.612
Yellow Fever	57	18	24.000
Totals	1213	494	28.940
Mean of percentages for individual poems			29.081
Mean of percentages for individual poems with a total of at least 10 words in the second and third columns			29.489
Night Before Xmas	25	29	53.704

In this case, results for every poem have been tabulated, but statistical analysis is restricted to those that afford at least ten test words. It needs no t-test to prove that the two authorial groups of poems are utterly distinctive. Livingston's mean of 60.814 for individual poems with at least ten test words is more than twice Moore's of 29.489. The percentage of 53.704 for "The Night Before Christmas" lies just outside Moore's actual range of 14.583–53.333 for such poems but well within Livingston's of 30.000–89.474. These ranges closely match the two-standard-deviation ranges (9.189–49.789, inferential standard deviation 10.145 for Moore; 32.632–88.996, inferential standard deviation 14.091 for Livingston). Of course, even though the poems offering fewest data have been discarded from these analyses, the fact that Livingston's poems are, on average, much shorter than Moore's, leads to his having both theoretical and actual wider ranges of percentages. But once again "The Night Before Christmas" sits comfortably among Livingston's poems (at 0.505 standard deviations from his mean), but would be abnormal for Moore (at 2.387 standard deviations from his mean). This would be so, even if we were to include the poems with fewer than ten test words.

Notably, those poems by Moore that score most highly in Table 17.1—"Cowper," "Gloves," and "Petrosa"—all had low scores in Table 16.2, those for "Gloves" and "Petrosa" being especially low. "Old Dobbin," the poem by Moore that had the highest percentage of Livingston-favored words in Table 16.2, has a markedly low percentage in Table 17.1. Also notable are the poor performances of "The Pig and the Rooster" and "From Saint Nicholas," so often invoked as analogous to "The Night Before Christmas." In their use of medium-high-frequency words they are quintessentially Moore-like, while "The Night Before Christmas" patently is not.

Criticizing Donald Foster, Joe Nickell warns of "the dangers of subjectivity and bias" when citing "subtleties of vocabulary and phrasing" and points out that, on Moore's side of the ledger, "The Night Before Christmas" contains a lot of similes, such as "his nose like a cherry," and that "The Pig and the Rooster" also contains several, whereas the letter to "Mistress Van Kleeck" has none.[2] Nickell combats selective bias with selective bias. In the test described in this chapter, the similes in "Visit" are fully taken into account, because "like" is counted among the objectively chosen Moore-favored words, and "Visit" uses it as many as eight times. Even so, the poem emerges as more akin to verse by Livingston than to verse by Moore. It is obvious, however, that the similes in "Visit" serve the particular function of conveying a vivid picture of the elfin St. Nick. Without those eight instances of "like"—six of them crowded into a mere nine lines, in a manner unique within either poet's work—the percentage of Livingston-favored test words in Table 17.1 would be 64.043, even further outside Moore's range. The other word that can introduce a simile, "as" (or "As"), happens to be used by Livingston at higher rates than by Moore.

At any rate, the measure of authorship described in this chapter is entirely free from "subjectivity and bias," the relevant data having been compiled according to mathematical criteria specified in advance.

18

Checking the Tests:
Moore's Manuscript Poems

On every one of our tests, "The Night Before Christmas" belongs with Livingston's poems, not with Moore's. Poems by Moore that achieve Livingston-like rates in one or more tests are like Moore rather than Livingston on other tests. "Nymphs," for example, is Livingston-like on Tables 10.1, 12.1, and 13.1, but its Table 11.1 figures are typical of Moore, while in Table 15.1 it has as many as five Moore markers (where "Visit" has none). In Table 16.2 "Old Dobbin," "Birthday," and "Farewell" exceed "Visit" in their percentages of Livingston-favored words, while both "Old Dobbin" and "Birthday," which are short, are devoid of the Moore markers. But all three of these poems are closer to Moore than Livingston on other tests, while the "that" rate for "Farewell" is as high as 28.037—a figure strongly associating it with Moore. Even the very short "To Clem," which is like Livingston in Tables 11.1 and 13.1 and has no Moore markers in Table 15.1, is most unlike Livingston and typical of Moore in Tables 16.2 and 17.1, as is the similarly short "To Fanny," which, like "To Clem" is among the more Livingston-like poems in its Table 13.1 percentage and has no Moore markers in Table 15.1. "The Organist," which is the Moore poem with figures closest to "Visit" in Table 11.1, is not only unlike Livingston in features displayed in other tables but also has as many as eight Moore markers. In short, no poem by Moore is even remotely as Livingstonian as "The Night Before Christmas," which is repeatedly and consistently associated with Livingston's, rather than Moore's, corpus.

However, we have deliberately been holding in reserve the unpublished poems in Moore's manuscript notebook, and it is to these that we must now turn.[1] Might any one of them be mistakenly classified by our tests as Livingston's?

Moore's collection of *Poems* (1844) was published two decades after he is alleged to have composed "The Night Before Christmas," and the poems in his manuscript notebook are dated 1843–52, so the last was written thirty years after the Christmas poem appeared in the *Troy Sentinel*. A poet's style may develop over such a period of time. "Charles Elphinstone" is a long pseudo-autobiographical "epic" blank-verse narrative about the struggle between the powers of heaven and hell for the hero's "immortal soul." It is so remote in manner and matter from "The Night Before Christmas" that breaking it down into sections and offering counts of all the authorial data is scarcely warranted. The other twelve original poems, in a lighter vein, mostly addressed to young women, and averaging 290 words in length, have been referred to in defenses of Moore's authorship of "The Night Before Christmas" as establishing his capacity for composing such popular verse.[2] So they require investigation. Their aging author's outlook on the world appears to have mellowed somewhat, but are there any significant changes in his lexical and stylistic habits?

We may begin by considering the "Moore markers." "Charles Elphinstone" has no fewer than 53 altogether: "some" 21, "at length" 9, "in vain" 3, "many a" 2, "oft" 12, and "that's" 6. Moore reserves "at length" for narrative. The rate for Moore markers in "Charles Elphinstone" is one per 258 words.

Results for the shorter poems (with the word length in parentheses) are as follows:

Valentine-MS (269): "that's" 1
Irish Valentine (590): "that's" 1
West Point (486): "some" 2, "many a" 1, "oft" 1
Caroline's Album (181):—
Catherine's Album (147): "many a" 1
For a Kiss (198): "some" 1, "oft" 1
Theresa's Flower (147): "many a" 1, "that's" 1
Jeanette New Year (465): "many a" 2, "in vain" 1, "that's" 1
Eliza in England (272):—
Margaret (155): "many a" 1, "some" 1
Basket of Flowers (262): "many a" 1
Newport Beach (307): "oft" 1

Ten of the twelve poems—listed in the order in which they appear in the notebook—are differentiated from "The Night Before Christmas" by their inclusion of one or more of the Moore markers. The two exceptions are one-third and half the length of the Christmas poem. Besides, "Eliza in England" contains "various," which—as we shall see in Chapter 21—is used on eleven other occasions in printed or manuscript verse by Moore (three times in "Charles Elphinstone") but never in Livingston's poems.

The results for high-frequency words more favored by Moore or Livingston also associate the manuscript poems firmly with Moore's published poems and distinguish them from "The Night Before Christmas." In the lengthy "Charles Elphinstone," Livingston-favored words occur 809 times, Moore-favored words 1,024 times, giving a percentage of Livingston-favored words of 44.135, far below the percentage of 60.920 for "The Night Before Christmas." Figures for the shorter poems are shown in Table 18.1. They are similar to figures for Moore's published poems, as tabulated in Table 16.2. "Caroline's Album" and "Eliza in England," which contained no Moore markers, are on the present test clearly differentiated from "The Night Before Christmas" (60.920), which is close to the Livingston mean of 61.417.

TABLE 18.1: High-frequency words more favored by Moore or Livingston, as in Table 16.2

Moore manuscript notebook poems

	Moore-favored	Livingston-favored	Percentage L/L+M
Valentine-MS	11	14	56.000
Irish Valentine	52	51	49.515
West Point	28	32	53.333
Caroline's Album	15	11	42.308
Catherine's Album	12	10	45.455
For a Kiss	26	8	23.529
Theresa's Flower	16	10	38.462
Jeanette New Year	27	32	54.237
Eliza in England	21	19	47.500
Margaret	14	7	33.333
Basket of Flowers	24	18	42.857
Newport Beach	15	9	37.500

Results for medium-high-frequency words are given in Table 18.2. Although these poems of 1843–52 are more Livingston-like on this measure than Moore's earlier poems, only "Irish Valentine" has a (slightly) higher percentage of Livingston-favored words than "The Night Before Christmas," though "Theresa's Flower" runs it close. But these two poems, particularly the latter, fall well short of "The Night Before Christmas" and Livingston's mean in Table 18.1. The percentage for "Charles Elphinstone" on the present measure is 40.000.

TABLE 18.2: Medium-high-frequency words more favored by Moore or Livingston, as in Table 17.1

Moore manuscript notebook poems

	Moore-favored	Livingston-favored	Percentage L/L+M
Valentine-MS	12	11	47.800
Irish Valentine	23	29	55.769
West Point	17	15	46.875
Caroline's Album	5	3	37.500
Catherine's Album	9	4	30.769
For a Kiss	10	2	16.667
Theresa's Flower	6	6	50.000
Jeanette New Year	24	16	40.000
Eliza in England	11	7	38.889
Margaret	14	7	33.333
Basket of Flowers	16	15	48.387
Newport Beach	10	5	33.333

The most effective of all discriminators between Moore and Livingston have been the phoneme pairs, as displayed in Table 12.1. These are a measure of how the poets combine words and sounds within lines. Their choices are both lexical and phonetic. Table 18.3 shows the data for the twelve short notebook poems. The percentages of Livingston-favored phoneme pairs consort well with those for Moore's published poems. The mean for the twelve is 40.783, close to that for Moore's poems in Table 12.1 (42.912) and far from the mean for Livingston (66.654) and the percentage for "The Night Before Christmas" (64.912), which, on this test too, remains as unlike Moore's notebook verse as it is unlike his published verse.

The long narrative poem "Charles Elphinstone" is also typical of Moore in its phoneme pairs. The overall percentage of Livingston-favored pairs is 45.714 and the seven parts into which it is divided have percentages of 46.008, 46.226, 46.875, 46.667, 45.149, 42.623, and 46.711. The consistency is remarkable.

Less reliable, but nevertheless useful, discriminators were the categories of phoneme pairs more favored by Moore or by Livingston, as shown in Table 11.1. Results for the twelve short poems in Moore's manuscript notebook are presented in Table 18.4. The percentages for all but three of the poems—"Irish Valentine," "Caroline's Album," and "Eliza in England"—are closer to Moore's mean (44.647) in Table 11.1 than to

TABLE 18.3: Phoneme pairs more favored by Moore or Livingston, as in Table 12.1

Moore manuscript notebook poems

	Moore-favored	Livingston-favored	Percentage L/L+M
Valentine-MS	13	11	45.833
Irish Valentine	38	16	29.630
West Point	19	18	48.649
Caroline's Album	12	7	36.842
Catherine's Album	12	8	40.000
For a Kiss	13	8	38.095
Theresa's Flower	16	10	38.462
Jeanette New Year	22	21	48.837
Eliza in England	16	8	33.333
Margaret	6	4	40.000
Basket of Flowers	9	9	50.000
Newport Beach	15	11	42.308

TABLE 18.4: Categories of phoneme pairs more favored by Livingston or Moore, as in Table 11.1

	Moore-favored	Livingston-favored	Percentage L/L+M
Valentine-MS	34	32	48.465
Irish Valentine	102	117	53.425
West Point	72	61	45.865
Caroline's Album	22	33	60.000
Catherine's Album	26	15	36.585
For a Kiss	33	28	45.902
Theresa's Flower	22	15	40.541
Jeanette New Year	79	67	45.890
Eliza in England	28	45	61.644
Margaret	24	21	46.667
Basket of Flowers	42	31	42.466
Newport Beach	43	42	49.412

Livingston's (55.175), and none of the three exceptions is quite as distant from Moore's mean as "The Night Before Christmas" (63.483).

The three notebook poems that were most Livingston-like on the immediately previous test (though far from being so on the test before that) are typical of Moore in their rates of use of "that," displayed in Table

18.5. In Table 14.1, counts for "that" were derived from blocks of text of at least 500 words. So it is not surprising that there is considerable variability in the rates for the notebook poems. But they are all above the Livingston mean in Table 14.1 (6.319) and far above the rate for "The Night Before Christmas" (1.845). The rate for the combined block of twelve poems, with 59 instances of "that" in 3,479 words is 16.959, somewhat higher than the Table 14.1 mean rate for Moore poems of 12.210. The overall rate for "Charles Elphinstone," with 200 instances of "that" in 13,670 words, is 14.631. Again, Table 18.5 reveals nothing to alter our conclusions that no poem by Moore is as consistently Livingston-like, on a two-poet comparison, as "The Night Before Christmas."

TABLE 18.5: Instances of "that" per 1,000 words in poems from Moore's manuscript notebook			
	Words in poem	**Instances of "that"**	**Rate**
Valentine-MS	269	3	11.152
Irish Valentine	590	13	22.034
West Point	486	9	18.519
Caroline's Album	181	6	33.149
Catharine's Album	147	2	13.605
For a Kiss	198	3	15.152
Theresa's Flower	147	1	6.803
Jeanette New Year	465	12	25.806
Eliza in England	272	2	7.353
Margaret	155	1	6.452
Basket of Flowers	262	3	11.450
Newport Beach	307	4	13.029

Table 10.1 displayed Moore's and Livingston's contrasting uses of phoneme pairs with phonetic AH and phonetic T as the first element, with Livingston using higher percentages of AH. Table 18.6 gives the results for Moore's manuscript notebook poems.

The mean of 46.273 for the individual notebook poems is marginally closer to Moore's (39.998) in Table 10.1 than to Livingston's (52.661), but the range from 30.769 to 65.383 is wide. Evidently Moore's unpublished pieces associated with young women called for more instances of the definite and indefinite article—the major contributors to phoneme pairs beginning with AH—than did his published poems. All the same, "Newport Beach" is the only notebook poem to score more highly than "The Night

TABLE 18.6: Phoneme pairs with phonetic AH and phonetic T as first element, as in Table 10.1

Moore manuscript notebook poems

	AH	T	Percentage AH/AH plus T
Valentine-MS	19	18	51.351
Irish Valentine	58	73	44.275
West Point	42	55	43.299
Caroline's Album	24	22	52.174
Catherine's Album	8	18	30.769
For a Kiss	16	21	43.243
Theresa's Flower	10	14	41.667
Jeanette New Year	31	55	36.047
Eliza in England	23	16	58.974
Margaret	8	13	38.095
Basket of Flowers	17	17	50.000
Newport Beach	34	18	65.385

Before Christmas" (60.577), and seven of the poems are, on this test, decidedly more Moore-like than Livingston-like. The seven include "Theresa's Flower" and "Margaret," which had the lowest rates of "that" and so were the least clearly associated with Moore on the previous test. The percentage for AH/AH plus T in "Charles Elphinstone" is 42.572, and T is higher than AH for each of the seven parts.

As expected, Table 18.6's totals for AH as the first element in a phoneme pair are closely matched in the combined totals for "a" and "the," as shown in Table 18.7, where the last column gives these totals as percentages of all the words in each poem.

It is clear that in these late occasional pieces Moore does indeed use the definite and indefinite articles more frequently than in his published *Poems* (1844). For two of the notebook poems, "Caroline's Album" and "Newport Beach" the percentages are outside his range in Table 13.1, in the case of the former of these far outside. And the mean of 7.928 percent for these twelve notebook poems is higher than that for Moore's poems in Table 13.1 (6.127 percent), and more in line with the unpublished "To Fanny" (8.824 percent) and "To Clem" (8.738 percent) in Table 13.1. The percentage of 13.260 for "Caroline's Album" is a salutary reminder that once in a while an author may write a poem in which he or she uses some word, phoneme, or other linguistic unit at a rate that statistical analysis of his other works would find highly improbable. It remains true, however, that "Caroline's Album" is

TABLE 18.7: Definite and indefinite articles in
Moore's manuscript notebook poems

	Total words	"a"	"the"	"a"+"the"	percent "a" + "the"
Valentine-MS	269	2	17	19	7.063
Irish Valentine	590	30	25	55	9.322
West Point	486	9	32	41	8.436
Caroline's Album	181	3	21	24	13.260
Catherine's Album	147	2	6	8	5.442
For a Kiss	198	3	13	16	8.081
Theresa's Flower	147	5	5	10	6.803
Jeanette New Year	465	5	24	29	6.237
Eliza in England	292	0	22	22	8.088
Margaret	155	2	6	8	5.161
Basket of Flowers	262	5	12	17	6.489
Newport Beach	307	4	29	33	10.749

the only one of these poems that, like "The Night Before Christmas," attains a rate above 11.000 percent, whereas fourteen of Livingston's poems do. Besides, the shorter the poem, the more likely it is to be anomalous, because of purely random factors, and "Caroline's Album" is short, only a third the length of "The Night Before Christmas." The percentages in Table 18.7 are not matched by the long "Charles Elphinstone," in which Moore reverts to a rate of use of "a" plus "the" even lower than in *Poems*. In "Charles Elphinstone" 669 of 13,670 words, or 4.894 percent, are "a" or "the."

Table 7.1 presented rates of occurrence of nouns modified by attributive adjectives, with poems of fewer than 500 words amalgamated with others to form blocks of text of at least that size. Rates were expressed as per 550 words, the approximate length of "The Night Before Christmas" (542 words). Table 18.8 shows the rates for Moore's twelve notebook poems. Since they range from 147 to 590 words, we can anticipate a wider random spread than in Table 7.1's blocks of 500 or more words.

The rates for eight of the poems are well above the mean of 41.286 for Livingston's blocks in Table 7.1. Those for "Irish Valentine" and "For a Kiss" are considerably higher than that for "Visit" (16.2) but not far above the lower limit of Livingston's Table 7.1 range (24.1) and "Irish Valentine" is of block-size length. Both "Irish Valentine" and "For a Kiss" are in anapests. So it seems likely that the meter militates against the liberal use of adjectives. The rates for the anapestic "The Pig and the Rooster" and "From Saint Nicholas" were 39.4 and 36.0 respectively. It would be rea-

Table 18.8: Nouns modified by attributive adjectives per 550 words in Moore's manuscript notebook poems		
	Size of text in words	Rate
Valentine-MS	269	65.4
Irish Valentine	590	28.0
West Point	486	71.3
Caroline's Album	181	54.7
Catharine's Album	147	63.6
For a Kiss	198	27.8
Theresa's Flower	147	59.9
Jeanette New Year	465	65.1
Eliza in England	272	40.4
Margaret	155	56.8
Basket of Flowers	262	37.8
Newport Beach	307	66.3

sonable to infer that Livingston's lower rates than Moore's are in part due to his much greater use of anapests, and that Moore could conceivably have written a poem in anapests that was as sparing of adjectives as "The Night Before Christmas." Nevertheless, although the adjective-plus-noun test evidently points less clearly to Livingston's authorship of "Visit" than appeared in Chapter 7, the extremely low rate in "Visit" does speak in his favor. Among individual Livingston poems, the rate for the "Monarchs Rebus" (157 words) is as low as 10.5; for "German Spa" (125 words), 17.6; for the "Sages Rebus" (274 words), 18.1; and for the "Deity Rebus" (172 words), 19.2.

Consideration of Moore's two notebook poems that are in anapests brings us to another point. "For a Kiss" has twenty tetrameter lines. It contains only three disyllabic words in metrically unstressed positions, so the rate of 15 per hundred lines in this very short piece is close to that for "The Night Before Christmas" (14.3, as in Table 5.1). The sixty-eight-line "Irish Valentine" is in alternating tetrameters and trimeters, the equivalent of a fraction under 60 tetrameter lines. It has thirteen metrically unstressed disyllables, a rate of 21.7 per hundred lines, which is much closer to Moore's average for "The Pig and the Rooster" and "From Saint Nicholas" (25.7) than to Livingston's average (12.6). In his later years Moore was still not handling the anapestic meter as adeptly as it is handled in "The Night Before Christmas." In fact, "Irish Valentine," which aims to be rollicking, is merely gawky.

Moore's notebook poems share two rhymes with "The Night Before

Christmas": "below"–"snow" in "Irish Valentine" and "elf"–"self" (in the form "thyself") in "Caroline's Album." *Literature Online* shows the first of these to have been very common in the period; "elf"–"self," as noted in Chapter 8, is much less so, though also used by Livingston. However, "Caroline's Album" is dated 1845, the year after Moore had published "The Night Before Christmas" among his own *Poems*, so it might well be argued that his choice of this rhyme in "Caroline's Album" was influenced by its presence in "The Night Before Christmas," without his necessarily being the author of the Christmas poem. In Tables 18.1, 18.2, and 18.3 "Caroline's Album" is clearly aligned with Moore's verse and differentiated from Livingston's.

Another characteristic of the rhyme words in "Visit," as noted in Chapter 8, is that as many as 75 percent of them are nouns. In several poems by Livingston, but none by Moore, the percentage is almost as high. Among Moore's shorter notebook poems "Theresa's Flower" has the highest percentage, namely 62.5. No other poem has 60 percent or more, and the overall figure for all twelve is exactly 50 percent. A sampling of "Charles Elphinstone" suggests that its percentage is appreciably lower.

We saw in Chapter 15 that "The Night Before Christmas" has the collocations "To the" and "With the" beginning lines, and that Livingston's poems contain 14 instances of "To the" and 13 of "With the" while Moore's poems contain none. Moore's avoidance of these line beginnings continues in his notebook poems, even in the two anapestic pieces. "Charles Elphinstone" does however have one instance of "And the" and "Irish Valentine" has two instances. "And the," which also occurs in "The Night Before Christmas," had been found in Chapter 15 to occur twenty-eight times in Livingston's verse, only once in Moore's. In the same chapter it was noted that on forty occasions Moore begins a line with "And," (the conjunction followed by a comma) and that Livingston never does. Moore's habit is continued into the notebook poems, all in his own handwriting, with twenty-five instances in "Charles Elphinstone," two in each of "Valentine," the anapestic "Irish Valentine," and "Jeanette's New Year," and one in "Theresa's Flower." This is further confirmation that Moore's use of a comma after "And," absent from "The Night Before Christmas," is a personal characteristic, not an artifact of the printer of his *Poems* (1844), and that the difference between him and Livingston in this respect is not solely a consequence of Moore's much less frequent recourse to anapests.

Also discussed was Livingston's liking for, and Moore's almost complete avoidance of, a particular type of rhetorical pattern involving the exact repetition of two or more consecutive words in the midst of parallel phrase constructions. There are, however, four instances among Moore's notebook poems. "Irish Valentine" affords "With a purse *full of* shiners; and heart *full of* joy"; "Till the back of your head seem'd *beginning to* frown, / And the folk were *beginning to* stare"; and "And I thought it was best, at the top *of my* letter, / Just to give you a sketch *of my* phiz"; while "Health *to the* body, vigor *to the* mind" occurs in "Newport Beach." But in this last example there is a crucial difference from the fourteen examples in Livingston's poems and one in "Visit." Moore likes to write of "the mind": the collocation can be found ten times in his *Poems*. In the notebook it occurs six times in "Charles Elphinstone," twice in "West Point," and once in "Theresa's Flower," as well as in "Newport Beach." It turns up only twice in Livingston's verse. Its incorporation into the repetitive structure of the "Newport Beach" line robs that line of its otherwise Livingstonian character. Further, of the three items in "Irish Valentine" only one is of the single-line type, which is found ten times in Livingston's poems, once in "Visit," and never in Moore's *Poems* or three loose-leaf pieces.

Of the two other categories of repetition that were discussed in Chapter 15 and shown to associate "Visit" with Livingston—(a) simple repetitions within a single line and without further parallelism, and (b) strings of the same part of speech linked by "and" within a single line—neither is represented in the verse of Moore's notebook.

Finally, nowhere among Moore's notebook poems does he use a nasal near-rhyme of the kind favored by Livingston and exemplified in "Vixen"–"Blixem" of "The Night Before Christmas," and nor can there be found an instance of the anomalous placement of the exclamation mark characteristic of Livingston and so conspicuous in the original *Troy Sentinel* punctuation of the couplet naming St. Nick's eight reindeer.

It seems clear that when, as in "Irish Valentine," the aging Moore attempted anapestic verse, long after he is alleged to have composed "The Night Before Christmas," he became somewhat more Livingston-like in certain respects—the use of head-of-line collocations and of repetitions within parallelism, for example, and also in such important tests as categories of phoneme pairs, articles, and medium-high-frequency words. But "Irish Valentine" is glaringly non–Livingston-like in its favored phoneme pairs, its high-frequency words, and its rate of use of "that," and fails to match "Visit" in avoidance of disyllables in unstressed positions, avoidance of adjective–noun combinations, and liking for phoneme pairs in which the first element is AH rather than T. It contains the Moore marker "that's." Unlike several of Livingston's poems, it does not approach "Visit" in its percentage of nouns as rhyme words ("Visit" 76.8; "Irish" 47.1).

In short, if we did not know whether the poems in Moore's manuscript notebook were by him or by Livingston, our full range of tests would, in combination, categorize every one of them as much more probably Moore's. In this they contrast sharply with "The Night Before Christmas," which is *consistently* associated more closely with Livingston.[3]

19

The Moore Creation Myth

The earliest written account of Clement Clarke Moore's supposed composition of "The Night Before Christmas" and explanation of how the poem reached the *Troy Sentinel* of 23 December 1823 is to be found in documents held by the New-York Historical Society and published anonymously in the *New-York Historical Society Quarterly Bulletin* in 1919, under the title "Original Documents from the Archives of the Society. The Autograph Copy of the 'Visit from St. Nicholas.'"[1] A letter, dated 15 March 1862, from T. W. C. Moore to the Society's Librarian, George H. Moore, explains that Clement Clarke Moore had provided an autograph copy of "Visit." It is reproduced in facsimile, with Clement Clarke Moore's annotation "1862, March 13th. originally written many years ago." George H. Moore was no relation to Clement, but T. W. C. Moore and Clement, though not related by blood, were both nephews of the same aunt and uncle. T. W. C. Moore writes that "these lines were composed for his two daughters, as a Christmas present, about 40 years ago.—They were copied by a relative of Dr. Moores [*sic*] in her Album, from which a copy was made by a friend of hers, from Troy, and, much to the surprise of the Author, were published (for the first time) in a Newspaper of that city.—" In a new paragraph he adds: "In an interview that I had yesterday with Dr. Moore, he told me that a portly, rubicund, Dutchman, living in the neighbourhood of his fathers [*sic*] country seat, Chelsea, suggested to him the idea of making St. Nicholas the hero of this 'Christmas piece' for his children" (111, 114).

The article expands on the letter, identifying the "relative" as Harriet Butler, specifying no album, and naming the editor of the *Troy Sentinel*:

> The story of this charming Christmas poem runs, that Miss Harriet Butler, daughter of the Reverend David Butler, rector of St. Paul's Episcopal Church,

Troy, New York, was visiting the Moore family in New York City in 1823, when she met with the poem. Delighted with its rhythm and happy conceptions she requested the privilege of making a copy of it. On her return to Troy she sent it to the Editor of the *Troy Sentinel*, Orville L. Holley, who published it in the issue of December 23, 1823 with an introductory paragraph in which he thanked the unknown sender and complimented the unknown author. It is recorded that the publication of it caused Professor Moore regret and chagrin as he did not wish it to be published. (114–15)

These remarks, however, date from 1919. They probably derive from whatever source of information served William S. Pelletreau for his biography of Moore published in 1897, with an account of "The Night Before Christmas":

> This little poem ... was written in 1822, as a Christmas present for his children, which was highly appreciated. Among their many friends was the family of Rev. Dr. David Butler, then rector of St. Paul's church, in the city of Troy. The eldest daughter of Dr. Butler, while visiting the Moore family, saw the poem and quickly copied the verses into her "album" (an article which every young lady at that time was supposed to possess), intending to read them to the children at the rectory. She was so impressed with their value that she sent a copy to an editor, and they were first printed in the "Troy Sentinel," of December 23, 1823, accompanied with a cut illustrating Santa Claus on his rounds, and preceded by an introduction by the editor. Strange to say the name of the author did not then appear. It is said that Dr. Moore was displeased at first, as in his opinion the poem has slight literary merit.[2]

Pelletreau also mentions the "rubicund Dutchman." Noting George H. Moore's obtaining of the autograph copy, which Pelletreau reproduces, he writes: "The venerable author stated in a letter, that when a boy, he first heard the story of St. Nicholas from a rubicund Dutchman who lived near his father's residence."

There are interesting minor discrepancies between these accounts, which must ultimately, through whatever intermediaries, derive from Clement Clarke Moore himself. The New-York Historical Society letter specifies two copyists—the "relative" and "a friend of hers." Both Pelletreau and the *Quarterly Bulletin* article that accompanies the letter replace Moore's vague "relative" with Harriet Butler and have her sending the poem to the *Sentinel* herself, though, since both state that she had copied it into her personal "album," which she would hardly have released to the newspaper, a further copy is implied: indeed Pelletreau says that she first copied the poem into her album and then "sent a copy" to an editor.

However, by 1862 Moore had known for eighteen years—through a letter sent him by *Troy Sentinel* owner Norman Tuttle on 23 February

1844—that the newspaper's editor, Orville Holley, had received copy for his printing of "Visit" in 1823 from Sarah Sackett, whose husband's crockery store was within a few meters of his office, a fact not, however, mentioned by Tuttle.[3] If either Harriet Butler or some unidentified "relative" were instrumental in conveying a text of "Visit" in Moore's house to the *Troy Sentinel*, Sarah Sackett would have to have been the "friend of hers" who completed the chain of transmission.

In the light of Tuttle's information, Donald Foster employed Occam's razor and simply dismissed the Harriet Butler story. But other believers in Livingston's authorship of "Visit," aiming to account for the poem's becoming associated with Moore, also invoke it, in one version or another—a matter to be explored after we have finished discussing the material cited above. Harriet Butler and Sarah Sackett were indeed neighbors and acquaintances, as we shall see.

The accounts of unsanctioned copies that reached the *Sentinel* raise a question. Why, when he came to include the poem in his *Poems* of 1844, did Moore have no holograph, whether rough draft or fair copy, from which to prepare copy for the printer? He clearly relied on the broadsheet that Norman Tuttle posted to him in response to his query earlier that year about the provenance of the manuscript from which the poem had first been printed.[4]

In the letter, the rubicund Dutchman, who lived in the neighborhood of Moore's father's country seat, Chelsea, is said to have "suggested" to Moore "the idea of making St. Nicholas the hero" of "Visit." The word "suggested" is ambiguous. It might naturally be interpreted to mean that, as Pelletreau states, it was from the Dutchman that Moore "first heard the story of St Nicholas." Pelletreau's statement that this happened when Moore was "a boy" reinforces such an interpretation, and the fact that even in the letter of 1862 Moore is reported as saying that the Dutchman lived near his *father's* house seems to carry the implication that Moore himself was young at the time. By the time he is supposed to have written "The Night Before Christmas" his father was dead and the house was his. When does a boy become a youth or a young man? Surely not later than the age of sixteen. That would mean Moore (born 15 July 1779) had heard the Dutchman's story by about 1796. But the Dutch *Sint-Nicolaas* was a gaunt and severe saint, not the "right jolly old elf," round-bellied and ruddy, imagined, without precedent, in "The Night Before Christmas."

Subsequent writers chose to believe that the Dutchman "suggested" to Moore the idea of making Saint Nicholas the hero of "Visit" in the sense that this "portly, rubicund" man served as a model, and they have tended to bring Moore's encounter with him forward in time, so as to make him an immediate stimulus to the writing of the poem. Even Foster writes as though it was Moore's sighting of the rubicund Dutchman on 24 December 1822 that supposedly induced the "epiphany" that resulted in the "Christmas piece."[5]

Pelletreau not only gets the year of Moore's birth wrong (1781, instead of the correct 1779), but says, again incorrectly, that in the *Sentinel* of 23 December 1823 "Visit" was "accompanied by a cut illustrating Santa Claus on his rounds." If this misconception emanated from Moore, it reinforces the evidence that he believed the copy of the broadsheet sent him by Norman Tuttle when he enquired who had delivered the poem to the *Sentinel* was the original printing. Of course it was not. Tuttle had sent the 1830 broadsheet, which was indeed accompanied by an illustration of "Santa Claus on his rounds."

The tale of the turkey first enters the documentary record in 1920, when Moore's grandson, Casimir de R. Moore, secured two depositions from Maria Jephson O'Conor (Mrs. John C. O'Conor, née Post). The first is dated 20 December, the second 23 December.[6] They are almost identical, though the information is given in slightly different order. Mrs. O'Conor explains that her grandfather, Elliot Taylor, was a brother-in-law of Clement Clarke Moore, and that her late father, Colonel Henry V. A. Post, married her grandfather's daughter, Maria Farquhar Taylor. So her father, who was "very well acquainted with Moore," gleaned from him the following account of the circumstances under which "Visit" came to be written. On Christmas Eve Mrs. Moore was packing baskets of provisions to be sent to the neighborhood poor and found she was one turkey short. Moore set off to the market to buy one. "On his return with the turkey he was struck by the beauty of the moonlight on the snow and the brightness of the starlit sky. This, with the holiday season, suggested to him the idea of writing a few lines appropriate to St Nicholas." The second version adds that Moore told Mrs. O'Connor's father that "he immediately went to his study and wrote the poem" and also "when he came to publish the same, with some of his other poems, he only made two slight changes in the lines as originally written by him." The first version had worded this last sentence differently, reporting Moore as having said that when the poem "was published, without his knowledge ... there were only two errors in the printed copy."

In Mrs. O'Conor's deposition the rubicund Dutchman is replaced by moonlit snow and a starlit sky, viewed during a trip for a turkey, as Moore's sources of inspiration. The claim patently alludes to the poem's lines, "The moon on the breast of the new fallen snow, / Gave the lustre of mid-day to objects below." But, as we have seen, the imagery and wording there have close parallels in the verse of Livingston. One suspects that the detail, reported by Mrs. O'Conor, of the brightly moonlit snow was prompted by the poem, rather than the other way around.

The two depositions differ crucially about Moore's "changes," the first saying that he corrected two errors in the text as (presumably originally) printed, the second saying that he made two revisions to the text *as he had composed it*. In fact the text of "Visit" in *Poems* (1844) has, if one counts a line of alterations from roman to italic as a single variant, some fifty variants in "incidentals" from the *Troy Sentinel* text of 1823—variations in spelling, punctuation, capitalization, italicization, and the like—and five "substantive" variants: "sprang" for "sprung" in line 10, "*Blitzen*" for "Blixem" in line 22, "leaves that before" for "leaves before" in line 25, "he had flung" for "was flung" in line 35, and "sprang" for "sprung" in line 53. Since the changes to "sprang" had already been made in the 1830 broadsheet, *Poems* made only the other three substantive changes from it, plus the correction of the obvious misprint "look'd liked" to "look'd like" in line 36. All four of these alterations are made in handwriting on the Museum of the City of New York copy of the 1830 broadsheet that Tuttle evidently sent Moore in 1844. We can be almost certain that the new variants are in Moore's own hand: "that" and "he had," in particular, look remarkably similar to the same words in his later handwritten transcripts and in his manuscript notebook; Seth Kaller refers without proviso to "Moore's autograph corrections."[7]

In neither of the two deposition statements about changes are the remarks attributed to Moore strictly accurate. If for his *Poems* Moore corrected two substantive errors in the text as originally printed, then he also made three revisions. If he made two changes to the text as he composed it, then the *Troy Sentinel* of 1823 contained three errors. But if Moore wrongly supposed that the 1830 broadsheet corresponded exactly to the first printing, he might conceivably have claimed the insertion of "that" and the correction of "liked" as eliminating errors and the alterations to "*Blitzen*" and "he had flung" as revisions to the poem "as originally written by him." The minor contradictions in Mrs. O'Conor's account of Moore's statements about his textual changes cannot fairly be held to indict him of misappropriation of a poem not his, but neither do they encourage confidence in anything he is reported as having said about the poem's origins and history.

Even T. W. C. Moore's report in 1862, after talking with Clement Clarke Moore, that "Visit" was composed "about 40 years ago"—a dating upon which all subsequent Moore-party creation myths about a portly Dutchman and a Christmas Eve turkey are based—is highly suspect in view of the fact that in August 1853, at the end of an earlier handwritten copy of the poem (held by The Strong National Museum of Play in Rochester, New York) Clement had declared "Written many years ago; I cannot say exactly when."[8] Those last five words seem strangely circumspect. If in 1853 he could not say "exactly when" the poem was written, how in 1862, now nine years older, did he suddenly remember that it was about 1822, twelve months before it was printed, to his alleged chagrin, in the *Troy Sentinel*?

Besides extracting the two depositions from Mrs. O'Conor, Casimir de R. Moore replied in a letter to an enquiry from Henry Litchfield West. His remarks are very general, simply repeating that Moore wrote "The Night Before Christmas" "for the enjoyment of his children and had no intention of publishing it" but that a "connection of the family saw it on a visit to my grandfather, copied it, and had it published in a Troy paper, I believe," and that Moore eventually succumbed to the urging of others to acknowledge his authorship. Casimir's information is derived from what he has been told by "my father, uncle and aunts." He concludes: "What became of the original manuscript I cannot say."[9] Indeed, nobody ever claimed to have seen it.

No turkey (or snowy, moonlit night) features in Casimir's remarks. But later accounts—like a series of "Chinese whispers"—enthusiastically embroider the dubious statements made up until 1920. For instance, in his 1956 biography of Moore, Samuel White Patterson romances about the "unknown workman" as "the model that Clement Moore took for St. Nick" and speculates: "Was he a tiller of Chelsea soil or just a good neighbor? Did he ever trim the poet's lovely old trees, or mend his fences? Did he ever even so much as glimpse what the kindly spoken gentleman he used to meet was to make of him?"[10] This is all the product of Patterson's benign imagination. Significantly, in quoting from T. W. C. Moore's letter of 1862, Patterson refers to Clement Moore's supposed "model" as "a portly, rubicund Dutchman living in the neighborhood of … Chelsea," the ellipsis concealing the absence of "his father's country seat," which tends to undermine Patterson's interpretation of the reported remarks. Accounts of the genesis of "Visit" with Moore as author are enveloped in fantasy.

20

The Livingston Version

The Livingston counterpart to the story of Moore's returning on Christmas Eve 1822 from an expedition to procure a turkey and shortly afterward emerging from his study to read to his children the newly composed "The Night Before Christmas" is the assertion that Henry Livingston's son Edwin and "his brothers and sisters remember distinctly their father coming from out his 'den' as he called the study in the old Manor House at Locust Grove … and reading this poem to the children just before Christmas," as the major's great great-granddaughter Cornelia Griswold Goodrich wrote in a letter of 3 January 1900 to Henry Livingston of Babylon, Long Island, adding that already she had letters in her possession "testifying to this."[1] Descendants of the poet Livingston's eldest son Charles and his wife Elizabeth née Brewer, in particular, who as a child had lived next door to Locust Grove and was a constant playmate of the Livingston children, repeatedly make the same assertion: "Uncle Charles—according to his daughter, Cousin Jeannie Hubbard [Jeanne Hubbard Denig]—remembered perfectly when his father brought up the freshly written paper from his Sanctum, with the ink still wet upon it, and read it to the family" (Gertrude Fonda Thomas to Cornelia Griswold Goodrich, 23 October 1912).

Cornelia Griswold Goodrich and a few relatives began collecting the recollections of Livingston descendants in the late nineteenth century, and William Sturges Thomas and his son William Stephen Thomas continued the quest. The result was a substantial collection of "witness letters," bequeathed to Stephen Livingston Thomas and now presented, in both scanned and transcribed form, on the website of Mary Van Deusen, Henry Livingston's great-great-great-great-great-granddaughter. In combination these documents establish beyond reasonable doubt that Livingston's eldest son Charles claimed to have heard his father read "Visit" as his own long before Moore is alleged to have composed it and that Charles and his wife often read the poem to their children as their grandfather's. Indirect testimony from Charles's brother Sidney, as well as that from Edwin cited above, is also recorded (Henry Livingston of Babylon, Long Island, to Cornelia Griswold Goodrich, 10 January 1900). Both Sidney and his sister Susan Gurney told Livinia L. Haugan that their father wrote "Visit," as she reported to W. S. Thomas in a letter dated 22 March 1917. It is hard to assess the degree to which all the amassed recollections are independent, but it is undoubtedly the case that belief in Henry Livingston's authorship of "The Night Before Christmas" was widespread in the extended family. Moreover, the eminent Dutchess County historian Helen W. Reynolds, in conversation with Mrs. Augustus Doughty née Margaret Livingston Crooke (born 1842), elicited from her a declaration that she heard when she was young (which would have been in the 1850s) that Henry Livingston had written "Visit" and that both she and her oldest sister, Julia, were "very much surprised" to find it ascribed to Clement Clarke Moore (record of 4 May 1920, copied by W. S. Thomas).[2] Margaret Crooke was related to the beautiful Nancy Crooke whose name is the solution to a Henry Livingston rebus, "Dance" or "A Rebus (on the Name Nancy Crooke)." Mrs. Doughty's is significant testimony—coming from a woman outside the family by way of a distinguished historian—that Moore's authorship of "The Night Before Christmas" was being contested, at least in conversation, not long after he included it in *Poems* (1844).

In Nancy Marshall's *Descriptive Bibliography* of editions of "Visit" the first thirteen printings listed are anonymous. The ascription to Moore in Charles Fenno Hoffman's *New-York Book of Poetry* and the *New-York Mirror* in 1837 is followed by eleven printings, six of which contain the attribution. Then, after the inclusion of "Visit" in Moore's *Poems* (1844), attributions to Moore outweigh anonymous publications by twenty-one to ten up until 1865 (items 28–61, with the three holographs excluded), and within the period 1858–62 all eight printings (items 47–55, ignoring the 1860 holograph, item 49) are ascribed. It is within the years 1858–62 that the crediting of "Visit" to Moore would have been least likely to have escaped Jane Livingston's attention. In a letter to W. S. Thomas dated 14 March 1917, Jeanne Hubbard Denig writes that "in 1859 a paper covered edition of ['The Night Before Christmas'] was put upon the market & it was then grandmother Livingston saw it & was indignant" that it was misattributed. The edition mentioned there could be Marshall's item 47, dated "ca. 1858" and described as "in green paper wraps" with an engraving. Henry

Livingston of Babylon, Long Island, said in a letter of 10 January 1910 to Cornelia Griswold Goodrich that, to his knowledge, the question of authorship was "not brought up ... until after 1862, when it was ... credited to Clement C. Moore." Though these two witnesses differ slightly, they both place the Livingston family's discovery of the alleged misattribution within the period that is on other grounds most probable. And the date sorts well with Eliza Livingston Thompson Lansing's statement (in her letter of 4 March 1879 to Anne Livingston Goodrich): "I well remember our astonishment when we saw it claimed as 'Clement C Moore.'" A discovery made about twenty years ago would be spoken of in these terms ("I well remember").

Those who defend Moore's claim to "Visit" make sport of contradictions and inconsistencies in and between certain "witness letters." Different dates are given for Livingston's first reading of the poem, though "about 1808" is now regarded as most likely. It is said to have been published in some Poughkeepsie or other newspaper or journal years before it appeared in the 1823 *Troy Sentinel*, but some of the suggested venues are impossible—for example, the *Knickerbocker* magazine, suggested by Henry Livingston of Babylon on 10 January 1900, was founded as late as 1833—and no printing earlier than 1823 has ever been discovered. Had it been published a decade or more before then, why in the intervening years was it not reprinted with the same zeal as from 1823 onward? (A possible answer might be that publication was in a journal with a much smaller circulation than the *Sentinel*.)

There is also uncertainty about the date of the fire in which Livingston's manuscript of "Visit" is supposed to have burned. On 10 January 1900 Henry Livingston of Babylon put its destruction at Susan Gurney's home in "Kaskaskia, Wis.," along with her brother Edwin's "personal effects," as about 1847 or 1848. But Edwin was not in Kaskaskia (Illinois) at that time (though Charles was there at an earlier period), Susan's home was in Wisconsin, not in Kaskaskia, Illinois, and she did not move to it until the early 1850s. However, the Gurneys "were burned out two or three times" (Jeanne Hubbard Denig to W. S. Thomas, 2 October 1920), and Susan's daughter Jeannie Gurney wrote to W. S. Thomas on 5 October 1921 that her mother had a book in which Henry Livingston had written several of his poems, but "it was burned when our house burned in 1869." Since Jeannie would have been nineteen in 1869, this memory can be trusted. By 1869 Edwin had been dead for six years, but some of his belongings could conceivably have been left with his sister. The book feared burned survived in a bookcase in the house of Gertrude Fonda Thomas, who had, however, previously testified to W. S. Thomas (as he recorded in a note) that "Aunt Sue [Livingston's daughter Susan Gurney] had two books of her father's poetry—one bound, though in his own handwriting, the other written on the old-fashioned large sheets." When she made that statement she thought they had both perished in "the first fire," and "Visit" could have been among the loose sheets, which were in fact destroyed. It has not been established when "the first fire" occurred, but it is clear enough that there were indeed fires in which Livingston manuscripts could have burned. The book that survived was passed to W. S. Thomas (Gertrude Fonda Thomas to W. S. Thomas, 30 March 1917) and remains a valuable source of Livingston texts. The majority of the poems in his established corpus are inscribed within it. But it covers poems only of the period 1776–90. We can be sure that Livingston remained no less productive as a poet over the ensuing decades, till his death in 1828, and yet hardly any verse that he composed after 1790 has survived in manuscript, and that small residue belongs almost exclusively to his final two or three years and his daughter Jane's "poetry book." Dismissing Livingston's claim to "The Night Before Christmas," Nancy Marshall notes that "not a single line of the poem has ever been found among his papers nor with any of his other poetical works."[3] But this is to ignore the fact that the same could be said of numerous other poems that Livingston must have written in the thirty-seven-year period 1791–1828.

Some Livingston family narratives about how "Visit" came to be associated with Moore include a governess's taking it from Locust Grove to Moore's Chelsea home. Neils Sonne, Joe Nickell, and others object that in 1808 Clement Moore had no children, his first, Margaret, having been born in 1815.[4] But (a) it is not absolutely necessary to this explanation that transfer of the poem took place any earlier than 1822, and, in any case, (b) there is no agreement in the Livingston family accounts that the alleged governess was about to assume that role in Clement Moore's household: in one witness letter she was joining a Moore family "down South" (Cornelia Griswold Goodrich, 3 January 1900). "Aunt Gertrude" (Gertrude Fonda Thomas), interviewed by Henry Livingston of Babylon on 19 October 1920, affirmed that Henry Livingston "regularly employed a governess in his own family when there were children there," her mother (Jane Patterson Livingston) having told her about one of whom the family were particularly fond. In any case, rumors about how a Livingston poem might have been mistaken as by Moore are peripheral to the central claim.

A letter by Mary Goodrich Montgomery to William Sturges Thomas, dated 3 March 1917, has been badly distorted by Moore's apologists. The sender was named (correctly enough) as "Mrs. Edward Livingston" in Henry Litchfield West's 1921 *Bookman* article. Referring to it, Nickell, the latest of the mockers, writes that "a great-granddaughter of Livingston said that her grandmother Catherine (Livingston's eldest daughter) had told her about the origin of the poem," Livingston being said to have "read it one Christmas morning to his family and a female guest," who "went directly to the home of Clement C. Moore, where she filled the position of governess to his children." Nickell comments: "Unfortunately the source of this tale, Catherine, died in 1808, at which time Clement Moore remained a bachelor."[5] But Mary Goodrich Montgomery, alias Mrs. Edward Livingston, nowhere states that Livingston's daughter, Catherine (who did indeed die in 1808) was the "source" of the story: she writes that it was *related* to her (Mary) by her grandmother, Catherine Walker Griswold, who would have heard it from Livingston's younger children. West and Nickell confused Catherines of different generations. Even the letter's evidently mistaken detail that the young lady who heard the poem read at Locust Grove was currently a governess at Clement Clarke Moore's home, is followed by the more plausible alternative that "on leaving Locust grove, she went to join Mr. Moore's family in one of the Southern states."

It is only to be expected that mistakes and contradictions should exist in a large collection of statements made by Henry Livingston's descendants and their relatives, of varying ages, over several decades. After all, none of the anomalies, unlike those in the Moore stories, emanate from the poet himself. What is abundantly clear is that there was a long-standing tradition that Livingston had been the author of "The Night Before Christmas."

Furthermore, one scrap of evidence appears to confirm that at least one of Henry Livingston's children was familiar with the poem before December 1823, when it was printed in the *Troy Sentinel*, and before December 1822, when Moore is alleged to have composed it. Henry's great-granddaughter, Jeanne Hubbard Denig offered some intriguing information, which has been overlooked in the debate about authorship. In a letter to William S. Thomas dated 25 March 1917 she states that "Uncle Edwin Livingston wrote rhymes," mentions a letter of his of July 1821, and quotes from it some lines of an anapestic tetrameter poem, which she says she will decipher in full and have typewritten, adding that it is torn and "difficult to read." Neither the typed copy nor Edwin's original letter can now be located. But the quoted fragment is in the epistolary vein of Edwin's father's "To my dear brother Beekman I sit down to write." As transcribed, it reads:

Jane, Helen & Pa tomorrow set sail
And anxiously await the glad summons to hail
That calls all a board, & off to New York!
The tight Sally-Frances plies shrewdly to work,
A fortnight at least they'll stay in the city,
Or anxious to see strange things new & pretty
di-di-
Your Uncle Stephs family's hearty & fat
And he, although feeble, is full of his chat
The House at the River is about status-quo,
All very well, the old lady "So So,"

Moreover, Jeanne Denig must have kept her promise, because in his biographical article of 1919 William S. Thomas published a larger extract, and only five of the lines overlap with those that she first provided him. Thomas gives the date of Edwin's letter, from Locust Grove to his brother Charles in Kaskaskia, Illinois, as 11 June 1821, and explains that "after assuring the absent one that true fellowship continued to exist at home," Edwin writes that:

With seeing our friends and returning their calls,
No care intervenes or trouble enthralls.

and goes on to tell of a party at which:

Our sisters, myself, with about thirty more
Made as social a group as e'er crowded a floor,
We parted at twelve and soundly at one,
Slept I in the famous old mansion of stone;
The visions of gaiety cheering till morn,
When the magic is broke by the loud breakfast horn.
Jane, Helen and pa tomorrow set sail,
And anxiously wait the glad summons to hail
That calls all on board and off for New York;
The tight "Sally Frances" plies shrewdly to work.
A fortnight at least they'll stay in the city.

Pa returns in a week, for naught at his age
Amuses—the fashions and gay equipage;
Far dearer to him is the still country shade
Than the bustle of cities, their pomp and parade.[6]

Thomas omits the line that rhymes with city, "Or anxious to see strange things new & pretty": either "Or" is a mistranscription (perhaps for "All") or the sense was completed in the next line or lines. Presumably in the slightly clumsy phrase "the glad summons to hail" word order is inverted for the sake of the rhyme, the sense being "to hail the glad summons."

Jeanne Denig thought that "back in Edwin's brain sang the words 'While visions of sugar plums danced in their heads,' and so he wrote, 'The visions of gaiety, cheering the morn.'" She might reasonably have suspected another echo: "plies shrewdly to work" reminds one of St. Nick, who "went straight to his work," "work" forming an end-of-line rhyme in each case. Even more germane is her observation that the influence of "The Night Before Christmas" may perhaps be detected in the presence in Edwin's poem of "visions," "lustre," and "hoof." The suggestion is that already by 1821 Edwin had "Visit," in which these three words are brought together, somewhere in his subconscious mind. Of course only "visions" is in the passages that survive, but we can be sure that "lustre" and "hoof" were within the poem as sent and received in 1821.

Edwin's rhyming letter is unlikely to have been much longer than "Visit." Three items of vocabulary, the same anapestic meter, and a couple of echoes of cadence may seem to constitute a rather tenuous link between the two poems, but a check of *Literature Online* (*LION*) for works in which Mrs. Denig's three specific words plus "work" are conjoined within a fairly short space—using the search "visions NEAR.600 lustre NEAR.600 hoof NEAR.600 work"—turned up only three instances in the whole of the enormous database (poetry, drama, and prose from the fifteenth century to the present), namely in "Visit" and in two iambic pentameter poems by the Englishman Richard Polwhele, "Epistle to a College-Friend" (1791) and "The Vision of Sir Aaron" (1806).[7] And a further search, of *LION* poetry published up till 1850 for poems in which the phrases "visions of" and "to [possessive pronoun] work" occur within some sixty lines of each other, yielded only "Visit," while substituting Edwin's variant "to work" yielded only three more instances, in Fulke Greville's *A Treatise of Monarchy* (of about 1600), John Hamilton Reynolds's "The Romance of Youth" from *The Garden of Florence* (1821), and Egerton Brydges, *The Lake of Geneva* (1832).[8] All these poems are in iambic pentameters, not anapests, and in no case does "work" end a line, let alone supply a rhyme.

This is by no means irrefragable proof that Henry Livingston's son Edwin was familiar with "The Night Before Christmas" at least a year and a half before Clement Clarke Moore is supposed to have composed it, but it is evidence of some substance to that effect. Jeanne Denig's belief that in 1821 Edwin still had his father's poem ringing in his head receives solid support.

Thirty years later the poem was certainly well known to Henry Livingston Thomas (1835–1903), Major Henry's grandson, son of his daughter

Jane. He told W. S. Thomas that his (HLT's) grandfather wrote the poem. W. S. Thomas himself had memorized it as a boy from his (HLT's) dictation, and recalled his own "indignant surprise" when he saw it attributed to Moore (recorded in an undated note by W. S. Thomas). Whether or not Henry Livingston Thomas also had "Visit" by heart he could, quite casually, quote from it in his youth. In a letter to his exact contemporary Abraham Lansing, dated 15 December 1851, the sixteen-year-old Henry remarks on the extremely cold Poughkeepsie weather and "lowering sky" and hopes that conditions will "allow an easy passage to Santa Claus with his 'eight tiny reindeer.'"[9] The naturalness of his allusion to "Visit," with the obvious expectation that his cousin will recognize it, lends further credence to the family traditions about their proprietary interest in the poem. And the letter was written long before any campaign to collect "witness letters."

An anecdote told by Gertrude Thomas to W. S. Thomas on 13 October 1920 also involves Henry Livingston Thomas. He was, according to her, "teaching at Mr. Churchill's school Singsing" when, "The Night Before Christmas" having been mentioned, he said, "My grandfather wrote that" and a boy in his class said, "No, my grandfather did." A colorful tale of this kind invites skepticism. But Henry was Gertrude's brother and she averred that she had the story from him. Moreover, Henry's son William gained corroboration from a "Mr. Stuyvesant Fish at his Garrison house" that Casimir de R. Moore, Clement Clarke Moore's grandson, had been a contemporary of Fish's at "Churchill's Academy at Sing Sing" and been taught Latin by Henry Livingston Thomas. He wrote to Casimir (W. S. Thomas to Casimir de R. Moore, 12 December 1920), and received an immediate reply (13 December 1920). Casimir well remembered having been taught by Henry Livingston Thomas, but declared that neither he nor his brother could recall the incident, though he conceded that after more than fifty years memories of his schooldays had faded. If the exchange occurred— and the teacher is less likely to have recalled something that did not happen than the pupil to have forgotten something that did—it would be the first public statement of Livingston's authorship, because Churchill School of Sing Sing (now Ossining), New York, founded by Marlborough Churchill in 1843, was sold in 1869, when it became St. John's Military School.[10]

Whatever we may think of some of the more peripheral gossip surrounding the family tradition that Henry Livingston wrote "The Night Before Christmas," the "witness letters," from a variety of sources and covering a considerable chronological range, cannot be lightly set aside.

21

Further Considerations: Claims and Connections

Those who ascribe "The Night Before Christmas" to Livingston must concede that Moore was linked to the poem at least as early as 1829, when Orville Holley broadly hinted at his authorship, and belief in it may have arisen even earlier. In a letter, dated 24 December 2000, to the editor of the *Washington Post Outlook*, Paul H. Smith noted that among a collection of Clement Clarke Moore's correspondence with Jonathan Odell, in the Odell papers owned by the New Brunswick Museum and Archives at St. John, New Brunswick, is a manuscript copy of "A Visit from St. Nicholas," as it is headed, on paper with an 1824 watermark.[1] Jonathan Odell, Loyalist poet and Church of England minister, was Clement's godfather. Born in 1737, he died in 1818, having migrated to Canada in 1784. Smith remarks that the copy must have been acquired by one of Jonathan's children after his death, but that "the existence of the manuscript of the poem among the Moore letters certainly suggests that someone in the Odell family believed that Moore wrote it." That someone was evidently Jonathan's unmarried daughter Mary (1773–1848), since the copy of "Visit" is in her handwriting, as are, in the same Odell collection, copies of Clement Clarke Moore's "Lines Written after a Snowstorm" and "From a Husband to his Wife." Signed examples of Mary's handwriting are included in the Odell papers.

The source for Mary's copy of "Visit"—which could have been made any time between 1824 and her death in 1848—is a mystery. It contains a set of variants that has not been traced to any known printing, and yet it cannot, of course, have preceded the first extant version, published in the *Troy Sentinel* of 1823. A collation with that printing reveals the following variants:

	1823	**Odell**
6	sugar plums	sugar plumbs
	danced in	danc'd thro'
8	winter's nap	winter nap
21–22	"Now! Dasher, now! Dancer, now! Prancer, and Vixen	
	On! Comet, on! Cupid, on! Dunder and Blixem"; (1823)	
	"Now Dancer and Prancer—now Dasher and Vixen	
	On Comet, on Cupid—on Donder and Blixen—" (Odell)	
25	dry leaves before	dry leaves that before
30	prancing and pawing	pawing and prancing
35	was flung on	was slung over
42	like a wreath	in a wreath
55	ere he drove	as he drove

All "-'d" verbal endings in the *Sentinel* become "-ed" in Mary Odell's copy, and there are many differences in punctuation, though marks in the manuscript are in places hard to make out. But they include dashes at the ends of lines 12, 22, 24, and 56, and a sprinkling of short midline dashes, not only within lines 21–22 but also 23, 24, 50, and 56. Yet where the *Sentinel* does have a dash, after "Toys" in line 28, there is none. It is unclear whether the spelling is "jirk" or "jerk" in line 50, but, as in the *Sentinel*, it appears to be "sprung" (rather than "sprang") that is used in both line 10 and line 53.

Mary's version can hardly have come from Clement Clarke Moore, who was reported by Maria Jephson O'Conor as saying that for *Poems* (1844) he made either (a) only two corrections to "Visit" as printed or (b) two revisions to the poem as he composed it. The insertion of "that" in line 25, to read "dry leaves that before" is the only Odell variant that appears in Moore's *Poems*, apart from the spelling "Donder." The bastard form "Blixen," neither Dutch nor German, had first appeared in print in David McClure's *United States National Almanac* (1825), and it was in Charles Fenno Hoffman's *New-York Book of Poetry* (1837), which perpetuated this change, that "Dunder" was first altered to "Donder." In 1844 Moore of course named the eighth reindeer "Blitzen." Hoffman added "that" in line 25 but deleted "dry." Hoffman, and later Moore in *Poems*, regularized the slightly odd grammar of line 35 and turned an iambic foot into an anapest by changing "A bundle of toys was flung on his back" to "A bundle of toys he had flung on his back." Moore would hardly have adopted this variant, had he ever written "A bundle of toys was slung over his back." In fact, if this were proved to be the authentic reading, then it would tell against Moore's authorship, since in 1844 he would have been misled by a misprint, as the original author would almost certainly not have been. Nor, as I have argued, is Moore ever likely to have twice used "sprung" as a preterit. The punctuation of lines 21–22 deviates markedly both from the Livingston-like punctuation in the *Sentinel* and the normalized punctuation of subsequent editions. And Mary Odell's consistent use of "-ed" endings contravenes the conventions adopted in Moore's *Poems* and his unpublished poems.

Although several of the minor variants found in the Odell copy ("plumbs" and "thro'" in line 6, "that" in line 25, "in" in line 42, "as" in line 55) crept into one or other of the innumerable reprints of "Visit," the full combination is otherwise unknown, and no parallel for the reordering of the names Dasher, Dancer, Prancer, and Vixen has yet been found. It is conceivable that Mary relied on memory, as might be suggested from her writing "up the chimney he goes" in line 52, before crossing out "goes" and replacing it with the correct "rose."

There seems to be no way of ascertaining either the source or the date of the copy. But the company it keeps undoubtedly affords strong evidence that Mary Odell believed the poem to be Moore's. The fact that such friends or acquaintances as Robert Walter Weir and William Cullen Bryant did so, after Hoffman had published the poem under Moore's name in 1837, is not compelling as evidence of Moore's authorship. Holley's belief in it by 1829 is potentially of more consequence, and Mary Odell may, or may not, have shared this belief even earlier. But Moore's practice of "neither confirming nor denying" that "Visit" was his, until he was induced to include it in his *Poems* of 1844, would inevitably have allowed rumor that he was the author, once initiated, to have flourished and spread even among friends, without any one of them having independent confirmation from Moore himself.

Like stories of how "The Night Before Christmas" was published in the *Troy Sentinel* without Moore's knowledge, explanations of how a poem composed by Major Henry Livingston could have come to be attributed to Clement Clarke Moore also invoke intermediaries, with Harriet Butler a possible suspect. A copy of Livingston's poem found its way, it is conjectured, into Moore's home and so was assumed to be his by a person who, reading it there, conveyed it—or began the process of conveying it—to the *Troy Sentinel*. Henry Noble MacCracken, for example, points out that there were loose ties by marriage between the Livingston and Moore families and that Judith Livingston Moore was not only the first cousin and next-door neighbor of Henry Livingston but also grandmother of Frances Livingston Hart, who married Harriet Butler's young brother, Clement Moore

Butler (1810–90).[2] He might have added that Henry Livingston's uncle, Pierre Van Cortland, was the brother of Clement Moore's wife's great-grandfather, Stephen Van Cortland.[3] This may seem little more than the proverbial "six degrees of separation" that unites us all. But, as MacCracken observes, "marriage and blood ties were much more important in those days" and the web of connections between "Moores, Livingstons, and Butlers proves ... that it would have been perfectly easy for a young lady of any one of these families to turn up as visitor at Mrs. C. C. Moore's, and either to bring or to find an album there, with St. Nick in it."[4]

MacCracken proposes that the following "route of *A Visit from St. Nicholas* in its album" can be traced "with some degree of probability." The first step is from Livingston's homestead, Locust Grove, to Judith Livingston Moore's children. One of her daughters "leaves an album containing the poem at the home of Dr. C. C. Moore. There a Miss Butler finds and copies it. She takes it to Troy in 1823, though without the Doctor's permission, for anything in an album is 'in the public domain.' When asked where she got it, she tells the editor of the *Troy Sentinel*, 'at the house of Dr. Moore.'" The editor surmises that the poem is by Moore but, since it has reached him indirectly, publishes it anonymously. Later, in introducing a reprint of 1829, when the poem has become popular, his original surmise materializes as broad hints. "Moore, at some later date, unknown, hears of the newspaper piracy, but lets the matter go. The poem is trivial and worthless. He is deep in a new Hebrew lexicon. Time goes on, and greatness is thrust upon him when the American public takes the poem to its heart."[5]

This is all pure speculation, and MacCracken is badly mistaken in suggesting that Moore was "deep in a new Hebrew Lexicon" at any time after the publication of "Visit," since the lexicon was published in 1809. But it is certainly the case that a copy of a "Visit" could have traveled from Livingston's house to Moore's and that a visitor encountering it might have mistakenly assumed that Moore was the author. It is true too that albums were miscellanies, in which poems of diverse provenance could nestle side by side. The "poetry book" of Livingston's daughter Jane Patterson Livingston contains verses by Byron, songs, hymns, and popular pieces, along with poems by her father, inscribed by his own hand.

But to Harriet Butler as conveyor of "Visit" to the *Sentinel* office must be added Sarah Hackett. And an association between the two women did exist. Honor Conklin has discovered that not only was the Sackett store in the vicinity of the Reverend David Butler's St. Paul's Episcopal Church, but that Butler, Sackett, and Holley were all officiating members of the same antislavery group, the Troy Colonization Society.[6]

It is possible also that Moore was somehow credited with the wrong "Christmas piece," to use his own term, as reported by T. W. C. Moore in 1862. Moore is commonly said to have been influenced by "Old Santeclaus" an anonymous poem featured in a little booklet called *The Children's Friend*.[7] It represents Santa as driving his reindeer "this frosty night" over "chimney-tops, and tracks of snow" to bring "his yearly gifts." But he comes less in the spirit of Christmas Cheer than of the Last Judgment, in which the sheep are drafted from the goats. Good children will receive toys, naughty ones the "birchen rod." Donald Foster was sure that these moralistic lines, which were accompanied by an illustration of Santa in a one-reindeer sleigh, were by Moore. As biographers have demonstrated, Moore had dealings with William Gilley, who not only published *The Children's Friend* along with more weighty works by Moore's favorite writers, but "was also publisher for the Protestant Episcopal Church of New York and a sometime neighbor of the Moore family."[8] We will examine Foster's theory in the next chapter.

22

"Old Santeclaus" and Moore

Old SANTECLAUS with much delight
His reindeer drives this frosty night,
O'er chimney-tops, and tracks of snow,
To bring his yearly gifts to you.

The steady friend of virtuous youth,
The friend of duty, and of truth,
Each Christmas eve he joys to come
Where love and peace have made their home.

Through many houses he has been,
And various beds and stockings seen;
Some, white as snow, and neatly mended,
Others, that seem for pigs intended.

Where e'er I found good girls and boys,
That hated quarrels, strife and noise,
I left an apple, or a tart,
Or wooden gun, or painted cart.

To some I gave a pretty doll,
To some a peg-top, or a ball;
No crackers, cannons, squibs, or rockets,
To blow their eyes up, or their pockets.

No drums to stun their Mother's ear,
Nor swords to make their sisters fear;
But pretty books to store their mind
With knowledge of each various kind.

But where I found the children naughty,
In manners rude, in tempers haughty,

Thankless to parents, liars, swearers,
Boxers, or cheats, or base tale-bearers,

I left a long, black birchen rod,
Such as the dread command of God
Directs a Parent's hand to use
When virtue's path his sons refuse.

Donald Foster claims that "the 1821 Santeclaus poem has the Professor's stylistic fingerprints all over it." He is confident enough in this diagnosis to assert: "In fact, if 'Old Santeclaus' was not written by the original Grinch, Professor Clement Clarke Moore himself, then call me 'Rudolph' and never let me play in reindeer games."[1] He adduces several parallels with Moore's verse in thought and expression. As he says, the imagination, for Moore in "To Southey," is a place "Where all things strange and monstrous make their home," while a good family, for the "Old Santeclaus" poet, is one "Where love and peace have made their home." Moore asks in "Saratoga," "Why should we not store our minds … ?" while "Old Santeclaus" promises good children "books to store their mind." In a poem written in 1813 to commemorate his marriage and quoted by his biographer Samuel White Patterson, Moore describes his youthful self as having a "well-stored mind."[2] *Literature Online* (*LION*) cannot find another poet who, in his or her published work of 1800–1850 used both "make/made their home" and "store … mind(s)." Further, Moore, as Foster notes, "complains obsessively" of "bustle, noise, and rout," "the strife, the tumult, and the noise," "bustle, heat, and noise," "playful, strife and noise."[3] The last of these phrases rhymes with "boys," who create the "noise." The "Old Santeclaus" poet uses the same rhyme: for him "good girls and boys" hate "quarrels, strife and noise."

Likewise in Moore's holograph Christmas poem, "From Saint Nicholas," "a good child" will be "quietly lying" in bed, while "some naughty ones would be fretting or crying." Little Sis's "screeches and screams, so loud ev'ry day" drive Saint Nicholas away. As in "Old Santeclaus," good, quiet behavior throughout the year is rewarded, but gifts are withheld from those who disrupt the peace.

In fact Old Santeclaus leaves them only "a long, black birchen rod," foreshadowing "long, black boots" and "a birchen rod" in Moore's *Poems*, though the rod is mentioned in a short poem by Moore's late wife, who complains of having to discipline her progeny. Moore writes (in a translation from Aeschylus) of "Jove's dread command" and the "Santeclaus" poet of "the dread command of God." As Foster remarks, Moore "is big on dread": for him it "is the sinner's ticket to salvation, the child's motivation to be good."[4]

In "Old Santeclaus" the good children may receive "a pretty doll" or "pretty books." In "From Saint Nicholas," Moore's little daughter will "have something pretty," perhaps "some books," when she learns to control her "screeches and screams." Then Saint Nicholas will write her "a prettier letter." The "Old Santeclaus" poet speaks of "various beds and stockings" and of books containing "knowledge of each various kind." As Foster observes, when Moore is not "recycling descriptive phrases picked up from his reading" he "quickly runs out of modifiers" and settles for "various," an adjective which occurs eight times in his *Poems*, three times in "Charles Elphinstone," and once in the manuscript piece "Eliza in England," but is never used by Livingston.[5] Moore's vague "various" is like his vague "some," to which, as we have seen in Chapter 15, he is addicted and which is used no fewer than three times in "Old Santeclaus."

There is another significant similarity between "Old Santeclaus" and Moore's "From Saint Nicholas." The latter is nominally spoken or written by Saint Nicholas but his voice merges with that of the father of "little Sis," Moore himself. Likewise, the first three stanzas of "Old Santeclaus" employ a third-person narrative, with the pronouns "His," "he," "he," but after the complaint, in the last line of the third stanza, about beds and stockings "that seemed for pigs intended," the poem shifts into the first person, with five examples of "I," beginning with the first line of the fourth stanza, as Santeclaus's censorious attitude blends with Moore's own.

In fact the judgmental vocabulary of "Old Santeclaus" everywhere recalls Moore's and strikingly contrasts with Livingston's. Santeclaus is "The steady friend of virtuous youth, / The friend of duty, and of truth." Moore rhymes "youth" with "truth" six times and "youths" with "truths" once. Livingston uses the rhyme only once, when he characteristically rhymes "passion and youth" with "beauty and truth." "Old Santeclaus" reviles children "In manners rude, in temper haughty." Moore uses "rude" five times, twice about the roughness of nature, but three times about rude behavior: children must not show themselves "gluttonous and rude," but those "boys" who were of an age to revel in "playful strife and noise" were (we are told within the same lines) "rude in mind." As Foster quips: "Moore's poetry, like 'Old Santeclaus,' denounces rude boys and pigs"[6]; Moore's pig in "The Pig and the Rooster" and the "pigs" in "Old Santeclaus" epitomize squalor, whereas Livingston's pigs—in "A Tenant of Mrs. Van Klerk"—produce piglets. Moore also writes of the "temper of our mind."

Livingston's context for "temper" is positive—"tempers benign"—and "rude" he uses only in his blessing upon his niece: let "No rude winds around her howl." "Strife" for Livingston is political and military, not domestic: he tenderly contrasts his infant daughter back home with his soldier self, "Amid the din of arms and strife." The last word in "Old Santeclaus," "refuse," appears three times in Moore's poems, but never in Livingston's.

"Old Santeclaus" contains two instances of "that," a rate of 9.569 per thousand words, which is marginally closer to the mean for Moore's poems (12.210) than to the mean for Livingston's (6.319). Its four instances of "the" and six of "a" work out at 4.785 per one hundred words which is much closer to Moore's mean of 6.127 than to Livingston's of 8.551. Its rates of Moore-favored phonemes (58.824 percent) and Moore-favored words (60 percent) are less Moore-like than Livingston-like, though comfortably within Moore's two-standard-deviation range. The rate of occurrence of nouns preceded by an adjective (nineteen, or 50.000 per 550 words) aligns the poem with Moore (whose mean is 54.668), not with Livingston (39.66). Of course Livingston is not a candidate for the authorship of "Old Santeclaus," but the fact that on these tests the poem is, unlike "The Night Before Christmas," repeatedly characteristic of Moore, not Livingston, is at the very least consistent with Moore's authorship.

Old Santeclaus is a very different personality from St. Nick in "Visit." The simile "white as snow," applied to some stockings in the Santeclaus poem, does have a counterpart in St. Nick's beard's being "as white as the snow" in "Visit," and both Moore and Livingston use the common compound "snow-white." And it so happens that Livingston, like the "Old Santeclaus" poet, rhymes "rockets" with "pockets," but the rhyme is not rare, occurring at least thirty times in *LION* poetry of the nineteenth century.

We can be tolerably certain of one point about "Old Santeclaus": the poet who wrote this piece had indeed read Washington Irving's *History of New-York* in the 1812 or later edition: there were reprints in 1820 and 1821.[7] In the first stanza Santeclaus is said to travel "To bring his yearly gifts to you." Irving writes of Saint Nicholas that "he brings his yearly presents to children." Neither *LION* nor the electronic database *Early English Books Online-Text Creation Partnership* finds any parallel to these two instances of anybody bringing his yearly gifts/presents to people[8]; although there are some examples of "yearly gifts" and "yearly presents," they lack the verb, pronoun, and preposition. And Irving and the "Old Santeclaus" poet are, of course, each referring to the same gift-bearer.

It seems highly probable that Foster is right—that "Old Santeclaus" was a Christmas poem to which Moore could legitimately lay claim. If Moore and Livingston were rival candidates for its authorship, we would have no trouble at all assigning it to Moore. In this respect, it stands in stark contrast to "The Night Before Christmas," which test after test classifies, not with Moore's poems, but with Livingston's.

23

Summary and Conclusions

By 1829 Orville Holley, editor of the *Troy Sentinel*, in which "The Night Before Christmas" is first known to have been published, clearly believed that Clement Clarke Moore was the author of the poem, and gossip to that effect may even have begun earlier. Several of Moore's acquaintances shared that belief before Moore included "The Night Before Christmas" in his *Poems* (1844). There is no record, until that point, of Moore's personally either claiming or disclaiming authorship. Dedicating *Poems* to his children, he explained that the volume was published "in compliance with your wishes," that it contained verses "written by me at different periods of my life," including "mere trifles" that had been "found by me to afford greater pleasure than what was by myself esteemed of more worth."[1] Although he prefaced "The Pig and the Rooster" with an account of the occasion of this "piece of fun," "A Visit from St. Nicholas" was printed unheralded. Within the volume were four poems that were not his but were duly credited—two to his late wife Eliza, and one each to his friends William Bard and Philip Hone; there were also three acknowledged translations, two from the Italian and one from the Greek. Later accounts of the genesis of "Visit," ultimately emanating from Moore, are riddled with small contradictions. In 1853, he knew that it was written "many years ago" but could not "say exactly when," but by 1862 he was reported as telling his interviewer that it was written "about 40 years ago," placing its composition the year before its publication. He evidently had no manuscript of the poem to give to his printer in 1844. He had to ask Norman Tuttle, former owner of the *Sentinel*, how the newspaper came by it, and in preparing copy for *Poems* relied on a *Sentinel* reprint that Tuttle sent him. A slight air of evasiveness hangs over his statements, with their passive constructions—"was written," rather than "I wrote"—and allusions to "the Christmas piece" rather than the specific "A Visit from St. Nicholas." He had, after all, written at least one other Christmas poem, "From Saint Nicholas," and had probably written "Old Santeclaus" as well.

Donald Foster's theory is not inherently implausible—that once Moore's name had been associated with "The Night Before Christmas" he simply allowed rumor to prevail, to the point where he lacked the courage to correct it. How, he may have felt, could he bear to disabuse his children? Trivial sins of omission can gather momentum. Moore was doubtless a man of strong religious convictions, high principles, and unsullied reputation, but many thousands of upright citizens have been guilty of far more serious fraud, deception, and fudging of the truth. Priests and presidents have not been immune. Good men partake of our common human frailty. Moore's inclusion of "The Night Before Christmas" in his *Poems* establishes a prima facie case for his authorship, but not a watertight one.

Doubts over Moore's claim to the poem would, however, never have arisen had not descendants of Henry Livingston been convinced that their forebear had composed it and read it to his children more than a decade before 1822. The tradition has been passed down through several family lines. Assertions that the ascription to Moore was mistaken were made by the late 1850s or early 1860s, when his name was first being attached to several reprints. There are minor contradictions in the Livingston accounts, but the number of independent voices testifying to Livingston's authorship of the poem is impressive. And apparent confirmation comes from evidence that by 1821, two years before "The Night Before Christmas" was published in the *Troy Sentinel*, Livingston's son Edwin was so familiar with it as to be influenced by its wording in some verses of his own.

Seth Kaller is dismissive of the "campaign" waged by the Livingston "clan," hinting that their motives were suspect, or that, muddle-headed, they believed what they wished to believe.[2] So it is worth remarking that the clan included not only remarkably accomplished women but numerous men who achieved the highest distinction in law, education, medicine, commerce, government, the army, the navy, and the church.[3] The campaign was motivated by the desire to right what they saw as an injustice.

This does not, of course, mean that they were correct. Whatever we may privately think of the external evidence, with its claims and counter-claims, the reasonable conclusion must be that it fails to settle the question of the poem's true provenance one way or the other.

In contrast, once it has been shown that there are insufficient grounds for supposing that "The Night Before Christmas" is indebted to Washington Irving's *History of New-York*, as revised in 1812, the internal evidence is unequivocal. No experienced reader of poetry who was familiar with the verse of the two rival candidates could fail to recognize that "The Night Before Christmas" is as uncharacteristic of Moore as it is characteristic of Livingston, with his proven ability to take a child's view of things, his intense awareness of flying creatures, and his fascination with the miniature. Livingston's work, like "Visit," is informed by a lively imagination, a vein of whimsy, and an energizing gusto that are absent from Moore's.

There are passages in "Visit," discussed in Chapter 9, that combine several Livingstonian images or usages within a short space, in ways that cannot be paralleled in Moore's verse. Particularly telling is that three times in his acknowledged verse Livingston uses the idea, also found in "Visit," of the moon converting day to lustrous noon. Further, in "Visit" "the breast of the new fallen snow" is drawn into the complex of images, and Livingston elsewhere links "breast" and "snow" and uses the phrase "new fall'n snows." Moreover, in the form in which "Visit" was published in the *Troy Sentinel*, the reindeer names, "Dunder and Blixem," variants of the Dutch oath meaning "Thunder and Lightning," are of the kind that would have been chosen not only by a Dutch Saint Nicholas but also by Dutchess County's Livingston, whose mother was Dutch along with three of his grandparents. When in 1844 Moore included "Visit" in his *Poems* he altered "Blixem" to the German "Blitzen." It is unlikely that he was revising a name that he himself had originally conceived as the much more apposite "Blixem." Why, if he had purposely given the reindeer a Dutch name, appropriate to its driver, would he change it to a less pertinent one? Besides, "Blixem" rhymes in the poem with "Vixen," and Moore avoided such nasal ("n"–"m") near-rhymes, whereas Livingston employed dozens of them. Yet it is equally improbable that in making the alteration to "Blitzen" Moore was restoring his own original reading, which had been corrupted in the *Sentinel*, because textual corruption ought not to have created the manifestly superior reading, "Blixem" (a common spelling of the modern Dutch *Bliksem*). The more natural inference is that Moore did not appreciate the pertinence of "Blixem" in a poem that Livingston had composed, especially since the couplet in which the "little old driver" calls his eight reindeer "by name" is punctuated in an idiosyncratic manner typical of Livingston but not of Moore.

Livingston, much of whose verse is, like "Visit," in anapestic tetrameter, was more adept than Moore at handling the meter. Counts of the number of times a two-syllable word occupies a metrically unstressed (or "non-ictic" or "weak") position in a line register this difference, since all two-syllable words in fact carry a stress. Figures for "The Night Before Christmas" are like those for Livingston's anapestic verses, not Moore's.

"Visit" is relatively uncluttered with attributive adjectives, with which Livingston is more sparing than Moore. In relation to the sizes of Moore's and Livingston's verse corpora, "Visit" shares more rhymes and more trigrams (three-word sequences) with Livingston than with Moore, and the links to Livingston involve rarer items. Several poems by Livingston come closer than any by Moore to matching the high percentage of nouns used as rhyme words in "Visit." Parallels between "Visit" and Moore's poems have been cited, but these are unimpressive in comparison with those that can be found with Livingston's poems. Besides, to be truly evidential searches must have been comprehensive and identical for each of the two candidates. This requirement was met in the gathering of shared rhymes and trigrams.

For an important part of the present study the poems of both Livingston and Moore were transcribed into the phonetic alphabet, Arpabet, designed for General American English. Computerized analysis of the consequent mass of data revealed that the two poets differed significantly in their rates of use of certain "phoneme pairs." These consisted of the Arpabet symbols ending one word and beginning the next within a line. An author's choices of sequences of both words and sounds are reflected in these pairings. Three kinds of classification were made of pairs more favored by one or other poet. These were fully discussed in Chapters 10, 11, and 12, with the results presented in Tables 10.1, 11.1, and 12.1. In each case "The Night Before Christmas" was unequivocally aligned with Livingston's poems, not with Moore's. For example, all phoneme pairs in either poet's top hundred, in terms of overall frequency, were tested by chi-square to determine which were used by either man at statistically significant higher rates than by the other. It so happened that this objective means of selection produced ten phoneme pairs more often used by Moore and ten more often used by Livingston. Frequencies of "Livingston" pairs were then calculated, for all poems containing at least twelve relevant pairs, as percentages of the total frequencies of "Livingston" and "Moore" pairs combined. There was almost complete separation between Moore's poems and Livingston's, only four of Livingston's forty scored less than 54 percent and only two of Moore's thirty-two scored more than 54 percent. The mean for individual poems by Livingston was 66.654 percent; the mean for individual poems by Moore was 42.912 percent. The score of 64.912 percent for "The Night Before Christmas" fell near the middle of Livingston's range and outside Moore's.

Among tendencies registered by the counts of phoneme pairs it was clear that Livingston had a much greater liking than Moore for the definite and indefinite articles, "the" (especially) and "a," a measure of his greater reliance on concrete nouns. Rates of use of "the" and "a," calculated as percentages of the total number of words, distinguished between the poems of Moore and Livingston. At 11.439 "Visit" fell comfortably within Livingston's range of 2.521–15.882 but outside Moore's of 2.952–9.354. The chances of a sizable poem by Moore having a score so distant from his mean of 6.127 are about one in 1,400.

Tests of frequencies of other high-frequency words—a staple of modern authorship attribution studies—yielded similarly decisive results. Of the most common English words of all, apart from "the," only "that" was used by the two poets at rates so dissimilar as to render it effective as a stand-alone discriminator. Verse blocks of at least 500 words averaged a rate per 1,000 words of 12.210 for Moore, little more than half that, namely 6.319, for Livingston. The low rate of 1.845 in "Visit" again situated it more comfortably among Livingston's poems than among Moore's.

In Chapter 16 further analyses of common function words also allied "Visit" with Livingston, rather than with Moore. For the most sensitive test, from computerized lists of word counts in the two men's bodies of verse the most frequently occurring fifty in the work of either author were singled out and those used at rates at least 1.2 times greater by either Livingston or Moore, but not participating in word tests described in other chapters, were classed as either Livingston-favored words (there being eighteen) or Moore-favored words (there being twenty-two). The percentages of instances of Livingston-favored words among instances of all forty were computed for all poems by either author. At 60.920 percent "The Night Before Christmas" was very close to Livingston's mean of 61.417 percent, but far above Moore's of 36.295 percent. It was thus right in the middle of the distribution of scores for Livingston's poems and an outlier among scores for Moore's poems. A similar test of words somewhat less common but still occurring quite frequently was also shown in Chapter 17 to place "The Night Before Christmas" well within Livingston's range but just outside Moore's.

An attentive reader of Moore's verse soon becomes aware of his fondness for locutions such as "some," "at length," "in vain," "many a," "oft," and "that's." Since they occur no fewer than 160 times in his verse, but only nine times in Livingston's, they can be regarded as Moore "markers." "The Night Before Christmas" contains none. The only five poems by Moore (outside his manuscript notebook) without any of his markers are all less than a third of its length.[4] The anapestic "The Pig and the Rooster," included in Moore's *Poems* (1844), has two instances of "some," two of "at length," and one of "many a," while the manuscript piece "From Saint Nicholas" has three instances of "some" and one of "oft." In its total lack of Moore markers, "The Night Before Christmas" would be anomalous as a poem by Moore but normal as a poem by Livingston.

Two-word collocations beginning lines tell the same story. For example, "The Night Before Christmas" has "To the," "With the," and "And the," which together occur fifty-five times in Livingston's poems, whereas "To the" and "With the" are absent from Moore's, and "And the" appears only once. Livingston's much greater number of anapestic poems doubtless has a bearing on this discrepancy, but cannot adequately explain it. A detail of Moore's syntax furnishes another indicator. After an initial "And" his sentence structure often requires a comma, duly supplied on forty occasions. None of Livingston's 241 instances of "And" is punctuated with a comma and nor are any of the twelve in "The Night Before Christmas."

The exact repetition of two or more consecutive words in the midst of parallel phrase constructions occurs fourteen times in Livingston's verse and once in "Visit." Moore has only six examples of this class of repetition, two among his *Poems*, and four in his manuscript notebook. Only three fall within single lines, as do ten of Livingston's, and the example in Moore's notebook piece "Newport Beach" is rendered un–Livingston-like by its incorporation of the words "the mind," which Moore uses twenty-one times, if we include his notebook poems, but Livingston uses only twice. Two other relatively rare kinds of repetition in "Visit" are far more common in Livingston's verse than in Moore's.

Every attribution test summarized above classified "The Night Before Christmas" as belonging with Livingston's poems, not Moore's. The chief discriminators had not been cherry-picked so as bring about such a result. They were selected according to predetermined mathematical rules. It is hard to see why "The Night Before Christmas" should consistently be linked to Livingston in these one-on-one contests if it were really written by Moore.

When Donald Foster published *Author Unknown*, in which he argued that Livingston was the true author of "The Night Before Christmas," Moore's champions objected that he had ignored Moore's unpublished manuscript verses, several lightheartedly addressed to young folk. For the present investigation, all but three loose-leaved pieces, "From Saint Nicholas," "To Clem," and "To Fanny," were excluded from the analyses and reserved in order to check the tests themselves. The question to be answered was then whether any of these poems—the massive "Charles Elphinstone" and twelve short offerings—performed like "The Night

Before Christmas" on the battery of tests. In other words, when applied to this set of thirteen poems (all dated 1843–52), did the tests produce "false positives" by associating one or more of the set with Livingston? The answer was an unequivocal "No." Poems that emerged as conceivably Livingstonian on one or more of the tests were definitely ruled out by others. In the late poems Moore did use more articles ("the" and "a") than in *Poems*. But the most potent of all sets of discriminators—phoneme pairs more favored by Moore or Livingston—remained especially efficacious. Scores had been calculated as percentages of Livingston-favored phoneme pairs in relation to the combined totals of pairs favored by either author. These created almost complete separation between the works of the two men. Livingston's mean score of 66.654 was far above Moore's 42.912 but closely matched by 64.912 for "The Night Before Christmas." None of Moore's twelve short notebook poems yielded scores approaching that for "The Night Before Christmas." They averaged 40.783, while that for "Charles Elphinstone" was 45.714. The results for high-frequency words and medium-high-frequency words were scarcely less decisive.

Graphs will clarify, in vivid pictorial terms, the statements in the last seven sentences. Figure 3 combines results from Tables 12.1 and 18.3 for phoneme pairs. In other words, Moore's notebook poems are now included, along with the other poems with enough data to qualify for inclusion in

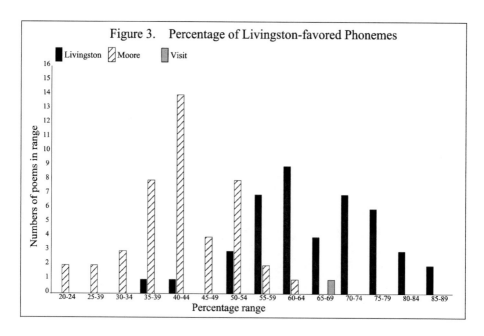

Figure 3.   Percentage of Livingston-favored Phonemes

Table 12.1. Percentages of Livingston-favored phoneme pairs are rounded off to the nearest whole number, and the numbers of poems by Moore and by Livingston that fall into the various ranges of percentages (20–24, 25–29, 30–34, and so on) are displayed in bar-graph form. It is clear that there are two authorial distributions of scores, with the peak number for Moore falling within the 40–44 percent range and the peak number for Livingston falling within the 60–64 percent range. "Visit" is placed in the 65–69 percent range, beyond Moore's overall span, but near the middle of Livingston's.

Figure 4 combines results for high-frequency and medium-high-frequency words, as tabulated in Tables 16.2, 17.1, 18.1, and 18.2.[5] Figures for "that" are also included. Those for individual Moore notebook poems are from Table 18.5, but those for Livingston are derived from the counts for individual poems that lie behind the amalgamations of Table 14.1. The graph is constructed in the same way as that in Figure 3. Again there are two overlapping authorial distributions, with Moore's highest peak in the 40–44 percent range, Livingston's in the 60–64 percent range. "Visit" is placed in the 55–59 percent range, beyond Moore's overall span, but not too far from the middle of Livingston's. In fact, the specific percentage for "Visit," namely 58, places it fairly close to the median score of 60 for Livingston, and well clear of the highest percentage for a poem by Moore, namely 50. That Moore poem is "Old Dobbin," which is not included in

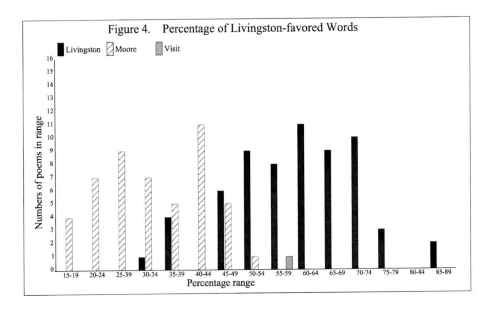

Figure 4.   Percentage of Livingston-favored Words

Figure 3, because it contains fewer than twelve relevant phoneme pairs, but of the ten that it does contain, six are Moore-favored, two Livingston-favored, giving it a score of 25 percent Livingston-favored, within the lower reaches of Moore's figures and well short of even the lowest-scoring Livingston poem. And, as we have seen, "Old Dobbin" is decisively categorized with Moore's verse, not Livingston's, on measures such as categories of phoneme pairs (Table 11.1) and definite and indefinite articles (Table 13.1).

In short, no poem by Moore, whether published in *Poems* (1844) or preserved in manuscript, comes close to equaling "The Night Before Christmas" in the consistency with which quantitative data associate it, not with Moore, but with Livingston.[6] Noteworthy also is the stability of Livingston's measurable poetic style over the years. As pointed out, most of his surviving poems, preserved in his handwritten volume, can be dated 1776–90, but, on the tests behind Figures 3 and 4, the dozen clearly datable to 1802–27 are not distinguishable from the earlier ones.

Burton E. Stevenson, believing that Moore wrote the poem, pointed out "that *Alice in Wonderland* was written by a professor of mathematics and that the *Nonsense Novels* and *The Elements of Political Science* are by one and the same hand."[7] But this is neither here not there. The Anglican deacon, mathematician, and logician Charles Dodgson could, under the pseudonym Lewis Carroll, write the classic story for children and its sequel *Through the Looking Glass*, and Stephen Leacock could publish weighty books on politics, history, and economics while also being one of the English language's great humorists. Similarly the classical, oriental, and biblical scholar, Clement Clarke Moore could both compile a *Hebrew Lexicon* and compose poems, some for young people. That kind of versatility is not so very rare. The pertinent issue is whether it is at all credible that Moore wrote one poem so unlike all his others as is "The Night Before Christmas." No doubt a writer may have a flash of inspiration that enables him or her to achieve a unique literary success that seems in a sense "out of character." But to postulate that Moore enjoyed such a serendipitous episode will hardly account for the nature of "The Night Before Christmas." We would still have to explain why Moore, on the solitary occasion in which he created something that was to catch the world's imagination, slipped into a style that was not only utterly atypical of his own verse but utterly typical of the verse of the very man who, according to his descendants, was the true author. It must be emphasized that the most significant tests conducted here are not of lexical items whose presence or absence depends on content. They are of the frequencies of common words such as "the," "on," "as," "at," "to," "that," "would," and "some"; locutions such as "many a" and "in vain"; and phoneme pairs composed of the last phonetic symbol in one word and the first in the next. These elements of composition are not readily subject to imitation. Their rates of use are largely beyond a writer's conscious control. They distinguish Moore's verse from Livingston's and they classify "The Night Before Christmas" with the latter. The reasonable conclusion is that "The Night Before Christmas" was composed by Henry Livingston.

Appendix I. Henry Livingston: Selected Poems and Prose

Poems have been chosen in order to illustrate the different kinds that Livingston wrote. They have been transcribed from Livingston's handwriting, or from the early printed texts when no manuscript copy is available. Titles have been standardized, as in Appendix II. Ampersands and abbreviations such as "wd" for "would" have been silently expanded, and misplaced or absent apostrophes have been moved or added. Spellings that are no longer standard have been retained when they can be paralleled in other texts of his time. Livingston's punctuation often seems to be more concerned with rhythm and tempo than with syntax, and he frequently uses the end of a line as substitute for a comma or heavier stop; a few small adjustments have been made where the punctuation or lack of punctuation is confusing or where omissions are clearly accidental. Livingston adopted four ways of indicating new stanzas or other breaks: sometimes he separated them by a line of space; sometimes he also numbered them; sometimes he indented the first line of a new stanza; and sometimes he began a stanza or section with a long dash. I have imposed uniformity by always taking the option of a line of space. Livingston's dashes are of various lengths, but have here been regularized. Livingston mostly employs capitals for emphasis but on occasions simply writes a word at double the normal size. In cases of the second sort I have used capitals. Underlined words have been rendered as in italics.

The sources of all but two of the poems are Livingston's autograph, and all but four of these are from his manuscript notebook, with "A Fable," "Scots Wha Hae Wie Wallace Bled," "God is Love," and "Without Distinction" from his contributions to his daughter Jane's poetry book. "On My Little Catherine Sleeping" was composed in 1775 and enclosed in a letter to his wife, while Livingston's commission as major in the Third New York Regiment of the revolutionary army forced his absence from his infant daughter. The letter is in the Chief Justice Sidney Breese Collection in the Illinois State Archives. "Carrier's Address 1803" is from the *Political Barometer* of 1 January 1803 and "On the Late Mr. Gilbert Cortland"—which reworked Livingston's epitaph on his wife, "To the Memory of Sarah Livingston," and was in turn reworked as "Catherine Livingston Breese"—is from the *Country Journal and Poughkeepsie Advertiser* of 6 December 1786. Livingston notes that the inspiration for "Scots Wha Hae" is the patriotic song by Robert Burns. I have excluded the charming "To My Little Niece Anne Duyckinck. Aged 7 Years" because it is printed in full in Chapter 2. "To My Little Niece Sally Livingston" is "on a little serenading wren she admired."

The poems are in chronological order, so far as this can be determined. Those from Livingston's manuscript book are in the order in which they appear there and belong to the period 1784–89, though some were published a few years later. The "Carrier's Address 1803" is the only piece that intervenes between these early works and the four entries in Jane's book, which are as late as 1827.

The sample of Livingston's prose is much more selective, consisting mainly of products of his whimsical fancy. His actual range is wide, including pieces on archaeology, history, anthropology, law, local and national issues, and curiosities of science, especially biology and botany. He kept a vivid diary of his army life.

Livingston's full titles and preambles to his prose works have been retained as indicating the way he wished to present them. Otherwise the transcriptions adhere to the same principles as for the poems.

Poems

On My Little Catherine Sleeping

Sweet Innocent lye still and sleep,
While chearfull seraphs vigils keep,
To ward off ev'ry shaft of death
That may be wing'd to seize thy breath.

Dear Infant how serene you lay,
Nor heed the bustle of the day!
Thy little bosom knows no care,

For guilt ne'er lay and wrankled there;
In thee all troubles die and cease,
And all is quiet all is peace.

How much unlike thy Father's life
Amid the Din of Arms and strife!
The tumult and the noise of war
Forever thundring in his ear.

Thy mother too has shed her tears
Has heav'd her sigh and known her fears.
Her lips hath not forgot to press
The bitter cup of keen distress.

And Thou sweet Babe will soon perceive
That to be mortal is to grieve;
That as the spark will upward fly,
So man still lives to mourn and dye.

Easter

WHEN JESUS bow'd his awful head
   And dy'd t'avert our fatal doom,
His friends the sacred corpse convey'd,
   To the dark region of the tomb.

The Angelic host, with wonder saw,
   Their sov'reign leave his bright abode,
To vindicate the righteous law,
   Promulged by th' Eternal GOD.

They view'd him in the sinner's stead
   Obey the precepts man forsook;
While woes unnumbered o'er his head,
   Like an unbounded ocean broke.

But when they saw the fatal tree,
   And there, the son of GOD expire!
(Unknown the ineffable decree,)
   Amazement fill'd the heav'nly choir.

And the dejected friendless train,
   Who fondly dream't of empire here;
Now mourn'd each expectation vain,
   And every hope dissolv'd in air.

Their foes exult, and scoffing cry,
    "And is your boasted leader gone?"
"His pow'r! the power but to die?"
    "His kingdom! but a narrow tomb?"

Let earth rejoice, let heav'n resound!
    Behold the conquering MONARCH rise!
From the *dark* mansion under ground,
    To the *bright* empire of the skies!

Resplendant, now each promise shines;
    Divinely bright each varying scene.
The great TRANSACTION how sublime!
    And LOVE how infinite! to men.

The Angels bow before their *KING*
    But never hail'd a SAVIOUR'S name:
'Tis Man, can a REDEEMER sing;
    And dying love exalts *his* theme.

An Invitation to the Country

The winter all surly is flown,
    The frost, and the ice, and the snow:
The violets already have blown,
    Already the daffodils glow.

The forests and copses around,
    Their foliage begin to display;
The copses and forests resound
    With the music and disport of May.

E'er Phoebus has gladded the plains,
    E'er the mountains are tip'd with his gold!
The sky lark's shrill matin proclaims,
    A songster, harmonius as bold.

The Linnet, and Thrush, thro the day,
    Join notes with the soft cooing dove;
Not a bush, but can witness a Lay;
    Or the softer endearments of Love.

At eve, when the shadows prevail;
    And night throws her mantle around;

The nightingale warbles her tale
  And harmony dwells in the sound.

The grasshopper chirps at our feet,
  The butterfly wings it along,
The season and love will compleat,
  What they want in the raptures of song.

Not an insect that flits o'er the lawn
  But gambols in pleasure and play,
Rejoicing the winter is gone,
  And hailing the pleasanter May.

Let us join in their revels my dear!
  To innocent joy give a loose!
No surfeits, or harm can we fear
  The pleasures we cannot abuse.

What is all the gay town can bestow?
  What all its inhabitants share?
But trifles, and glitter, and show,
  That cloy and displease as they glare.

These snares may entangle the weak;
  But never the rational soul;
The flimsy enchantment will break
  Where reason can ever control.

By the side of a murmuring stream,
  Where willows the margin imbrown;
We'll wander, unheeded, unseen,
  Nor envy the taste of the town.

In scenes, where confusion and noise
  And riot's loud voice is unknown;
We'll humbly participate joys,
  That ever from greatness have flown.

Let avarice smile o'er its gain,
  Ambition exult at its height,
Dissipation unloose every rein,
  In pursuit of forbidden delight.

We'll cling to our cottage my love,
  There a meeting with bliss we ensure.

The Seraphs who carol above
Must smile on enjoyments so pure.

To My Little Niece Sally Livingston

Hasty pilgrim stop thy pace
Turn a moment to this place
Read what pity hath erected
To a songster she respected.

Little minstrel all is o'er
Never will thy chirpings more
Soothe the heavy heart of care
Or dispel the darkness there.

I have known thee e'er the sun
Hath on yonder mountain shone;
E'er the sky-lark hath ascended,
Or the Thrush her throat distended;
Cheerful trill thy little ditty
As the singer, blithe and pretty.

Labour stood half bent to hear,
Study lent a list'ning ear,
Dissipation stop'd a while,
Grief was even seen to smile,
Ambition—but the gushing tear
O'erwhelms the stone and stops me here.

Letter Sent to Master Timmy Dwight

Master Timmy brisk and airy
Blythe as Oberon the fairy
On thy head thy cousin wishes
Thousand and ten thousand blisses.

Never may thy wicket ball
In a well or puddle fall;
Or thy wild ambitious kite
O'er the Elm's thick foliage light.

When on bended knee thou sittest
And the mark in fancy hittest

May thy marble truly trace
Where thy wishes mark'd the place.

If at hide and seek you play,
All involved in the hay
Titt'ring hear the joyful sound
"Timmy never can be found."

If you hope or if you run
Or whatever is the fun,
Vic'try with her sounding pinion
Hover o'er her little minion.

But when hunger calls the boys
From their helter skelter joys:
Bread and cheese in order standing
For their most rapacious handling
Timmy may thy luncheon be
More than Ben's as five to three.

But if Hasty pudding's dish
Meet thy vast capacious wish—
Or lob-lolly's charming jelly
Court thy cormorantal belly
Mortal foe to megre fast
Be thy spoonful first and last.

Letter to My Brother Beekman

To my dear brother Beekman I sit down and write
Ten minutes past eight and a very cold night.
Not far from me sits with a vallancy cap on
Our very good couzin, Elizabeth Tappen,
A tighter young seamstress you'd ne'er wish to see
And she (blessings on her) is sewing for me.
New shirts and new cravats this morning cut out
Are tumbled in heaps and lye huddled about.
My wardrobe (a wonder) will soon be enriched
With ruffles new hemmed and wristbands new stitched.
Believe me dear brother tho women may be
Compared to us, of inferiour degree
Yet still they are useful I vow with a fegs
When our shirts are in tatters and jackets in rags.

Now for news my sweet fellow—first learn with a sigh
That matters are carried here gloriously high
Such gadding—such ambling—such jaunting about
To tea with Miss Nancy—To sweet Willy's rout
New Parties at coffee—then parties at wine
Next day all the world with the Major must dine
Bounce all hands to Fishkill must go in a clutter
To guzzle bohea and destroy bread and butter
While you at New Lebanon stand all forlorn
Behind the cold counter from ev'ning to morn
The old tenor merchants push nigher and nigher
Till fairly they shut out poor Baze from the fire.

Out out my dear brother Aunt Amy's just come
With a flask for molasses and a bottle of rum
Run! help the poor creature to light from her jade
You see the dear lady's a power afraid.

Souse into your arms she leaps like an otter
And smears your new coat with her piggin of butter
Next an army of shakers your quarters beleager
With optics distorted and visages meagre
To fill their black runlets with brandy and gin
Two blessed exorcists to drive away sin.

But laugh away sorrow nor mind it a daisy
Since it matters but little my dear brother Bazee
Whether here you are rolling in pastime and pleasure
Or up at New Lebanon taffety measure
If the sweetest of lasses CONTENTMENT you find
And the banquet enjoy of an undisturb'd mind
 Of friendship and love let who will make a pother
 Believe me dear Baze your affectionate brother
 Will never forget the fifth son of his mother.
P.S. If it suits your convenience remit if you please
To my good brother Paul an embrace and a squeeze.

The Vine and Oak

A vine from noblest lineage sprung
And with the choicest clusters hung,

In purple rob'd reclining lay
And catch'd the noontide's fervid ray:

The num'rous plants that deck the field
Did all the palm of beauty yield,
Pronounc'd her fairest of their train
And hail'd her empress of the plain.

A neighb'ring Oak whose spiry height
In low-hung clouds was hid from sight,
Who dar'd the winds in all their forms
And brav'd a thousand howling storms;
Conscious of worth, sublimely stood
The pride and glory of the wood.
He saw her all defenseless lay
To each invading beast a prey,
And wish'd to clasp her in his arms
And bear her far away from harms.
'Twas love—'twas tenderness—'twas all
That men the *tender passion* call.

He urg'd his suit but urg'd in vain,
The vine regardless of his pain
Still flirted with each flippant green
With seeing pleas'd, and being seen
And as the syren Flattery sang
Would o'er the strains ecstatic hang
Enjoy'd the minutes as they rose
Nor fears, her bosom discompose.

But now the boding clouds arise
And scowling darkness veils the skies;
Harsh thunders roar—red lightnings gleam,
And rushing torrents, close the scene.

The fawning, adulating crowd
Who late in thronged circles bow'd
Now left their goddess of a day
To the o'erwhelming flood a prey.
Which swell'd a deluge poured around
And tore her helpless from the ground;
Her rifled foliage floated wide
And ruby nectar ting'd the tide.

With eager eyes and heart dismay'd
She look'd, but look'd in vain for aid.
"Are all my lovers fled," she cry'd,
"Who at my feet this morning sigh'd,
"And swore my reign would never end
"While youth and beauty had a friend?
"I am unhappy who believ'd!
"And they detested who deceived!
"Curse on that whim call'd *maiden pride*
"Which made me shun the name of *bride*,
"When yonder oak confess'd his flame
"And woo'd me in fair honor's name.
"—But now repentance comes too late
"And all forlorn I meet my fate."

The oak who safely wav'd above
Look'd down once more with eyes of love
(Love higher wrought with pity join'd
True mark of an exalted mind,)
Declar'd her coldness could suspend
But not his gen'rous passion end.
Beg'd to renew his am'rous plea—
—As warm for union now as he,
To his embraces, quick she flew
And felt and gave sensations new.

Enrich'd and graced by the sweet prise
He lifts her tendrils to the skies;
Whilst she, protected and carest
Sinks in his arms completely blest.

To Spadille

Thou little four-leg'd paltry varlet
It makes my colour rise like scarlet
To see thee jump upon a knee
Where I would give the world to be;
Nay, I could name the very time
When I beheld that nose of thine
Approach those lips which once to kiss
I felt the height of all my bliss.

These eyes have seen thy head at rest
Upon my lovely Delia's breast;
—A breast from beauty's model made
Where all the loves and graces play'd.
I've seen thee gaze upon those eyes
Where roguish Cupid ever lyes
And meet a glance so soft—so kind
That envy fill'd my aching mind.
Spadille, in pity of my pain
Attempt thy pertness to restrain—
—It hurts my soul to see a waste
Of fondness thou canst never taste.

Could I but take they envied place
I'd gaze upon her lovely face
Till all inflamed with her charms
Around her neck I'd throw my arms
And riot in a sea of blisses
While giving and receiving kisses.

A Rebus on … (War Rebus)

Take the name of that hero who dreadful in war
Spread the terror of Rome thro the nations afar,
With the King of the fairies that sly jealous sprite
Who sleeps all the day but who gambols all night
Green Caty-dids draw him—a nut shell contains him,
His kingdom a meadow and a dewdrop sustains him.

What the peasant enjoys when his labour is o'er
And the seaboy embraces the hurricane's roar.

What the pretty girls cry tho their meaning is yes
When swains at their feet ask the boon of a kiss.

That period of day when gay Phoebus retires
To the arms of his Thetis to meet keener fires.

That passion delightful which thrilling imparts
Feelings more than ecstatic to congenial hearts,
Which arouses to fury—and lulls to repose
Is keen as the thorn yet as sweet as the rose.

The goddess white-robed by whom unbefriended
Even beauty and wit pass along unattended.
That region where heav'n-born freedom resides
Where each shepherd is true and each maiden is kind.

That goddess refulgent whose glance pours the day,
Where midnight, and error, and ignorance lay.

The chief who rush'd bold thro the Granican flood
While the fates pale with fear on the shore trembling stood.

What each one pursues tho but few can obtain
And ever repays its possession with pain.

What wrings the kind heart when distress is in view
And what each observer discovers in you.

And lastly that word which no lover can bear
Nor I from this charmer with patience can hear.

The initials of these ye lads and ye lassess
Will show you a girl that description surpasses.
The lily combin'd with the new open'd rose
In her bosom's displayed—on her cheek sweetly glows.
Her pencil e'en fancy throws by in despair
When fondly attempting to copy my fair.

On the Late Mr. Gilbert Cortland

BEYOND where billows roll or tempests vex
Is gone! the best, and loveliest of his sex!
His brittle bark on life's wild ocean tost,
In the unequal conflict soon was lost.

Tho' short its struggle, much alas it bore,
Then sank beneath the storm, and rose no more.

But when th' Arch-angel's awful trump shall sound
And thunder, LIFE, thro' all the vast profound,
The renovated vessel will be seen;
Transcendant floating on the silver stream!
Its joyful Ensigns waving in the air,
The tides propitious, and the zephyrs fair!
'Tis safe within the destin'd port of bliss,
Each sail is furl'd, and all around is peace.

Letter from a Tenant of Mrs. Van Kleeck

My very good landlady, Mistress Van Kleeck
(For the tears that o'erwhelm me I scarcely can speak)
I know that I promis'd you hogs two or three
(But who knows his destiny? certain not me!)
That I promis'd three hogs I don't mean to deny
(I can prove that I had five or six upon sty.)

Three hogs did I say? three sows I say then
Pon' honour I ne'er had a male upon pen.

Well Madam, the long and the short of the clatter
For mumbling and mincing will not better the matter;
And murder and truth my dear mammy would say
By some means or other forever saw day;
And Daddy himself, as we chop'd in the wood
Would often observe that lying wan't good.

Tell truth my sweet fellow—no matter who feels it:
It ne'er can do hurt to the man who reveals it.

But stop!—While my Dady and Mammy's the subject
I am running aside of the original object–

The sows my sweet madam—the sows I repeat
Which you and your household expected to eat,
Instead of attending their corn and their swill
Gave way to an ugly He-sow's wicked will.

When 'twill end your good Lady-ship need not be told
For *Nature* is still, as she hath been of old;
And when he cries YES, mortals may not cry NO

So Madam farewell, with my holliday bow.

The Fly

As on a summer's fervid day
The youthful Delia slumb'ring lay,
A thousand Cupids flutt'red round
The guardians of the hallow'd ground.

Some clustered in her auburn hair
To keep the ringlets wreathed there;

While others form'd a canopy
With wing in wing enlock'd on high,
To ward each stragling solar ray
That thro the foliage found a way.
Another party took her breath
Replete with sweetness and with health,
To aid the elegant perfume
Of every charming flow'r in bloom.

But luckless girl! her snow-white breast
Which the inverted shawl confest,
A fly of taste had fondly chose
Whereon to riot or repose:

Him, a young sentinel espy'd,
And as his bow he bent he cry'd,
"Go sacrilegious catif go
To writhe with plund'ring Gnats below."

The winged shaft as lightning flew
And pierced the hapless insect thro
But stop'd not there—Roused by the smart
Poor Delia found it in her heart.

On a Lap-Dog of the Miss Loth, Called Belle

If ever 'twas proper and lawful and decent
To mourn for a death both untimely and recent,
It certain is now—Each grace and each muse
In the dear little creature a spice did infuse.
Like a sweet pretty lady she bridled her chin
And trip'd o'er the floor like another Miss Prim
And when the dear animal open'd its throat
Urania herself might have mother'd the note:
No coxcomb that pats o'er the rough-pebbled street
Or Beau-ling self pleased so smooth and so sweet
Could meet with a smile or even a simper
If Belle dearer Belle was observed to whimper.
But if in sweet blandishment Belle frisk'd around
E'en wits with the *beaux* in despair left the ground.

But she'd gone, lovely creature! the sweetest of curs
To weep is our LOT, but to slumber is hers.

To Miss (Roses)

SWEET as op'ning roses are
As th' expanded lilly fair
Blithsome as the breathing day
Smiling as the smiling May
Heav'n itself her feeling mind
Loveliest of the lovely kind
Is my Daphne! sweetest maid
That e'er sported in the glade.

When beneath the nodding grove
She inclines to muse or rove
Airs of Eden float around
Flow'rs spontaneous deck the ground
Cupids clap their wings about her
Life itself's not life without her.

News-Boy's Address (1803)

ALL hail to the season so jovial and gay,
More grateful to NEWS-BOYS than blossoms of May,
Than Summer's green gown, or Miss Autumn's brocade
Bespangled with gold, and with diamonds o'erlaid;
Give me surly Winter, bald-headed and bare,
Cold nights, frosty mornings, and keen piercing air,
With storms roaring round him; rain, hail, sleet and snow,
While hoarse, from the mountains the howling winds blow;
For Summer and Autumn and fair-bosom'd Spring,
With their pinks and their peaches, no holidays bring;
But now comes blithe Christmas, while just in his rear,
Advances our saint, jolly, laughing, NEW-YEAR,
Which, time immemorial, to us has been made
The source of our wealth and support of our trade,
For then, *cockahoop* with the magical song,
That charms from your purses the glittering *l'argent*,
With our pulse beating quick, and our breast void of pain,
We quit *types* and *shadows*, the *substance* to gain.

But what, on this festive occasion, to say,
Is a question which puzzles your poet, to day;
Since the storms which have ravag'd old Europe are o'er,

And the light'nings and thund'rings of war are no more;
Even Oglou, who Turkey's grand Seignior defied,
Has, at length, gain'd his point, and preferment beside;
Toussaint, the black chief, too, is trick'd by Le Clerc,
And in chains sent to limbo by king Bonaparte,
While General *Le Death*, to revenge such foul play,
Tricks Le Clerc and his minions in much the same way,
And Negroes, by plunder, and carnage, and flame,
Shew Frenchmen how well they their *rights* can maintain.

Well—since from abroad no great tidings are brought,
Let us see what at home there is, worthy of note;
Why here we find little to trouble our heads,
Except paper-battles 'twixt Demos and Feds;
Abusing and squabbling and wrangling and spite,
Though I, for my life, see not what they get by't,
Unless 'tis the pleasure their venom to spit
And make folks believe they've abundance of wit;
But in this they mistake, for abuse, 'tis well known,
Is the wit and the wisdom of blackguards, alone.

But to come to the point which I've long had in view,
My patrons attend, I've a few words for you;
You'll please to remember how, many months past,
While tempests roar'd loud and while shrill scream'd the blast,
When heat sing'd the earth and when cold froze the air,
And sometimes when suns shone serenely and fair,
With the news gather'd up from the wide world, all o'er,
True as time, ev'ry week, I arrived at your door;
And now, as old custom ordains, I appear,
To present you, my Patrons, a HAPPY NEW-YEAR,
The year which we name EIGHTEEN HUNDRED and THREE,
Which brings you a song and your Carrier a *Fee*,
At least I predict so, (with deff'rence to you)
As we all can *predict* what we *wish* to be true.
How cheerfully then will I stick to the press,
For a twelvemonth to come—be the same more or less,
To tell you if War his bold clarion shall sound,
Or Betsy's shrill voice Billy's bosom shall wound;
If fevers shall rage and their thousands destroy,
Or your poultry be kidnap'd by some thievish boy;

If hurricanes level both city and town,
Or Bragman, the bully knock Limberlegs down;
If lightnings, fierce blazings, cause hundreds to die,
Or Johnny be pierc'd by Miss Jenny's bright eye;
Or if congress shall make, or our state legislature,
Remarkable movements—by land or by water,
And many more *strange things* we'll tell you to boot,
As the seasons roll on and occasion shall suit.

But 'tis time that I bid you good bye, till next year,
By wishing you happiness, peace and good cheer;
To the ladies, the charms both of form and of face,
Expression, attraction, and each nameless grace,
Their tempers benign, ting'd with sentiment's fire,
Galants whom they love, and the swains they admire;
To the clergy meek charity, unmix'd with pride,
And *something* to wake us on Sunday, beside;
To the farmer fine crops; to the merchant much trade;
To the sexton small use for the mattock and spade;
To physicians, few patients; to lawyers, light fees;
But to printers, the *shiners*, as oft as you please;
In short, to conclude my nonsensical song
To all, what they wish, if they wish nothing wrong.

A Fable

WHEN time was young the story goes
The birds and beasts were mortal foes:
The Lion led the latter throng
The Eagle urg'd the birds along.
The Tyger flash'd his lightning eyes,
The Cock's loud clarion reach'd the skies:
Breathing defiance—Grimly here
Growl'd the relentless savage bear.
Now Turkeys gobbelled alarms
And Skunks and field mice rush'd to arms.
A regiment of Moles were brought
Where the heroic Linnets fought.
The ponderous Elephant was plac'd
Where the gigantic Ostrich pac'd;
The Zebras, rough resistance found

From Cassowarys' battle ground,
And Wrens would flutter peck and scratch
Where the prim ground squirrel kept his watch.

Neutral, the Bat here stood alone
And arms or panoply had none
Averring o'er and o'er again
He was no beast—'Twas very plain—
For he could fly—And stretch'd a wing
There could not be a simpler thing:
He could not be a bird was clear
By pointing to his ears and hair.

While still the rage of battle burn'd
Those subterfuges serv'd his turn;
But when at last the Eagle rose
Superior o'er his flying foes
The Bat was seiz'd to hear his doom
Unlucky culprit! Much too soon.

Sentence pronounced by Judge advocate Crow

Unworthy of meridian light,
Too base for even ebon night,
In twilight only dare to fly
To seize the beetle humming by;
Then hie thee to thy murky place
And muffle there thy recreant face.

Scots Wha Hae Wie Wallace Bled

In arts and arms Escotia stands
Foremost of European lands
Dear soil! from whence my fathers came
I bless and hail thy worth and fame.

Thy sturdy sons in martial pride
With their good broad-swords by their side
In tartan plaid and bonnets blue
A band of Heroes in review.

Scotland excels in peaceful arts:
—Her pulpits warm the coldest hearts;
In poetry her Thompson shines
And thrills us with his glowing lines.

Ramsey and Burns each in their day
Attune their lyres in sweetest lay,
While Scott ascends Parnassus heights
And all the listening world delights.

–But—useless grown my broken shell
I bid the land of cares farewell
Oppressed with the lapse of time
I faintly dream of AULD LANG SYNE.

God is Love

I LOVE my feeble voice to raise
In humble pray'r and ardent praise
Till my rapt soul attains that height
When all is glory and delight.

I LOVE to read the book of Heav'n
Which Grace to fall'n man has giv'n;
Where ev'ry page and ev'ry line
Proclaims its origen divine.

I LOVE that consecrated Fane
Where GOD has stamp'd his holy name:
United with my brethren there
We hear the word and join in pray'r.

I LOVE to join the pious few
And there the covenant renew,
Recount our joys, relate our grief
And jointly ask from GOD relief.

I LOVE on Pity's wing to fly
To sooth the deep expiring sigh.
To wipe the tear from wan distress
And light a smile on Sorrow's face.

I LOVE to view domestic bliss
Bound with the ligature of peace,
Where Parents—Children—All agree
To tune the lute of harmony.

I LOVE the morning's roseate ray,
I bless the glorious march of day,

And when the lulling ev'ning comes
I love the night amidst its glooms.

I LOVE to anticipate the day
When the freed spirit wings its way
To the Jerusalem above
Where reigns th' eternal SOURCE of LOVE.

Without Distinction

Without distinction, fame, or note
Upon the tide of life I float
A bubble almost lost to sight
As cobweb frail, as vapor light;
And yet within that bubble lies
A spark of life which never dies.

Prose

Astronomical Intelligence

The Editor of the POUGHKEEPSIE JOURNAL,
has permission to publish the following amazing Discoveries.   R—.

ASTRONOMICAL INTELLIGENCE.

IN the month of February 1789, a most excentric idea entered the head of
professor Zeritof Shoralow, of the royal academy for celestial observations
at Moscow. He caused a tube of 234 feet in length, and 29 feet in diameter,
to be constructed of planks; perfectly smooth and circular within as the
interior part of a fuzee. Instead of glass lens to furnish this enormous telescope, and which no vitrisical manufactory upon earth could supply, he
formed them from the purest, transparent ice, carefully cut from the river
Wolga. These pieces were five feet in thickness, and of the diameter of the
cylander. Their proper diminutions he effected by the application of warm
substances. It was not till after thirteen days unwearied attention that they
were perfectly finished and rendered fit for optical purposes.

This huge machine was constructed on a hill adjacent to the city of
Moscow, where the learned and ingenius professor Shoralow intended to
make his observations; and was suspended so mechanically nice, that with
ease he could turn it to any part of the heavens.

It was on the 25th of February, in a night uncommonly serene, that professor Zeritof Shoralow, wrapped in threefold thicknesses of fur, turned his gigantic tube full on the planet Jupiter; when, to his astonishment, he found that immense frozen globe brought as it were within the reach of his hand for inspection. The mountains, rivers, houses, men, women, and even the very hens and chickens were perfectly apparent.

Inured as the Muscovite was to ice and snow, the shivering appearance that every thing put on at near five hundred millions of miles distance from the sun frighted him. The sole employment of the men appeared to consist in procuring fuel, and of the women in heaping it on the fires. Lovers confabulated swathed in redoubled flannels; and frequently, when the mutual kiss was attempted a cement of ice completed the contact.

From these frigid scenes, the astronomer, shivering with sympathetic cold, turned his telescope to glowing Mercury. Every thing was in contrast to Jupiter. *There*, eternal frost held its dreary reign; every pulse beat low, and life was almost afraid to avow its existence. *Here*, all was glowing sunshine and hurly burly. Lawyers were worse than loquacious; coquets fidgeted in frenzy; and the very ducks danced on the mud. The heat appeared intense. Joints of meat were roasted before the sun as on our globe at a kitchen fire, and apple pyes and custards were baking on every stone wall. The professor had already thrown off two of his fur gowns when the planet Mars caught his attention.

Ye that delight in blue coats with white or scarlet facings, or gold or silver epaulets, red feathers with black tops, or black feathers with red tops; hats cocked, hats flopped, or infantry caps; muskets, small swords, broad swords, bayonets, howitzers, royals, long twelves and forty-eight pounders; behold a banquet for you all! In this region ever thing wore the appearance of hostility. Farmers plowed in gaters, dropped feed corn from cartouch boxes, and digged potatoes with spontoons. The very women flew about in the stile *militaire*. Their mops were made to resemble spunges, the rims of their spinning wheels looked like trucks, and their sapawn pots were thirteen inch shells.

Professor Zeritof Shoralow saw a love scene, where the lady resisted as a besieged citadel, and the gallant made his approaches by zig-zag and countermine.

"Hail happy region, where woman for once is the governing animal, and men appear, perhaps as they ever ought, tagging humbly in their rear! Charming Venus! thine is the realm where masculinity dares not rear its audacious front, but lovely femalism is all in all!" Thus exclaimed the Russian sage when the beauteus orb of Venus met his enraptured eye.

In an elegant dome, where every lattice and portal were thrown wide open, that all might see and hear (for ladies love to be heard and seen) were seated an assembly of matrons to legislate for the community. The speaker, in conformity to the order of the house, was dressed in a rich purple gown with a train of three yards in length; a petticoat most tastefully flounced, a camel's hair shawl glistening with undulated rows of diamonds, earrings of the purest pearls, and a tete and bishop protuberant and enchanting beyond description.

The secretary was observed to make her minutes with a quill from the wing of a sparrow, and dipped her ink out of a reservoir of real HORN.

They appeared to be in warm debate: and the professor by looking at a paper over the shoulder of a lady dressed in cross-barred muslin, found the subject to be, whether the men in future might be entertained as obsequious humble companions, or, be driven absolutely out of doors, and employed in unremitted drudgery. A major appeared for the latter measure; but the satirical Shoralow could not help remarking that several very engaging damsels offered their services as overseers of the poor Yahoos.

Love, and all its delectable concomitants was utterly unknown there; as that passion exists but where equality is found or understood. The dear viragos had thrust the wretched males too far from them to admit of even an artificial reciprocity of situation.

Many philosophers assert that love in the female œconomy acts as a powerful absorbent; and, that where it is genuinely felt a thousand disagreeable queer feelings and pettishnesses are perfectly unknown. Zeritof Shoralow it is said now inclines to this opinion from the multiplicity of not very bewitching freaks he observed among the Venusian ladies.

Besides caprice, petulancy and ill-nature, the want of personal attention was general. Where there was no admirer to please, nor rival to mortify, to what purpose even the affection of amiability?

The accurate Muscovite in the memoir addressed to his college has observed that the female on this planet from imperial women down to the humble mosquito had uncontended domination. The ferocious heifer gored the bull from the pastures: rams fled before heroic ewes; the tremendous goose stalked before the suppliant gander; and champion hens crowed over dejected he-biddies.

The enlightened Shoralow was going on with observations to gratify and enrich his native planet, when a southern breeze blew mildly on him—warm vapours floated far and wide—and a trickling stream was all that remained of materials that drew such unexpected information from our neighbour worlds.

Country Journal and Poughkeepsie Advertiser, 15 September 1789

Notes: In the opening paragraph, "lens" is a nineteenth-century variant plural meaning "lenses" and "Wolga" is the Dutch form of the "Volga." In the sixth paragraph, "sapawn pots" are presumably pots for "sapan" or "sappan," a red dyewood from an East Indian tree. In the ninth paragraph, a "tête" (here "tete") is a woman's head of hair or elaborate wig, and a "bishop" is a bustle, which is a contrivance for causing a skirt to hang back from the hips. In the penultimate paragraph, "he-biddies" are roosters.

Universal Hospital

For the NEW-YORK MAGAZINE.

Messrs EDITORS:

You may publish the following copy of an advertisement I lately met with in my sojournings.   R–.

UNIVERSAL HOSPITAL

The subscriber, with whose education no pains has been spared—who has the whole works of *Duns Scotus*, Jacob Behmen, and Dr. Sangrado, by heart—has long been an adept in the almost-forgotten, never-enough-to-be-applauded, golden science of astrology—who has analyzed the *Garcinia Mangostana* under the burning rays of a vertical sun, examined the *winteranea aromatica* upon the cliffs on which it grew within twenty degrees of the frozen pole, and from the gloomy caverns of Derbyshire surprised the world with the inestimable, miraculous, *terra ponderosa*—who, in pursuit of an Arabian nostrum among the ruins of Palmyra, was upon the brink of suffering an excruciating impalement as a spy—has investigated every university in Europe—was personally acquainted with Hannah Stevens, negro Cæsar, and Dr. Yeldal—and, at this moment corresponds with all the benevolent dames in America—who knew the difference between *motherworth* and *old man's pepper*, has erected a superb edifice for the purposes of an *universal hospital*; where, besides eradicating the host of maladies which human frames are heirs to, he effects cures for mental disorders in a manner not less wonderful than perfectfully efficacious.

To induce the public not to consider him in the light of a pompous pretender, he particularizes, in a few examples, his method of performing cures of infirm minds: for instance, if a young lady, deeply in love, applies for relief, he takes three or four sighs, warm from her heart, melts them in a soft pomatum gallipot, with a little rosin scraped from a violin and virgin wax, makes the whole into a salve; a small plaister of which, put upon the tip of her tongue, will extract all the venom from her bosom, and cause it to evaporate in colloquial nonsense.

Coquetry he relieves by a process diametrically opposite to the afore-going; by taking a few energetic declarations immediately as they fall from the lips, and forging them into the form of a magnet: this he applys under the stays next her heart—sympathy does the rest.

The *prude* is cured by simply bringing her mouth into contact with that of a coquette when the latter is above mediocrity in her character: this process is called in Cochin-China, *imbibition*.

Pride, in men or women, is eradicated, by mixing half a dozen whistles of the *humility*, (a meek little bird of the snipe kind) with an ounce of the honey of the *humble* bee, and cramming a pellet of it in each nostril, when in their haughtiest distension.

If a *husband* is *morose*, the kindest expostulations of his wife must be tied up in a small blue silk bag, and kept warm in his bosom; if he is *jealous*, he must take three scruples of Shakespeare's Othello, reduced to an impal-pable powder, and diet himself and spouse upon oat-meal gruel: if he is *hen-peck'd*, he may live a fortnight upon soup made of the hearts of Bantam cocks, and read *Catherine* and *Petruchio* twice every day.

He compels *inconstant* swains to employ themselves without the least intermission in building cages for turtle-doves; and nymphs afflicted with the same malady, to sit and look on the whole time.

That the under-written is exceedingly modest (although by his above professions, some might be led to suppose the contrary) appears by his openly declaring, that, bending as he is under the pressure of experimental and theoretical information, yet, he knows of no medicant that will operate upon a *shrew*; he has distilled every plant of every name—examined the whole kingdome of metals, ores and fossils, and put every element to the torture for this purpose, but all in vain. His *pay* is the *satisfaction* resulting from his agency in lightening some of the burdens incident to humanity, and eradicating a few of the thorns which but too plentifully spring up and mar the path of earth's poor pilgrims.

WIZARD.

New-York Museum; or, Literary Review, 4.2 (April 1791), 222.

Note: In the opening paragraph, Duns Scotus (c. 1266–1308) was among the fore-most medieval philosopher-theologians; "Jacob Behmen" is an archaic English vari-ant of the name of the German Christian mystic Jacob Boehme (1575–1624); Dr. Sangrado is a charlatan physician, whose remedies were copious bloodletting and administration of hot water, in Alain René Le Sage's picaresque novel *Gil Blas* (1715–35); Garcinia Mangastana or purple mangosteen is a tropical tree used in traditional medicine; the slave Negro Caesar's folk-medical antidote to poison secured him his freedom and an annuity of one hundred pounds from the South Carolina Commons House of Assembly in 1749; a Dr. Yeldal is named in the *Ency-*

clopedia Londinensis, volume 2, edited by John Wilkes (London: J. Adlard, 1812) as a follower of Mesmer and a user of magnetism (p. 497); *winteranea aromatica* (a tonic bark), *terra ponderosa* (barium sulphate), *motherworth* or *motherwort* (an herbacious perennial), and *old man's pepper* (yarrow) have all been used as medicines.

Description of the Baby House of Miss Biddy Puerilla

DESCRIPTION *of the* Baby House, *&c. of Miss* Biddy Puerilla, *intended to be constructed in the southwest corner of her Mamma's garden.*
By *Seignior* Whimsicallo Pomposo

The whole ground to be improved, is 16 feet from north to south, and 11 1-2 feet from east to west. On an eminence, made by one of nature's pioneers, a mole, is to be erected the principal edifice, for the accommodation of Miss Biddy's doll Fanny. The five architectural orders are to be stripped of their choicest beauties to decorate it; and obelisks, statues, and columns, are to stand centinels all around.

From a duck trough at the southeast angle, water is to be brought by hydraulic machines; so as to form, almost under the eaves of the palace, a cascade six inches wide and 9 3-4 inches in heighth. This was a desideratum long contemplated, and but lately compleated in the cerrebellum of the above ingenious artist.

The principal street leading from Miss Fanny's palace to that of Miss Clarinda, the next doll in favor; is to be 7 inches wide: and all the diverging lanes 4 1-2 inches broad.

Those parts of the map colored with deep red, are to be appropriated to a number of elegant purposes, too multifarious to be here enumerated.

Gigantic trees, of the whortle-berry and current tribes, are to shed a pleasing gloom over the most important avenues: while the river before mentioned, enriched with delightful tadpoles, is to meander thro' every part of the paradise. Melodious wrens are engaged to warble from a gooseberry bush, and several well-instructed frogs are to croak the bass. Two elegant kittens will bound along the streets, and Miss Biddy's pied lap-dog Cupie, is to stalk the mammoth of this new creation.

Upon the whole, Miss Biddy is determined, that her improvements shall be so stupendous; as would overwhelm the builders of Palmyra, the constructors of the Appian Way, and William Penn, himself, with shame and confusion were they present to behold them.

There are not wanting however some captious carping people, who arraign the economy and prudence of Miss Biddy's mamma, for going to such enormous expence to gratify a capricious little minx. This, they observe is to be her third baby house; [*a line of text is missing here*] into a fourth. Besides say they, the old lady should consider, that at the very moment she is fostering these dreams of puny splendor, the garden fence itself is by no means secure; for twice has the great black bull broke through, near the very spot where Miss Biddy is to be indulged in this wonderful wonder: and, add they, should he rush thro when the plan is perfected; adieu in a moment to the palaces, the temples, the obelisks, the naval pillar, the statues, the triumphal arches—and—the unfortunate gooseberry bush. R.

Country Journal and Poughkeepsie Advertiser, 19 January 1792.

Anticipation: The Battle of Miami

For the NEW-YORK MAGAZINE

ANTICIPATION.

Extract from Naponascon's celebrated history of the rise, declension, and renovation, of the empire of the west. Published in two folio volumes, with splendid engravings, at Qutagamis, *in* 1885.

The BATTLE *of* MIAMI.

IN the autumn of the year 1791, the pale men, to the number of five thousand, headed by one of their most experienced chiefs, with seven pieces of brass cannon, and every other implement of war in use at that time, began a march into our country along the banks of the lesser Miami.

Their avowed purpose was to erect fortresses every twenty or thirty miles—destroy our villages at the sources of the two Miamis—and, by keeping possession of that fertile territory, deprive the red men of their principal means of subsistence.

The confederated warriors, whose numbers did not exceed twelve hundred, were commanded by *Montolili*, grandson of the veteran *Pondiac*, whose wisdom and prowess would have done honour even to the present enlightened age. This wary chieftain with difficulty checked the ardor of his heroic followers, till the enemy had advanced within fifteen miles of the Maumee towns, when it became impossible to restrain it any longer.

In vain was it remonstrated that the enemy were encamped on advantageous ground, with a river in front, and other defences on the right and left wings: that they were well apprized of the neighbourhood of our warriors, and actually stood arrayed in expectation of an attack. The shout of war, terrible as thunder, and pregnant with death, drowned the whispers of ill-timed caution, and destruction rushed on the foe from every quarter.

Numbers fell by the well-aimed fire of the rifles, but many, many more, by that caterer for the grave, the tomahawk. The impetuosity of the red men, like a whirlwind, bore down opposition wherever it was directed.

The slaughter (for it could hardly be called a battle) lasted two hours; when the trembling remains of the vanquished army saved themselves by a flight, to which dreadful apprehension gave unusual precipitancy. Half a hundred leaders, and upwards of a thousand warriors of the foe, lay dead upon the plain; while the cries of a wounded multitude arose grateful in the ears of Areskoui.

And all the artillery—all the stores—and in short, every appendage of this well appointed army, fell into the conquerers' hands: and that every man was not destroyed, was entirely owing to the unwillingness our warriors manifested to butcher an unresisting enemy.

Thus terminated a conflict, not less honourable to the invincible lords of the soil, than disgraceful and humiliating to the palid despoilers of this beautiful garden of nature. R.

New-York Museum; or, Literary Repository, January 1792, 22–23.

Note: Pontiac (here Pondiac) or Obwandiyag was an Ottawa war chief who, in Pontiac's War (1763–66), led a confederation of tribes dissatisfied with British policies in the Great Lakes region. Livingston invents a future history book that tells of a later battle in the Miami or Maumee River area from the Native American point of view. On 4 November 1791 the U.S. Army under General Arthur St. Clair did indeed suffer crushing defeat by a coalition of Indian American nations, as described by Colin G. Calloway, "The Biggest Forgotten American Indian Victory," available at http://www.whatitmeanstobeamerican.org/ideas/the-biggest-forgot ten-american-indian-victory. Calloway's account confirms Livingston's, written 1792. Areskouis is a god of war.

Appendix II. Lists of the Poems of Livingston and Moore

The poetic corpora of Livingston and Moore that were investigated are listed below, in alphabetical order of the abbreviated titles used for the tables (though Table 5.1 has some slightly longer short titles to clearly identify the anapestic pieces).

Livingston's corpus is formed from poems in his own handwritten book, poems that he inscribed in his daughter Jane's "poetry book," poems attributed and owned by other descendants, and poems published under Livingston's pseudonym "R" in papers and journals to which he is known to have contributed. Poems that are only "possibly" by Livingston, designated "Henry Plus" on the Henry Livingston website (www.henrylivingston. com), have not been included in counts of features investigated for the present study, though a few of them are mentioned as doubtful sources of supplementary evidence. Livingston's fuller titles are listed here as they appear in his manuscript collection or as printed, but with some trivial editing. The ampersand is expanded and, in one or two cases, apostrophes are supplied, but in first lines archaic spellings have been retained.

I have standardized capitalization of both poets' titles, while retaining upper case for personal pronouns. Otherwise, Moore's titles are essentially those of the contents list in his *Poems* (1844), where some are slightly abbreviated from the titles within the body of the book; a few I have shortened a little more. Moore's loose manuscript pieces, "To Clem," "To Fanny," and "From Saint Nicholas," are given truncated versions of the handwritten headings. Titles of his manuscript notebook poems are those he provides, but again with a certain amount of abbreviation, since some occupy several lines of subsidiary information.

Livingston

(See "Henry Livingston's Poetry," http://www.henrylivingston.com/writing/
poetry/index.htm.)

Acknowledgment   The Acknowledgment
With the ladies' permission, most humbly I'd mention

Acrostic   Acrostic on Miss (Maria Martin)
Much I admire, thou loveliest of the fair

Alcmena   Rebus (Alcmena Rebus)
The son of Alcmena the champion of fable

American Eagle   Adventures of an American Eagle
In bleak Potosi's inmost cells

Anne   To My Little Niece Anne Duyckinck
To his charming black-ey'd niece

Apollo   A Rebus (Apollo Rebus)
The mount where old Homer has station'd Apollo

Arabella   To Arabella
Blooming as the youthful May

Bats (Fable)   A Fable
When time was young the story goes

Beekman   Letter to My Brother Beekman
To my dear brother Beekman I sit down to write

Belle   On a Lap-dog of the Miss Loth, Called Belle
If ever 'twas proper and lawful and decent

Carrier 1787   A New Year's Address of Richard and George (1787)
Before the friends of Mr. Power

Carrier 1803   News-Boy's Address (1803)
All hail to the season so jovial and gay

Carrier 1819   The Carrier of the Poughkeepsie Journal (1819)
Time, with his pinions broad and strong

Careless   The Soliloquy of a Careless Philosopher
I rise when I please, when I please I lie down

Catherine Breese L   Catharine Breese Livingston
We fondly nurs'd an op'ning rose

Catherine L Breese   Catherine Livingston Breese
Her little bark on life's wide ocean tossed

Catherine Sleeping   On My Little Catherine Sleeping
Sweet Innocent lye still and sleep

Country   An Invitation to the Country
The winter all surly is flown

Crane and Fox   The Crane and Fox
In long gone years a fox and crane

Dance   A Rebus (on the Name Nancy Crooke)
Take the name of the swain a forlorn witless elf

Death of Sarah   To the Memory of Sarah Livingston
Beyond where billows roll or tempests vex

Deity   Rebus (Deity Rebus)
Take the name of the Deity lovers obey

Dialogue   Dialogue Between Madame J. L. and her Children
Pray dearest mother if you please

Easter   Easter
When Jesus bow'd his awful head

Eliza Hughes   Acrostic (on Eliza Hughes)
Ev'ry grace in her combine

Fly   The Fly
As on a summer's fervid day

Frog King   The Frog King
The frogs of calm and quiet tir'd

Frontier Song   A Frontier Song
Let statesmen tread their giddy round

Frosts (Habakkuk)   Habakkuk III Chap. Verses 17 and 18
Tho frosts destroy or blasts invade

Gentleman   To a Gentleman on his Leaving Pakepsy
In summer the aerial musicians around

German Spa   Tune, German Spa
Shrewd remarkers often say

Gilbert Cortlandt   On the Late Mr. Gilbert Cortlandt
Beyond where billows roll or tempests vex

God is Love   God is Love
I love my feeble voice to raise

Henry Welles L   To the Memory of Henry Welles Livingston
A gentle spirit now above

Hero   Rebus on the Christian Name of a Gentleman
That hero whose great and magnanimous mind

Hezekiah   The Writing of Hezekiah
When blooming health and chearful days

Hogs   Letter from a Tenant of Mrs. Van Kleeck
My very good landlady, Mistress Van Kleeck

Isaiah   Isaiah, LXV Chap. 25. Verse
In that ecstatic, joyous day

Joanna   On My Sister Joanna's Entrance into her 33rd Year
On this thy natal day permit a friend

Job   Part of the 4th Chap. of Job, Versified
'Twas night. And thickest gloom prevail'd around.

Lo from the East   Lo from the East
Lo! from the east the sun appears

Marriage   Epithalamium
Robins! stop your whistling throats

Marriage Tax   An Apostrophe … Marriage License
With tears in my eyes I the other day saw

Midas   Midas
The miser Midas to his store

Monarchs   Rebus (Monarchs Rebus)
The wisest of monarchs yet weakest of men

Montgomery   Parody on the Death of General Wolfe
In a mouldering cave where the wretched retreat

Original Poems   Originals of Poems (Fragments)
A cool reflecting northern sage

Past is the Hour   Past is the Hour
Past is the hour, forever flown

Procession   A Procession
The legislators pass along

Queen   A Rebus (Queen of Love Rebus)
Fairer than the queen of love

Rispah   Apostrophe of Rispah
From morn to eve from eve to rosy morn

Sages   A Rebus (Sages Rebus)
Take the name of that planet which sages declare

Scots Wha Hae   Scots Wha Hae Wie Wallace Bled
In arts and arms Escotia stands

Settlement   Frontier Settlement (Answer to a Poetical Invitation)
Yes, yes my swain, thy faithful wife's prepar'd

Sisters   Rebus (Nine Sisters Rebus)
Take the name of nine sisters that romp on Parnassus

Spadille   To Spadille
Thou little four-leg'd paltry varlet

Tappen   An Elegy on the Death of Montgomery Tappen
The sweetest, gentlest, of the youthful train

Timmy   Letter Sent to Master Timmy Dwight
Master Timmy brisk and airy

To Miss   To Miss—on the Commencement of 1789
Hail! pride of each lass and the wish of each swain

To Miss Roses   To Miss (Roses)
Sweet as op'ning roses are

Valentine   A Valentine
Wellcome wellcome happy day

Vine   The Vine and Oak
A vine from noblest lineage sprung

War   A Rebus on ... (War Rebus)
Take the name of that hero who dreadful in war

Without   Without Distinction
Without distinction, fame, or note

Wren   To My Little Niece Sally Livingston
Hasty pilgrim stop thy pace

Among possible additions to the Livingston canon, categorized as "Henry Plus" on Mary Van Deusen's website, the most likely to be his, according to our tests, are "Carrier Address 1816," "Fair Adaline," and "The Filly and the Wolf." But there are several others that the tests do not clearly disqualify.

Moore

Ball   Apology for not Accepting an Invitation to a Ball
Full well I know what direful wrath impends

Birthday   To a Young Lady on her Birth-Day
To hail thy natal day, fair maid

Cholera   Lines on the Sisters of Charity
Ye sacred Sisters; not for you this strain

Cowper   On Cowper the Poet
Sweet melancholy Bard! whose piercing thought

Daughter's Marriage To My Daughter, on her Marriage
For you, my Margaret dear, I have no art

Farewell   Farewell—In Answer to a Young Lady's Invitation
My ear still vibrates with thy sweet command

Fashion   To the Fashionable Part of My Young Contrywomen
Who in the stream of fashion thoughtless glide

Flowers   Lines Accompanying a Bunch of Flowers
There is a language giv'n to flowers

Fragment Fair   Lines … Sent to a Fragment Fair
My merry friend, your balls are wound

From St. Nicholas   From Saint Nicholas
What! My sweet little Sis in bed all alone

Gloves   Lines Sent to a Young Lady, with a Pair of Gloves
Go envied glove, with anxious care

Muse   The Mischievous Muse—Translated
Bright God of harmony, whose voice

Natural Philosophy   To Young Ladies Who Attended Philosophical
                        Lectures
The beasts who roam o'er Libya's desert plain

Nymphs   To the Nymphs of Mount Harmony
An idle swain late chanc'd to roam

Old Dobbin   Old Dobbin
Oh Muse! I feel my genius rise

Organist   The Organist
The troubles of an Organist I sing

Paganini   On Receiving ... a Caricature Cast of Paganini
Accept, dear Doctor, my unfeigned thanks

Petrosa   To Petrosa
Thy charms, Petrosa, which inspire

Pig and Rooster   The Pig and the Rooster
On a warm sunny day, in the midst of July

Portrait   To My Children with My Portrait
The semblance of your parent's time-worn face

Sand   On Seeing My Name Written in the Sand
This name here drawn by Flora's hand

Saratoga 1–6   A Trip to Saratoga, Part First–Part Six
It was the opening spring-time of the year

Snow   Lines Written After a Fall of Snow
Come children dear, and look around

Song   A Song
Sweet Maid, could wealth or power

Southey   To Southey
Southey, I love the magic of thy lyre

To a Lady   To a Lady
Thy dimpled girls and rosy boys

To Clem   To Little Clem, from a Little Girl
While older people send their loves

To Fanny   For my Grandson Clement to Send to Fanny French
Now let us hope, my Fanny dear

Valentine   Lines to a Young Lady for Valentine's Day
Now when the breath of coming Spring

Water Drinker   The Water Drinker
Away with all your wine-fill'd casks

Wife   From a Husband to His Wife
The dreams of Hope that round us play

Wine Drinker   The Wine Drinker
I'll drink my glass of generous wine

Yellow Fever   Lines Written After a Season of Yellow Fever
Dread pestilence hath now fled far away

Moore Manuscript Notebook

Basket of Flowers   To a Young Lady Who Sent me a Basket of Flowers
A thousand thanks, my young and lovely friend

Caroline's Album   Written at Schooley's Mountain [for Caroline's] Album
Sweet maiden, could I on this page impress

Catharine's Album   Written for my Daughter Catharine [for an Album]
Dear Kate, these bright but short-lived flowers

Charles Elphinstone   Charles Elphinstone
I sing the strife maintain'd, by min'string powers

Eliza in England   To Eliza in England, from Her Grandfather
Old Chelsea once again looks gay

For a Kiss   To a Very Young Lady Who Sent me a Kiss
Thousand thanks, my sweet girl, for the kiss that you sent

Irish Valentine   A Valentine
The top of the morn to ye! this blessed day

Jeanette New Year   To Miss Jeanette McEvers
You ask me, gentle maiden, once again

Margaret   Fair Margaret
While at fair Margaret's placid brows

Newport Beach   A Morning on the Beach at Newport
'Twas an autumnal morn, celestial bright

Theresa's Flower   Written for my Daughter Theresa
While lib'ral wealth, from door to door

Valentine-MS
All Nature, bound in icy chain

West Point   West Point, Addressed to Miss Catherine Livingston
Fair maid, I'd quarrel with my Muse

Blocks of verse for Tables 7.1 and 14.1 were composed as follows. Moore: Saratoga 1; Saratoga 2; Saratoga 3; Saratoga 4; Saratoga 5; Saratoga 6; Fashion; Natural Philosophy; Ball; To a Lady; Yellow Fever; Nymphs; Organist; Pig and Rooster; Wine Drinker; Cholera; Marriage; Southey; Portrait + Muse; Snow + Sand + Cowper; Petrosa + Song + Old Dobbin + Fragment Fair; Wife + Flowers; Birthday + Paganini + Valentine; Gloves + Farewell + From St. Nicholas + To Fanny + To Clem. Livingston: Carrier 1803; Carrier 1819; American Eagle; Catherine Sleeping + Easter + Job +

Country; Sisters + Frosts (Habakkuk) + Isaiah; Lo from the East + Tappen + Death of Sarah + Henry Welles L; Queen of Love + Deity + Joanna + Wren; Settlement + Apollo + Timmy; Dance + Valentine + Gentleman; Hero + Beekman; Vine + Spadille; War + Sages; Carrier 1787 + Anne + Acknowledgment; Hogs + Montogomery + Fly; Careless + Belle + Frontier + Alcmena; Rispah + To Miss + Procession + To Miss Roses; Marriage + Bats (Fable) + Scots Wha Hae + Crane and Fox; Midas + God Is Love + Dialogue; Without Distinction + Catherine Breese L + Gilbert Courtland + Marriage Tax + Hezekiah; German Spa + Arabella + Past is the Hour + Acrostic + Eliza Hughes. Amalgamations were based on the order in which poems appeared in Mary Van Deusen's initial list of the accepted Livingston canon, beginning with those in his manuscript book.

Appendix III.
Printer's Copy for "Visit" in Moore's Poems (1844)

The evidence that the *Sentinel*'s broadsheet formed the basis for the manuscript of "Visit" sent to the printer of Moore's *Poems* (1844) is overwhelming. Both, unlike other versions up to 1844, print the names of the reindeer and the poem's final line in italics. The use in *Poems* of capitals and small capitals for "ST. NICHOLAS" in line 4 derives from the broadsheet, which carried through this practice, discontinued in *Poems*, in printing the name in lines 18, 28, and 32, and also in "SLEIGH" and "TOYS" in line 28. *Poems* did capitalize "Toys" in both line 28 and line 35. The broadsheet made some three dozen changes in punctuation from the 1823 printing. The punctuation of *Poems* closely follows that of the broadsheet, with only four changes: a comma to a period after "sash" at the end of line 12, a dash to a comma at line 28, a semicolon to a period after "pack" at the end of line 36, and a period to a semicolon after "myself" at the end of line 46.

Because the line 36 alteration has been indicated in pen on Moore's copy of the broadsheet, with a thick stroke after "pack," it is not perfectly clear what the period was replacing, but it seems to have been a semicolon. The alteration to line 12 is also marked in pen on Moore's copy of the broadsheet. At the end of line 46 the broadsheet appears to have a period, but there is some slight suggestion of a semicolon, as appears in *Poems*. Moore's copy of the broadsheet also has the changes from "*Blixem*" to "*Blitzen*," "leaves" to "leaves that," and "was flung" to "he had flung" marked in handwriting. Further, the title, "*ACCOUNT OF A VISIT FROM ST. NICHOLAS, OR SANTA CLAUS.*" has the first two and last three words bracketed off for deletion, and they do not appear in *Poems*.

Both Livingston and Moore made liberal use of "-'d," rather than "-ed" endings, when the meter did not require them to be sounded as an extra syllable. This is clear from their manuscripts, as well as from their verse as printed. In the broadsheet, seven of the 1823 "-'d" endings have been expanded to "-ed": "danced" in line 6, "called" in line 20, "dressed" in line 33, "tarnished" in line 34, "laughed" in lines 44 and 46, and "turned" in line 50. All these "-ed" endings are retained in *Poems*. This is despite the fact that elsewhere in the volume, "call'd" and "turn'd" appear seven and five times respectively, and "called" and "turned" only once each, while there are single instances of "danc'd" and "dress'd" and none of "danced" or "dressed." So outside "Visit," *Poems* clearly reflected Moore's own free choices in favor of "-'d" over "-ed" in these words—fourteen to two. "Visit" reflects the broadsheet printer's or editor's preferences. Other editions had altered several "-'d" endings to "-ed" endings, but the broadsheet and Moore's *Poems* seem to be the only versions in which only "look'd" (36) and "fill'd" (50) are retained. *Poems* also follows the broadsheet's spelling changes to the 1823 printing: "sugar-plums" for "sugar plums" in line 6, "Mamma" for "Mama" in line 7, "new-fallen" for "new fallen" in line 13, "bowlful" for "bowl full" in line 44, "jerk" for "jirk" in line 50.

Notes

Preface

1. W. H. Auden, "In Memory of W. B. Yeats." An account of the popularity of "The Night Before Christmas" in divers media can be read in the *Wikipedia* entry "A Visit from St. Nicholas," https.//en. wikipedia.org/wiki/A_Visit_from_St._N icholas.

2. Accurate information about Moore is provided in the *Wikipedia* entry "Clement Clarke Moore," https://en.wikipedia.org/ wiki/Clement_Clarke_Moore. The standard biography remains Samuel White Patterson, *The Poet of Christmas Eve: A Life of Clement Clarke Moore 1779–1863* (New York: Morehouse-Gorham, 1956). *Wikipedia* also gives the main facts about Henry Livingston: "Henry Livingston, Jr.," https://en.wikipedia.org/wiki/Henry_ Livingston,_Jr. For more details see Mary S. Van Deusen's website, "Henry Livingston, Jr.," http://www.henrylivingston. com. The site includes an index that gives guidance to the many subsites. William S. Thomas laid the foundations for a Livingston biography in "Henry Livingston," *Dutchess County Historical Society Yearbook* 5 (1919): 30–46. Further information about the two poets' work is supplied in Appendix II, and references for Moore's unpublished poems are given when they are first discussed. The basic textual sources are Clement Clarke Moore, *Poems* (New York: Bartlett & Welford, 1844) and "Henry Livingston's Writing," http:// www.henrylivingston.com/writing/index. htm. The latter includes images of manuscripts and the earliest printed texts of Livingston's poetry and prose. Photocopies of Livingston's bound autograph poems are held by the Dutchess County Historical Society in Poughkeepsie and the New-York Historical Society in New York.

3. Patrick Juola, "Authorship Attribution," *Foundations and Trends in Information Retrieval* 1, no. 3 (2008): 233–334. A useful guide is Harold Love's *Attributing Authorship: An Introduction* (Cambridge: Cambridge University Press, 2002). More technical is Michael P. Oakes, *Literary Detective Work on the Computer* (Amsterdam: John Benjamins, 2014).

4. Don Foster, *Author Unknown: On the Trail of Anonymous* (New York: Henry Holt, 2000).

5. Donald W. Foster, *Elegy by W. S.: A Study in Attribution* (Newark, DE: University of Delaware Press, 1989). MacDonald P. Jackson, "Editions and Textual Studies," *Shakespeare Survey* 43 (1991): 258–61.

6. Donald W. Foster, posted on "Shaksper: The Global Electronic Shakespeare Conference," http://www.shaksper. net, SHK 13.1514, 12 June 2002.

7. *Literature Online* (*LION*) is avail-

able to subscribing institutions at http://literature.proquest.com. Unless otherwise noted, my searches of this database were made in the period July–August 2013, before the creation of a new interface, which supplied the only version that could be accessed after 28 June 2014. *LION* continues to add texts, but it is now impossible to carry out some kinds of searches that could readily be carried out before.

8. Joe Nickell, "The Case of the Christmas Poem, Part 1 and Part 2," *Manuscript* 54, no. 4 (Fall 2002): 293–308, and 55, no. 1 (Winter 2003): 5–15; Seth Kaller, "The Authorship of The Night Before Christmas," https://www.sethkaller.com/about/education/tnbc/; Stephen Nissenbaum, "There Arose Such a Clatter: Who Really Wrote 'The Night Before Christmas'? (And Why Does It Matter)," *Common-Place* 1, no. 2 (January 2001), http://www.common-place.org/vol-01/no-02/moore/. Nissenbaum draws on his *The Battle for Christmas: A Cultural History of America's Most Cherished Holiday* (New York: Vintage, 1996).

Chapter 1

1. This is item 1 in Nancy H. Marshall's *The Night Before Christmas: A Descriptive Bibliography of Clement Clarke Moore's Immortal Poem with Editions from 1823 through 2000* (New Castle, DE: Oak Knoll Press, 2002).

2. Edwin G. Burrows and Mike Wallace, *Gotham: A History of New York City to 1898* (New York: Oxford University Press, 1999), 462–63.

3. The sons were Charles, born 18 May 1794; Sidney, born 4 October 1796; and Edwin, born 17 November 1798. The daughters were Jane, born 4 December 1800; and Elizabeth, born 17 March 1805. Elizabeth Clement Brewer, born 13 July 1798, was the neighbor who married Charles. Susan, born 23 April 1807, could not have been aware of any reading of "The Night Before Christmas" in 1808,

and even Elizabeth would probably have had to rely on the memories of her siblings. The claims passed down through different branches of the family are more fully addressed in Chapters 3 and 20.

Chapter 2

1. 1 January 1829 is the date cited by Arthur Nicholas Hosking, *The Night Before Christmas: The True Story of "A Visit from St. Nicholas," with a Life of the Author, Clement Clarke Moore* (New York: Rudge, 1934), 26. But the reprint was evidently the broadside with an illustration by Myron King, dated c. 1830 by Marshall, *Bibliography*, item 11. This exists in two slightly different forms, variant copies being preserved in the Museum of the City of New York (hereafter MCNY) and in the Anne Haight Collection at Carnegie Mellon University. They are reproduced and discussed at http://www.henrylivingston.com/xmas/poemvariants/troybroad.htm.

2. Neils H. Sonne, "'The Night Before Christmas': Who Wrote It?," *Historical Magazine of the Protestant Episcopal Church* 41, no. 4 (December 1971): 375.

3. *Ibid.*, 376; Marshall, *Bibliography*, item 41.

4. For details and one photographic reproduction (the Strong National Museum of Play in Rochester, New York, copy) see Marshall, *Bibliography*, xxv–xxviii.

5. Patterson, *Poet of Christmas Eve*, 3.

6. Jeanne Hubbard Dening to W. S. Thomas, 23 December 1918, Thomas Collection, http://www.henrylivingston.com/xmas/witnesses/index.htm. All "witness letters" are reproduced and transcribed on this website. Hereafter they are cited by sender, recipient, and date.

7. Eliza Livingston Thompson Lansing to Anne L. Goodrich, 4 March 1879.

8. Henry Livingston of Babylon to Cornelia Griswold Goodrich, 10 January 1900; Jeannie Hubbard Denig to W. S.

Thomas, 23 December 1918, 2 October 1920, and 28 October 1920; Jeannie Livingston Gurney to W. S. Thomas, 5 October 1920. Differences about the year of the relevant fire are discussed in Chapter 20. It is not, of course, claimed that Susan, an infant in 1808, recalled the first reading of "Visit," merely that she relayed the testimony of her older siblings.

9. These stories are assessed in Chapter 19.

10. This is the last of those cited in note 8 above.

11. It can be viewed at http://www. henrylivingston.com/music/index.htm.

12. Fables of the Elm and the Vine are found in Latin authors, including Ovid, and persisted throughout the centuries in European literature and art, usually as a trope for marital union. A version similar to Livingston's "The Vine and the Oak" was published anonymously in the *Gentleman's Magazine* 33 (October 1736): 510.

13. *The Goldfinch, or New Modern Songster* (Glasgow: J and M. Robertson, 1785; first published 1777). There was an Edinburgh edition of 1782. Available at https://archive.org/details/goldfin chornewmo00glas.

14. "From Saint Nicholas" (MCNY MS 54.331.4). "To Little Clem" (54.331.7) and "To Fanny" (54.331.6) are in the same collection.

15. Burkhard Bilger, "Waiting for Ghosts," *New Yorker*, 23 December 2002, 100.

16. "Strow'd" was a very common variant of "strew'd" or "strewn" in Livingston's time. *LION* yields scores of instances. In verse of Livingston's time the word "sublunary" was normally stressed on the first and third syllables: SUBlunAry.

17. Poems mentioned in this paragraph are included in the "Henry Livingston: Selected Poems and Prose" section of this book.

18. Livingston referred to Catullus's Carmen III in an essay entitled "Female Happiness" published in the *Country Journal and Poughkeepsie Advertiser*, 14 October 1788: "The mistress of Catullus wept for her sparrow many centuries ago." Available at http://www.henrylivingston. com/writing/prose/femalehappy.htm.

19. Henry Noble MacCracken, *Blithe Dutchess: The Flowering of an American County from 1812* (New York: Hastings House, 1958), 376. MacCracken gives a good account of "The Night Before Christmas" and the Livingston claim (370–90).

Chapter 3

1. Foster, *Author Unknown*, 260–61, 268.

2. Livingston refers to "dear Mamma" in a letter of 2 May 1802, to "Your/your Mamma" in letters of 2 July 1820, 5 August 1826, 25 May 1827, and 3 September 1827, to "Miss Biddy's mamma" and "her Mamma's garden" in his prose piece "Baby House," and to "Mammy" and "mammy" in "A Tenant of Mrs. Van Kleeck". These letters are available at http://www.henry livingston.com/writing/letters. All letters by Livingston subsequently referred to are transcribed on the Henry Livingston website, as given in this note. Letters by Moore to his mother from 29 August 1802 to 4 June 1812 (MCNY 54.331.9–54.331.16) start with the salutation "My dear Mother" or "Dear Mother." Patterson, *Poet of Christmas Eve*, quotes another to Moore's "dearest Mother," which also, as he requests money, calls her "Mama." But Moore seems never to have referred to his wife as "Mama/Mamma," as Livingston did in writing to even adult offspring.

3. *Early English Books Online–Text Creation Partnership* (http://quod.lib.umich. edu/e/eebogroup/) finds three examples of "happy Christmas" up to 1700, in 1676, 1687, and 1693, though not as salutations, as against thirty-one of "Merry/merry Christmas"; *Eighteenth Century Collections Online* (http://gdc.gale.com/products/eighteenth-century-collections-online/) finds no ex-

amples of "Happy/happy Christmas" but seven of "Merry/merry Christmas."

4. Foster, *Author Unknown*, 270–71; letter from Norman Tuttle to Clement Clarke Moore, 26 February 1844 (MCNY 54.331.17AB).

5. A Daniel Sackett died in Troy in 1845. He was married to Sarah Pardee. He was brother of Benjamin Sackett Jr. and son of Captain Benjamin Sackett and Phebe Davis. He lived in 7th Street. Sarah was the daughter of Calvin Pardee and Rachel Johnson, and, since she survived her husband, in 1844 when Moore's *Poems* were published she was still alive. This I gleaned from WeRelate.org; see http://www.werelate.org/wiki/Person:Daniel_Sackett_(5). The *Troy Sentinel* broadsheet has an imprint basing Tuttle and the Sentinel at 225 River Street, Troy. According to Google Maps the present 225 River Street is 5–10 minutes' walk from a small no-exit 7th Street. Honor Conklin, archivist and Manuscripts and Special Collections librarian at New York State Library, has further established that Sackett's crockery store was located at 221–22 River Street, and so was within less than a stone's throw of the *Troy Sentinel* (see Chapter 19, note 3).

6. See Chapters 19 and 21.

7. Moore's use of the broadside to furnish copy for the printer of "A Visit from St. Nicholas" in his *Poems* of 1844 is demonstrated in Appendix III.

8. MCNY 54.331.17A.

9. Foster, *Author Unknown*, 266.

10. Kaller, "Authorship," n.p. (under subheading "The Donder Party").

11. Patterson, *Poet of Christmas Eve*, 111. *Wikipedia* has entries for the Knickerbocker Group, the *Knickerbocker* magazine, and the New-York Historical Society.

12. Nissenbaum, "Such a Clatter," n.p. (in Section III). Nissenbaum gives information about the Knickerbockers here and in *Battle for Christmas*.

13. Fully discussed in Chapters 19 and 20.

14. Ted Mann, "Ho, Ho, Hoax" (see Bibliography for full title), *Scarsdale Magazine*, 1 December 2006; available at http://www.mediabistro.com/tedmann.

15. See the *Wikipedia* entry "Washington Irving," https://en.wikipedia.org/?title=Washington_Irving. A recent biography is Andrew Burstein, *The Original Knickerbocker: A Life of Washington Irving* (New York: Basic Books, 2007).

16. The Reverend Harold Livingston Reed Thomas (1877–c. 1941) told his parishioners that the Dutch equivalents were the names of horses in Henry Livingston's stable; see http://www.henry livingston/xmas/witnesses/index.htm. This piece of hearsay is better reckoned an embarrassment than worthwhile evidence, although it does indicate that the clergyman regarded the names as appropriate for Dutchess County horses of Livingston's time.

17. We also get such half rhymes as "strong"–"on," "upon"–"sung," "pushing"–"cushion," "ruin"–"wooing," and "climbing"–"Hymen."

18. Returning to the improbable alternative—that "Blitzen" was what Moore had written all along, and "Blixem" the result of scribal or editorial interference—we may doubt that even the "Vixen"–"Blitzen" near-rhyme would have come as naturally in original free composition to Moore as to Livingston.

19. *LION*'s two instances of "was slung on" both refer to an existing state: "was slung on his left shoulder," "was slung on his left hip." It is tempting to wonder whether "flung" in the *Troy Sentinel* of 1823 was a misprint. This newspaper did not use the ligature "fl" or the corresponding ligature for long "s" and "l" or one might conjecture that a foul case error had occurred. These barely distinguishable ligatures were standard in such journals as the *New-York Weekly Museum*, in which several poems by Livingston were published. It is conceivable in any case that "flung" was set accidentally instead of

"slung" under the influence of "of" earlier in the line. This would, of course, imply that Moore's change from "was" to "he had" was a miscorrection, as suspicious as the change from "Blixem" to "Blitzem." "A BUNdle of TOYS was slung OVer his BACK" would have made a metrically more normal line.

20. Some examples in Livingston's poems are "Continue dear nymph *as ev*er you've been," "It certain is now—*Each grace* and each muse," "Health dwells on her cheeks—*Love laughs* in her eye," "The shepherds in love *press fond*ly about her," "With the downy chin'd god *belov'd* by the lasses," "Graces hover around—*Love can't* live without her," "Would often observe *that ly*ing's not good."

21. I assume that in "As if all the world was on the look out," "world" would be given a disyllabic pronunciation.

22. In "Adventures of an American Eagle" "was flung" occurs twice, and "The Crane and the Fox" uses "flung" once.

23. Foster, *Author Unknown*, 265.

24. Letters from Henry Livingston to Charles Patterson Livingston, 24 August 1926; to Sidney Breese, 27 May 1821.

25. Nickell, "Christmas Poem," Part 2, 12.

26. Texts are from *LION*. Since Livingston composed several rebuses, it may be as well to explain that in these puzzle poems, popular at the time, each line or couplet presents a clue, the one-word answer to which begins with the letter that will form part of the overall solution. Thus in "Hero Rebus" the answers to the first six clues—Columbus, Oyster, No, Reward, Asses, Dullness—yield the forename "Conrad."

27. In line 10 of the 1823 *Troy Sentinel* text of "Visit," "sprung" has been wrongly rendered as "sprang" in Foster's *Author Unknown*. Pat Pflieger's website transcription from a facsimile provided by the Troy Public Library is now accurate; see http://www.merrycoz.org/moore/1823Troy.xhtml. The reading "sprung" becomes less

ambiguous under high magnification. It is confirmed by early reprints, all "from the *Troy Sentinel*," in the *Spectator* (New York), 1 January 1824, the *Essex Register* (Salem, MA), 5 January 1824, and Joshua Sharp's *Citizens and Farmers' Almanack for … 1825* (Philadelphia: Griggs and Dickinson, 1825), which all also retain the rare spelling "jirk" in line 50.

28. So when, as I argue in Appendix III, Moore prepared copy for his *Poems* from the 1830 broadsheet, he would have found the two corrections from "sprung" to "sprang" already made.

29. "Stephen," as printed in the *Weekly Museum*, was almost certainly a misreading of "Strephon," who appears 280 times in *LION* texts up to 1800 as a shepherd in Arcadian pastoral, sometimes wooing the shepherdess "Phyllis," as in "Past is the Hour" (where the spelling is "Philis"). A painting by Richard Westall (1764–1836) coupled "Strephon and Phyllis" (1794), who were to become characters in the Gilbert and Sullivan comic opera *Iolanthe* (1882). In his "Deity Rebus" Livingston has "poor Strephon by Phyllis discarded," and he couples "Strephon and Phillis" in his "Epithalamium."

30. "Lord of life, all praise excelling." It can be found on the Hymnary.org website at http://www.hymnary.org/text/lord_of_life_all_praise_excelling. It first appeared in the *American Prayer Book Collection* (1808), according to the appended note.

Chapter 4

1. Kaller, "Authorship," n.p. (under subheading "Santa Claus Didn't Come Out of Thin Air"). The extract from Irving is as Kaller quotes it.

2. Nickell, "Christmas Poem," Part 2, 8, also claims that the "Santa motif is not in Irving's original 'Knickerbocker' History (1809) but rather in a later revised edition of 1819." Like Kaller's "1821," Nickell's "1819" is wrong. Marshall, *Bibliography*, xxix, makes the same mistake.

The second edition is *A History of New-York from the Beginning of the World to the End of the Dutch Dynasty*, 2 vols. (New-York: Inskeep and Bradford, 1812). The relevant passage is in vol. 1, 106–7.

3. Irving, *History* (1812), 1:75.

4. *Ibid.*, 1:145.

5. Irving, *History* (1809), 1:126.

6. It is likely that Livingston had read Tobias Smollett as well, whose fiction not only affords one of the several precedents for the gesture of tapping of a finger on the side of the nose, but anticipates "The stump of a pipe" in "Visit": *LION* reveals that a Dutch sailor takes a "whiff of tobacco from the stump of a pipe" in Smollet's *Roderick Random* (1748).

7. See the *Wikipedia* entry "*Salmagundi* (periodical)," https://en.wikipedia.org/wiki/Salmagundi_(periodical).

8. On 8 August 1803 Irving was a guest of Judge Jonas Platt, Henry Livingston's brother-in-law and the mentor of his son-in-law Arthur Breese. Jonas and Helen Platt had at least one of Livingston's poems. See http://www.henrylivingston.com/slideshow/epilog-5arthurbreese.htm; also http://www.henrylivingston.com/xmas/arguments.htm (toward the end, after the link to Washington Irving).

9. Foster, *Author Unknown*, 263.

10. Henry Livingston to Charles Patterson Livingston, 25 May 1827.

11. Foster, *Author Unknown*, 263.

12. Livingston's prose pieces mentioned here are included in the "Henry Livingston: Selected Poems and Prose" section of this book.

13. These include both "Old Santeclaus," discussed in Chapter 22, and the "Sante Claus" verses that begin "Oh good holy man!" and were published in the New York newspaper the *Spectator* of 1 December 1815. See Marshall, *Bibliography*, xxii.

14. I have borrowed the word "re-inflated" from a private letter by Don Foster.

Chapter 5

1. Besides deploying the same meter with comparable sprightliness and dash, "The Night Before Christmas" and "Letter to Brother Beekman" are set within similar "frames," as William P. Tryon noted in a letter to W. S. Thomas, 8 May 1920: "In both cases you start with the poet and one of the women folks of his family as the principal figures. Then you have conjured up before you a third figure who is humorously described from the poet's viewpoint solely. In the case of the brother Beekman epistle, you have this third figure described as he appears indoors, then as he appears out of doors; in the case of the Christmas fantasy, you have the situation reversed, the third figure being described out of the house and then in."

2. Moore's elder son, Benjamin, four in 1822, would not have attended "grammar school" before the age of twelve.

3. Nickell, "Christmas Poem," Part 2, 10.

4. Since Livingston's fable poems were all written before "The Pig and the Rooster," any influence could only have been of Livingston on Moore.

5. It is probable that the "Spheres Rebus" ("The power which retains the bright spheres in their orbs," published in the *New-York Magazine; or, Literary Repository*, April 1791, is by Livingston. It had been rejected from the canon because a verse solution was published over the initials "N.H.W." But the editor states that this was chosen from the many verse solutions submitted, so that the solution is not by the author of the rebus itself. "Spheres Rebus" has 28 lines, without a single disyllable covering two metrically unstressed positions. It contrasts strikingly with the anapestic "A Song" ("No more glows") in the volume containing John Duer's Juvenal translation (New-York: E. Sargeant, 1806) and verse and prose contributions by Moore, as mentioned in the Preface above: its twenty

lines have eight disyllables in metrically unstressed positions, giving a percentage of 40. It is not signaled as by Moore, but (on pp. 131–32) is surrounded by his pieces, and at least serves to further highlight Livingston's relative avoidance of this license.

Chapter 6

1. The best introduction to statistics for nonmathematicians is Russell Langley, *Practical Statistics Simply Explained* (New York: Dover Publications, 1971). Though out of print, it is available from web-based bookshops. Also helpful is Anthony Kenny, *The Computation of Style: An Introduction to Statistics for Students of Literature and Humanities* (Oxford: Pergamon Press, 1982).

2. I have used the "VassarStats: Website for Statistical Computation" (http://vassarstats.net) and, for chi-square, K. J. Preacher's Vanderbilt University "Interactive Chi-Square Tests" (http://www.quantpsy.org/chisq/chisq.htm).

3. The symbol < means "less than" while > means "more than." So a chance probability (p) of less than one in twenty (or less than 5 percent) is indicated by $p < 0.05$, of less than one in a hundred by $p < 0.01$, and of less than one in a thousand by $p < 0.001$.

Chapter 7

1. See Appendix II for the composition of these blocks.

Chapter 8

1. John Jowett, "Henry Chettle and the Original Text of *Sir Thomas More*," in *Shakespeare and "Sir Thomas More": Essays on the Play and Its Shakespearian Interest*, ed. T. H. Howard-Hill (Cambridge: Cambridge University Press, 1989), 131–49; MacDonald P. Jackson, *Defining Shakespeare: "Pericles" as Test Case* (Oxford: Oxford University Press, 2003), 97–104.

2. *The Oxford Companion to English Literature: Fifth Edition*, ed. Margaret Drabble (Oxford: Oxford University Press, 1985), 66.

Chapter 9

1. An excellent assessment of the effectiveness in attribution studies of word strings of different lengths is by Alexis Antonia, Hugh Craig, and Jack Elliott, "Language Chunking, Data Sparseness, and the Value of a Long Marker List: Explorations with Word N-Grams and Authorial Attribution," *Literary and Linguistic Computing* 29 (2014): 147–63.

2. Kaller, "Authorship," appendix E.

3. Nickell, "Christmas Poem," Part 2, 7.

4. In the prose piece "Universal Hospital," *New York Magazine; or, Literary Repository*, April 1791. See the section of the present book entitled "Henry Livingston: Selected Poems and Prose."

5. Foster, *Author Unknown*, 255–56.

6. The solution to the "Hero Rebus" is Cornelia Tappen (Caesar, Oberon, Reward, No, Evening, Love, Iris, America, Thea, Alexander, Pleasure, Pity, No; a separate clue for "E" is missing, unless we are to understand Empathy after Pity), and to the "Sages Rebus" Mary Ann Wolcott (Moon, Alexander, Rose, Yes, America, Night, Newton, Woman, Oberon, Love, Canada, Olympus, Thea, Thrush); the forename in the "Apollo Rebus" appears to be "Otty" (Olympus, Thea, Thetis, Yes).

7. Edith Hamilton, *Mythology* (New York: Mentor Books, 1959; first published Boston: Little, Brown, 1940), 334.

8. I have not attempted to compile an inventory of all examples of chiasmus in the work of the two poets, because there is too great a subjective element in identifying them, especially when extraneous words complicate the simple abba structure. Among additional Livingston instances are "The violets already have blown, / Already the daffodils glow" (where the plural flower names precede and follow "already"); "From willing souls to souls as

willing"; "From morn to eve, from eve to rosy morn"; "Where lofty views and grand design, / Impress the grand and the sublime" (where the first "grand" is preceded by "lofty views" and the second is followed by "the sublime"). In Moore I have found "In search of pleasure, some, and some, of health"; this contains the repeated "some," a Moore marker almost entirely avoided by Livingston.

Chapter 10

1. There is a full description at https://en.wikipedia.org/wiki/Arpabet.

2. At http://www.speech.cs.cmu.edu/cgi-bin/cmudict.

3. Brian Boyd, *Why Lyrics Last: Evolution, Cognition, and Shakespeare's Sonnets* (Cambridge, MA: Harvard University Press, 2012), 41.

Chapter 11

1. The testing for significance of Stop/Fricative phoneme pairs will serve to illustrate the process. The 2 × 2 contingency table consisted of (a) numbers of Stop/Fricative pairs and (b) numbers of all other phoneme category pairs in (c) Moore's verse and in (d) Livingston's verse. The pair Stop/Fricative occurs 593 times among Livingston's 11,173 phoneme pairs and 1,135 times among Moore's 17,700. Hence 10,580 of Livingston's pairs and 16,565 of Moore's were not Stop/Fricative. Chi-square compared 593: 10,580 with 1,135: 16,565, yielding a results of chi-square = 14.685, 1 d.f., p < 0.0002, a chance probability of less than one in 5,000 that the two frequencies belong to a single population. A chi-square of at least 3.84, p < 0.05 (one in twenty) was accepted as denoting a significant difference.

Chapter 12

1. Again a significance level of p < 0.05 was accepted.

Chapter 14

1. Juola, "Authorship Attribution," discusses many articles employing high-frequency words. Influential has been J. F. Burrow, "'Delta': A Measure of Stylistic Difference and a Guide to Likely Authorship," *Literary and Linguistic Computing* 17 (2002): 267–86. Effective use is made of very common words by Hugh Craig and Arthur F. Kinney, eds., *Shakespeare, Computers, and the Mystery of Authorship* (Cambridge: Cambridge University Press, 2009).

2. At https//en.wikipedia.org/wiki/Most_common_words_in_English.

3. Significance was again tested by chi-square, where rows consisted, for each poet, of totals for the tested word versus totals of other words. Chi-squares for "to" and "that" were highly significant (for "to" 11.163 or 10.929 with Yates's correction; for "that" 28.469 or 27.872 with Yates's correction; 1 d.f. in each case).

Chapter 15

1. Livingston: "If ever 'twas proper and lawful and decent"; "And Negroes, by plunder and carnage and flame"; "Abusing and squabbling and wrangling and spite"; "The frost, and the ice, and the snow"; "But trifles and glitter and show"; "Such pulling and hauling and shoving and pushing"; "Love and truth and friendship join"; "She smil'd, and blush'd, and smiled"; "Where Captains and lawyers and jurymen join"; "Where midnight and error and ignorance lay." Moore: "I promise lasting peace and health and joy"; "These balls, so round and smooth and new"; "For Paganini's skull and claws and shanks"; "And, to keep his skin pleasant, and pliant, and cool"; "… and ev'ry morn, and night, and noon"; "With vanity and pride and pomp."

Chapter 16

1. The authorship attribution method employed here is essentially that of Albert

C.-C. Yang, C.-K. Peng, H. W. Yien, and Ary L. Goldberger, "Information Categorization Approach to Literary Authorship Disputes," *Physica A* 329 (2003): 473–83. Their "analysis is based on word rank order–frequency statistics" (473), though they show results in graphs (as in their figure 1, on p. 475), rather than giving Spearman's rank-order correlation.

2. Livingston-favored words are (in order of frequency): the, The, I, his, my, her, on, as, is, was, at, thy, will, day, When, me, Where, While. Moore-favored words are: to, that, from, your, That, for, they, be, With, this, our, not, which, so, would, For, it, heart, Of, are, we, some.

3. In the "You Decide!" section of the Livingston website, many poems in this genre are quoted: http://www.henryliving ston.com/xmas/livingstonmoore/index/ htm#decide.

Chapter 17

1. Livingston-favored words are: an, around, As, dear, do, fair, found, good, He, high, him, His, I'll, Is, lay, little, long, man, meet, My, name, never, o'er, upon, plain, rose, She, thy, Till, up, what, where, whose, wish. Moore-favored words are: At, away, eyes, have, How, If, joy, joys, know, let, life, light, like, may, mind, No, pure, rise, round, see, shall, she, should, soon, still, them, these, They, those, thought, thoughts, too, view, well, were, Who, will.

2. Nickell, "Christmas Poem," Part 2, 10–11.

Chapter 18

1. "Poetry Manuscript Book of Clement C. Moore" (MCNY 54.331.1 [7662]). Links to transcription of the notebook poems, and to Moore's other verse, are given under "All Clement C. Moore Poetry" at http://www.henrylivingston.com/xmas/living stonmoore/allmoorepoetry.htm.

2. I have ignored Moore's competent translation of number 346 of Petrarch's

Canzoniere, "Li angeli electi et l'anime beate."

3. Patterson, *Poet of Christmas Eve*, 61–64, quotes, with some cuts, a poem that Moore wrote in 1813 to commemorate his marriage. I have been unable to secure a copy of the whole poem, but nobody could mistakenly identify it as one of Livingston's. Moore's markers "many a" and "some" each appear once (compare Table 15.1); "that" is used at a rate, associated with Moore, of 20.942 times per 1,000 words (compare Table 14.1); occurrences of Livingston-favored high-frequency words (31) are outnumbered by Moore-favored words (41), giving a percentage of 43.056, typical of Moore (as in Table 16.2); and the combined total of 36 for "the," "The," "a," and "A" yields a percentage of 6.283, close to Moore's mean (as in Table 13.1).

Chapter 19

1. *New-York Historical Society Quarterly Bulletin* 2 (4 January 1919): 111–15.

2. William S. Pelletreau, *The Visit of Saint Nicholas by Clement C. Moore, LL.D. Facsimile of the Original Manuscript, with Life of the Author* (New York: G. W. Dilligham, 1897), 17–18. At Christmas 1822, when Moore is alleged to have composed the poem for "his children" ("two daughters," according to what Clement Clarke Moore told T. W. C. Moore), Margaret was seven, Charity six, Benjamin four, Mary three, Clement two, and Emily a mere eight months. Margaret and Charity were old enough to have been rapt listeners to Moore's supposed performance. They would be the "two daughters," though Benjamin and Mary could conceivably have taken some interest, if they were present.

3. As in Chapter 3, note 4. In an email to Mary Van Deusen, forwarded to me on 22 February 2014, archivist and Manuscripts and Special Collections librarian Honor Conklin of the New York State Library confirmed that Sackett's crockery

store and the *Troy Sentinel* office were neighbors. Drawing on the "earliest Troy directory we have" she cited "Sackett & Lane, crockery, 221 River [Street]"; the shop was damaged by fire 20 June 1820, but crockery dealers "Pierce, Sackett & Co., 1820–1827" were sited at 2 Lane's Row, which became 222 River Street, according to Arthur James Weise, *Troy's One Hundred Years, 1789–1889* (Troy, NY: William H. Young, 1991), 396. The *Sentinel* was stationed at 225 River Street.

4. This is established in Appendix III. As an explanation of why no prepublication autograph manuscript by Moore survives, Nickell suggests as a possibility "that his original was used for the larger manuscript of his *Poems* and was sent to his New York publishers (Bartlett & Welford) and never reclaimed" ("Christmas Poem," Part 1, 300). But this is wrong: a doctored copy of the 1830 *Sentinel* broadsheet served as the basis for the 1844 printing.

5. Foster, *Author Unknown*, 251–52.

6. MCNY 54.331.18–19 (the first of these being the deposition dated 23 December).

7. Kaller, "Authorship," n.p. (under subheading "Fact: Moore Celebrated Christmas and Also Wrote What Is Probably the First 'Letter' from Santa Claus").

8. Marshall, *Bibliography*, xxv–xxvii.

9. As reported by Henry Litchfield West, "Who Wrote 'Twas the Night Before Christmas'?" *Bookman* (December 1921): 302.

10. Patterson, *Poet of Christmas Eve*, 11.

Chapter 20

1. Thomas Collection; for letters by Livingston's descendants that are cited in this chapter see http://www.henryliving ston.com/xmas/witnesses/index.htm, where can also be found transcriptions of significant letters not specifically mentioned in my text: Gertrude Thomas to Cornelia Griswold Goodrich, 22 January

1905 (retailing information from Charles); Gertrude Thomas to Cornelia Griswold Goodrich, 18 October before 1909 (information from Charles); Jeannie Hubbard Denig to W. S. Thomas, 13 March 1917, writing that her mother, Charles's daughter, said that "all during her early childhood she often listened to 'The Night Before Christmas' recited to her by her parents who invariably told her that her grandfather Livingston had written the verses."

2. This can be viewed at http://www.henrylivingston.com/xmas/quest/images/margaretlivingstoncrookedoughtyinterviewwithhwr.jpg.

3. Marshall, *Bibliography*, xxix.

4. Sonne, "Night Before," 378; Nickell, "Christmas Poem," Part 1, 296. Kaller, "Authorship," makes the same mistake (under subheading "The Moore Things Change...").

5. Nickell, "Christmas Poem," Part 1, 296. Mary Van Deusen elaborates on the points made here in "The Livingstons' Governess Story": "Having a connection of both families traveling south to act as a governess in a Moore-connected household isn't that absurd. Henry Livingston's first cousin and next door neighbor was Judith Livingston, who was married to John Moore, the brother of Clement's uncle. In 1815, their daughter Lydia was married to a student of Moore's, Rev. William Henry Hart, and the couple moved to Virginia" (http://www.henry livingston.com/xmas/arguments.htm).

6. Thomas, "Henry Livingston," 44. See Preface, note 2, above.

7. Without "work," the other three words occur within a more restricted space ("vision NEAR.300 lustre NEAR. 300 hoof") only in "Visit" and in two other poems, of 1819 and 1854. The "600" or "300" stand for an interval of that many words, except that each line end is the equivalent of something like four words. These searches were carried out in July 2015.

8. The searches were for "visions of" NEAR.800 "to his work" (with "my," "your," "her," "its," "our," "their," or nothing at all successively replacing "his"). An interval of "620" retains "Visit" and rejects the Reynolds poem. This particular series of proximity searches was carried out before *LION* changed to a new interface, which became the only version available from 28 June 2014. The new version is unable to deal with proximity searches involving phrases that include very common words.

9. The letter, in the Lansing–Gansevoor Collection of the New York Public Library, can be seen at http://www.henry livingston.com/xmas/witnesses/ht-dec15-1851.htm.

10. Alfredo Jahn, "History of St. John's Military School," at http://www.jahnweb.com/ajj/stjohns.

Chapter 21

1. For information about Jonathan Odell see Alfred G. Bailey, "Odell, Jonathan," in *Dictionary of Canadian Biography*, Volume 5, University of Toronto/Université Laval, 2003, http://www.bio graphi.ca/en/bio/odell_jonathan_5E.htm. The relevant material in the New Brunswick Museum Archives and Research Library is Fonds ID3735–Odell family. The copy of "The Night Before Christmas" is identified as Odell Family Fonds F15–5. See also Ruby M. Cusack, "The Odell Family of Fredericton Had Connections to 'Twas the Night Before Christmas,'" http://www.rubycusack.com/issue257.html.

2. MacCracken, *Blithe Dutchess*, 389.

3. Genealogy at http://www.henry livingston.com/sackett-hart-livingston-moore.htm.

4. MacCracken, *Blithe Dutchess*, 389.

5. *Ibid.*, 390.

6. Honor Conklin, email to Mary Van Deusen, forwarded to me 22 February 2014.

7. *The Children's Friend Number III: A New-Year's Present to the Little Ones from Five to Twelve* (New York: William B. Gilley, 1821).

8. Foster, *Author Unknown*, 300, n.72.

Chapter 22

1. Foster, *Author Unknown*, 267 and 269.

2. "Minerva," quoted by Patterson, *Poet of Christmas Eve*, 61–64; "well-stored mind" is on p. 62. See Chapter 18, note 3, for more about this poem.

3. Foster, *Author Unknown*, 268.

4. *Ibid.*, 269.

5. *Ibid.*, 268.

6. *Ibid.*, 268.

7. Irving, *History* (1812), 1:106.

8. For *Early English Books Online–Text Creation Partnership*, see http://quod.lib.umich.edu/e/eebogroup/.

Chapter 23

1. Moore, *Poems*, v–viii.

2. Kaller, "Authorship," n.p. (under subheading "The Moore Things Change …").

3. See http://www.henrylivingston.com/genealogy/index.htm.

4. Moore poems without markers are: "Old Dobbin" (152 words), "Flowers" (150), "Birthday" (176), "To Fanny" (136), "To Clem" (103).

5. Livingston's "Catherine Breese Livingston" and "Without Distinction" and Moore's "Sand" were omitted from Table 16.2 as providing hardly any data. So they are excluded from Figure 4. For Figure 4, "Catherine Breese Livingston" has only three relevant items (Moore-favored 1, Livingston-favored 2, or 67 percent Livingston-favored). "Without Distinction" has ten (Moore 6, Livingston 4, 40 percent Livingston). "Sand" has six (Moore 6, Livingston 6, 50 percent Livingston).

6. In contrast, we may consider one tiny poem in Livingston's bound manuscript collection that happens not to have

been transcribed on Mary Van Deusen's website. It is entitled "On...." and reads: "Thy lips surpass the Ruby's glow / Roses thy cheeks invest / The water's smoothness on thy brow / Its calmness in thy breast." This contains one instance of a Livingston-favored high-frequency word ("on") and three instances of a Livingston-favored medium-high-frequency word (lowercase "thy" three times). There are no Moore-favored words of either category. So "On...." scores 100 percent for Livingston-favored words of each category. The definite article occurs twice, so that instances of "a" + "the" amount to 10 percent of all twenty words, aligning the poem with Livingston's mean of 8.661, rather than Moore's of 6.127.

7. Burton E. Stevenson, *Famous Single Poems, and the Controversies Which Have Ravaged around Them* (London: George G. Harrap, 1924), 79.

Bibliography

Antonia, Alexis, Hugh Craig, and Jack Elliott. "Language Chunking, Data Sparseness, and the Value of a Long Marker List: Explorations with Word N-Grams and Authorial Attribution." *Literary and Linguistic Computing* 29 (2014): 147–63.

"Arpabet." *Wikipedia*. https://en.wikipedia.org/wiki/Arpabet.

Bailey, Alfred G. "Odell, Jonathan," in *Dictionary of Canadian Biography*. Vol. 5. University of Toronto/Université Laval, 2003. http://www.biographi.ca/en/bio/odell_jonathan_5E.htm.

Bilger, Burkhard. "Waiting for Ghosts." *New Yorker*, 23 December 2002, 86–100.

Boyd, Brian. *Why Lyrics Last: Evolution, Cognition, and Shakespeare's Sonnets.* Cambridge, MA: Harvard University Press, 2012.

Burrow, John. "'Delta': A Measure of Stylistic Difference and a Guide to Likely Authorship." *Literary and Linguistic Computing* 17 (2002): 267–86.

Burrows, Edwin G., and Mike Wallace. *Gotham: A History of New York City to 1898.* New York: Oxford University Press, 1999.

Burstein, Andrew. *The Original Knickerbocker: A Life of Washington Irving.* New York: Basic Books, 2007.

Calloway, Colin G. "The Biggest Forgotten American Indian Victory." http://www.whatitmeanstobeamerican.org/ideas/the-biggest-forgotten-american-indian-victory/.

The Children's Friend Number III: A New-Year's Present to the Little Ones from Five to Twelve. New York: William B. Gilley, 1821.

"Clement Clarke Moore." *Wikipedia*. https://en.wikipedia.org/wiki/Clement_Clarke_Moore.

The CMU Pronouncing Dictionary. http://www.speech.cs.cmu.edu/cgi-bin/cmudict.

Craig, Hugh, and Arthur F. Kinney, eds. *Shakespeare, Computers, and the Mystery of Authorship.* Cambridge: Cambridge University Press, 2009.

Cusack, Ruby M. "The Odell Family of Fredericton Had Connections to 'Twas the Night Before Christmas.'" http://www.rubycusack.com/issue257.html.

Drabble, Margaret, ed. *The Oxford Companion to English Literature: Fifth Edition.* Oxford: Oxford University Press, 1985.

Duer, John. *A New Translation with Notes, of the Third Satire of Juvenal. To which are added Miscellaneous Poems, Original and Translated.* New-York: E. Sargeant, 1806.

Early English Books Online–Text Creation Partnership. http://quod.lib.umich.edu/e/eebogroup/.

Eighteenth Century Collections Online. http://gdc.gale.com/products/eighteenth-century-collections-online/.

Foster, Donald W. *Author Unknown: On the Trail of Anonymous.* New York: Henry Holt, 2000.

_____. *Elegy by W. S.: A Study in Attribution.* Newark, DE: University of Delaware Press, 1989.

The Goldfinch, or New Modern Songster. Glasgow: J. and M. Robertson, 1785; first published 1777.

Hamilton, Edith. *Mythology.* New York: Mentor Books, 1959; first published Boston: Little, Brown, 1940.

"Henry Livingston, Jr." *Wikipedia.* https://en.wikipedia.org/wiki/Henry_Livingston,_Jr.

Hoffman, Charles Fenno, ed. *The New-York Book of Poetry.* New York: George Dearborn, 1837.

Hosking, Arthur Nicholas. *The Night Before Christmas: The True Story of "A Visit from St. Nicholas," with a Life of the Author, Clement Clarke Moore.* New York: Rudge, 1934.

Internet Archive: Digital Library. https://www.archive.org.

Irving, Washington. *A History of New-York from the Beginning of the World to the End of the Dutch Dynasty.* 2 vols. New-York: Inskeep and Bradford, 1809; 2nd. ed. New-York: Inskeep and Bradford, 1812.

Jackson, MacDonald P. *Defining Shakespeare: "Pericles" as Test Case.* Oxford: Oxford University Press, 2003.

_____. "Editions and Textual Studies." *Shakespeare Survey* 43 (1991): 255–70.

Jahn, Alfredo. "History of St. John's Military School." http://www.jahnweb.com/ajj/stjohns.

Jowett, John. "Henry Chettle and the Original Text of *Sir Thomas More.*" In *Shakespeare and "Sir Thomas More": Essays on the Play and Its Shakespearian Interest,* edited by T. H. Howard-Hill. Cambridge: Cambridge University Press, 1989, 131–49.

Juola, Patrick. "Authorship Attribution." *Foundations and Trends in Information Retrieval* 1, no. 3 (2008): 233–334.

Kaller, Seth. "The Authorship of The Night Before Christmas." https//www.sethkaller.com/about/education/tnbc/.

Kenny, Anthony. *The Computation of Style: An Introduction to Statistics for Students of Literature and Humanities.* Oxford: Pergamon Press, 1982.

Langley, Russell. *Practical Statistics Simply Explained.* New York: Dover Publications, 1971.

Literature Online (LION). http://literature.proquest.com.

Livingston, Henry. Poems, Prose, Letters. All online at http://www.henrylivingston.com.

Love, Harold. *Attributing Authorship: An Introduction.* Cambridge: Cambridge University Press, 2002.

MacCracken, Henry Noble. *Blithe Dutchess: The Flowering of an American County from 1812.* New York: Hastings House, 1958.

Mann, Ted. "Ho, Ho, Hoax: Did Clement Clarke Moore Rip Off 'The Night Before Christmas'? Scarsdale Rare-Document Sleuth Seth Kaller Says He's Finally Solved the Mystery of the Poem's Authorship." *Scarsdale Magazine,* 1 December 2006.

Marshall, Nancy H. *The Night Before Christmas: A Descriptive Bibliography of Clement Clarke Moore's Immortal Poem with Editions from 1823 through 2000.* New Castle, DE: Oak Knoll Press, 2002.

McClure, David, *The United States National Almanac.* Philadelphia: R. Desilver, 1825.

Moore, Clement Clarke. *A Compendious Lexicon of the Hebrew Language*. New York: Collins and Perkins, 1809.

_____. *George Castriot, Surnamed Scandenberg, King of Albania*. New York: D. Appleton and Co., 1850.

_____. "Lord of Life, All Praise Excelling." http://www.hymnary.org/text/lord_of_life_all_praise_excelling.

_____. *Poems*. New York: Bartlett and Welford, 1844.

_____. "Poetry Manuscripts of Clement C. Moore." MCNY 54.331.1–7. Links to transcriptions of the notebook poems, and to Moore's other verse, are given under "All Clement C. Moore Poetry" at http://www.henrylivingston.com/xmas/livingstonmoore/allmoorepoetry.htm.

"Most Common Words in English." *Wikipedia*. https//en.wikipedia.org/wiki/Most-_common_words_in_English.

Nickell, Joe. "The Case of the Christmas Poem, Part 1 and Part 2." *Manuscript* 54, no. 4 (Fall 2002): 293–308, and 55.1 (Winter 2003), 5–15.

Nissenbaum, Stephen. *The Battle for Christmas: A Cultural History of America's Most Cherished Holiday*. New York: Vintage, 1996.

_____. "There Arose Such a Clatter: Who Really Wrote 'The Night Before Christmas'? (And Why Does It Matter)." *Common-Place* 1, no. 2 (January 2001). http://www.common-place.org/vol-01/no-02/moore/.

Oakes, Michael P. *Literary Detective Work on the Computer*. Amsterdam: John Benjamins, 2014.

O'Conor, Maria Jephson. "Depositions Sent to Casimir de R. Moore, 20 December and 23 December, 1920." Manuscripts. MCNY 54.331.18–19.

"Odell Papers." New Brunswick Museum Archives and Research Library, Fonds ID3735–Odell family.

"Original Documents from the Archives of the Society. The Autograph Copy of the 'Visit from St. Nicholas.'" *New-York Historical Society Quarterly Bulletin* 2 (4 January 1919), 111–15. Unattributed but contains material from Clement Clarke Moore, George H. Moore, and T. W. C. Moore.

Patterson, Samuel White. *The Poet of Christmas Eve: A Life of Clement Clarke Moore 1779–1863*. New York: Morehouse-Gorham, 1956.

Pelletreau, William S. *The Visit of Saint Nicholas by Clement C. Moore, LL,D. Facsimile of the Original Manuscript, with Life of the Author*. New York: G. W. Dilligham, 1897.

Pflieger, Pat. "An Account of a Visit from St. Nicholas (from *The Troy Sentinel*, December 23, 1823; p. 3; repro. Troy, NY: Troy Public Library, 1998)." http://www.merrycoz.org/moore/1823Troy.xhtml.

Preacher, K. J. "Calculation for the Chi-Square Test: An Interactive Calculation Tool for Chi-Square Tests of Goodness of Fit and Independence." http://www.quantpsy.org/chisq/chisq.htm.

"*Salmagundi* (periodical)." *Wikipedia*. https://en.wikipedia.org/wiki/Salmagundi_(periodical).

Sonne, Neils H. "'The Night Before Christmas': Who Wrote It?" *Historical Magazine of the Protestant Episcopal Church* 41, no. 4 (December 1971): 373–80.

Stevenson, Burton E. *Famous Single Poems, and the Controversies Which Have Ravaged around Them*. London: George G. Harrap, 1924.

Thomas, William S. "Henry Livingston," *Dutchess County Historical Society Yearbook* 5 (1919): 30–46.

Van Deusen, Mary S. "Major Henry Livingston, Jr." http://www.henrylivingston.com. See "Navigation" at the bottom of the home page for its many subsites.

"VassarStats: Website for Statistical Computation." http://vassarstats.net

"A Visit from St. Nicholas." *Wikipedia.* https.//en.wikipedia.org/wiki/A_Visit_from_ St._Nicholas.

"Washington Irving." *Wikipedia.* https://en.wikipedia.org/?title=Washington_Irving.

Weise, Arthur James. *Troy's One Hundred Years, 1789–1889.* Troy, NY: William H. Young, 1991.

WeRelate. http://www.werelate.org.

West, Henry Litchfield. "Who Wrote '"Twas the Night Before Christmas'?" *Bookman* (December 1921): 300–305.

Yang, Albert C.-C., C.-K. Peng, H. W. Yien, and Ary L. Goldberger. "Information Categorization Approach to Literary Authorship Disputes." *Physica A* 329 (2003): 473–83.

Index

References to tables are in **bold**; references to figures in *italics*.

adjective–noun combinations 38–40, 98, 100, 124
"Alcmena Rebus" 28, 67, 76
Almar, George 19–20
"American Eagle" 67
anapestic tetrameters 12, 31–2, **33**, 53, 112, 128
anapestic verse: collocations in 75; Edwin Livingston writing 114; iambic feet in 21–2; Moore's use of 97–8, 100
"And," at beginning of line 74–5
"and the" 75, 99, 131
"Anticipation: The Battle of Miami" 162–3
"Apollo Rebus" 46
Arpabet 8, 49, 54, 64, 129
"Astronomical Intelligence" 30, 156–9
attribution problems 2–3, 181*n*1
attributive adjectives 38, **39**, 97, **98**, 129

Bard, William 126
Bryant, William Cullen 9
Bulmer Lytton, Edward 15
Butler, Harriet 102–4, 118–19

"Caroline's Album" 92–3, 95–9
"Carrier Address" poems 42, 47–8, 138
"Catherine Breese Livingston" 58, 83, 138, 185*n*5
"Catherine Sleeping" 50
Catullus 14, 46, 177*n*18
"Charles Elphinstone" 91–3, 95–7, 99–100, 123, 131–2
Chelsea House 11
chi-square test 36–7, 53, 58, 182*n*3

chiasmus 47, 76–7, 181–2*n*8
The Children's Friend 120
Christmas, domestication of 17
Churchill School of Sing Sing 115
Cobbold, Richard 15
Cooper, James Fenimore 16, 19
Crooke, Margaret 109

definite articles 64–8, **65–6**, 75, 95–6, **97**, 124, 129–30, 186*n*6
"Deity Rebus" 68, 98
Denig, Jeannie Hubbard 108–10, 112–14
"Description of the Baby House of Miss Biddy Puerilla" 30, 161–2
Donder/Donner and Blitzen 17–19, **20**
dread 122–3
Duer, John 2, 180*n*5
Dunder and Blixem 5, 15–20, 23–4, 117, 128
Dutchman, rubicund 11, 103–5, 107

"Easter" 68, 139–40
"Eliza in England" 91–3, 123
exclamation marks 18, 22–4, 100

"A Fable" 137, 153–4
"Fair Margaret" 96
"Farewell—In Answer to a Young Lady's Invitation" 90
"The Fly" 149–50
"For a Kiss" 97–8
Foster, Donald: on authorship of "Visit" 3–4, 7–8, 127, 131; on exclamation marks 23–4; on "Old Santeclaus" 120, 122–5; on publication of "Visit"

104; on reindeer names 17; verbal
portraits of Moore and Livingston
14; on William King 46
freedom, degrees of 36–7
"From Saint Nicholas" 12–13; attributive adjectives in 40, 97; exclamation
marks in 24; favorite expressions in
73–4; medium-high-frequency words
in 89; meter of 32; Moore markers in
131; and "Old Santeclaus" 122–3;
phoneme pairs in 53, 55, 58; rhymes
in 21, 43
function words 69, 75, 130

"German Spa" 98
Gilley, William 120
"God Is Love" 137, 155–6
Goodrich, Cornelia Griswold 108–11
Griswold, Catherine Walker 112
Gurney, Susan 109–11

"Happy Christmas" 15, 38, 47, 77, 177–
8n3
"Hero Rebus" 69, 71, 181n6
"Hezekiah," rhymes used in 43
high-frequency words: in manuscript
poems 92; and phoneme pairs 64;
rates of 69–72, **79–80**, 85, **92**, 130,
134–5
History of New-York (Irving) 27, 124,
127
Hoffman, Charles Fenno 7, 9–10, 16–
17, 24, 109, 117–18
Holley, Orville 9, 16, 103–4, 116, 118,
126
Hone, Philip 126

indefinite articles **65–6**, 67; and
adjective-noun combinations 38; Livingston's use of 130; in Moore's manuscript poems 95–6, **97**; in "Old
Santeclaus" 124; in phoneme pairs
49–50, 68
Ingoldsby, Thomas 42
"An Invitation to the Country" 140–2
"Irish Valentine" 92, 97–100
Irving, Washington 16–19, 27–9, 124,
127, 179n2, 180n8

"Jeanette's New Year" 99
"jirk" 18, 25, 27, 117, 174, 179n27

Kaller, Seth 17, 27, 45, 106, 127
Kaskaskia, Illinois 110, 113
King, William 45–6
Knickerbocker Group 17, 19–20

"Letter from a Tenant of Mistress Van
Kleeck" 89, 123, 149
"Letter Sent to Master Timmy
Dwight" 142–3
"Letter to My Brother Beekman" 31, 71,
112, 143–4, 180n1
line-beginning collocations 75, 99, 131
LION (Literature Online):
"blixem/blitzen" in 4, 16, 19; finger
beside nose in 28; "flung" and "slung"
in 22, 178–9n19; "happy Christmas" in
15; "jerk" in 18; Livingston's characteristic rhymes in 41–2, 45, 124
Litchfield West, Henry 107, 112
Livingston, Charles 108–9
Livingston, Edwin 108, 112–14
Livingston, Henry: accounts of family
7, 10–11; and anapestic tetrameter 31;
anonymous publication by 2, 10; children of 176n3; early poems of 14;
images used by 128; list of poems
164–8; literary sources of 45–6; moral
tone of 123–4; and mythological tradition 29–30; novelists praised by 28–
9; phoneme pairs used by 50, 58–63,
61–2, 93, **94**, *132*, 133; repetitive
structures in 75–7, 99–100; rhymes
used by 20–1, 41–2; selected poems
and prose 137–8; topic addresses by
47–8; use of articles 67, 75; use of
variant past tenses 25; words favored
by 78, **80–3**, **85–8**, 89–90, **92–3**, 130,
133, 183n2, 186n6
Livingston, Jane 109, 119
Livingston, Sidney 109
Livingston and Moore families, marriage ties between 118–19
Locust Grove 9, 108, 111–13, 119

"Mama/Mamma" 15, 45, 174, 177n2
"Marriage Tax": articles in 68; rhymes
in 43
Marshall, Nancy 109, 111
medium-high-frequency words **85–8**,
89, 92, **93**, 100, 132–3
Merivale, John Herman 22
"Monarchs Rebus" 45, 98

Montgomery, Mary Goodrich 112
"Montgomery Tappen" 43
Moore, Casimir de R. 105, 107, 115
Moore, Clement Clarke 7; children
183*n*2; emendations to broadside text
of "Visit" 21–2, 70, 105–6, 117–18, 173;
favorite expressions of 73, **74**; governess 111–12; list of poems 164, 169–
70; manuscript poems of 90, **95–8**,
101, 131–2, 171–2; moral tone 11–14,
32, 122–3; phoneme pairs used by 50,
58–63, **61–2**, 93–5, **94**; poetic corpus
2, 8; repetitive structures in 76–7, 100;
rhymes used by 42–3; syntax 131; use
of anapestic tetrameter 32; use of
articles in 67, 96–7; use of Dutch 17–
18, 20–1; use of exclamation marks
24; words favored by 78, **80–3, 85–8**,
89, **92–3**, 124, 130, 183*n*2, 183*n*3
Moore, Judith Livingston 118–19
Moore, T.W.C. 102, 106–7, 120
Moore markers 60, 73, **74**, 85, 90–2,
100, 130–1, 182*n*8

nasal near-rhymes 21, 100, 128
The New-York Book of Poetry 7, 16, 22,
109, 117
New-York Historical Society 17–18,
102–3
*New-York Historical Society Quarterly
Bulletin* 102
New-York Weekly Museum 10, 178*n*19
"Newport Beach" 95–6, 100, 131
"News-Boy's Address" 151–3; *see also*
"Carrier's Address" poems
Nickell, Joe: on exclamation marks 24;
on Moore's moral tone 13; on narrative
of Livingston's composition 111–12; on
trigrams 45; on word frequencies 89
"The Night Before Christmas": anapestic rhythms in 21–2; attributive adjectives in 38–40; first public appearance
1; frame of 180*n*1; high-frequency
words in 78–80, 83; Livingston family
allusions to 113–15; medium-high-
frequency words in 88–9; narrative of
Livingston's composition 108–11, 118–
19, 127–8; narrative of Moore's composition 9–11, 16, 102–3, 105–7, 126–7;
Odell's copy of 116–18; phoneme pairs
in 52–3; poetic qualities of 32–3;
rhymes in 41–3, 98–9

nouns, rhyming 99, 129
"Nymphs of Mount Harmony" 90

Obama, Michelle 6–7
Oberon 29–30, 142
O'Conor, Maria Jephson 105–6, 117
Odell, Jonathan 116
Odell, Mary 117–18
Ogden, Mary Moore 9–10
"Old Dobbin" 83–4, 89–90, 133–4
"Old Santeclaus" 120–5, 127
"On a Lap-Dog" 150
"On My Little Catherine Sleeping" 137–
9
"On the Late Mr. Gilbert Cortland" 51,
66, 138, 148
"The Organist" 44, 90

parallelisms 76–7, 99–100, 131
past tense, of strong verbs 25
Patterson, Samuel White 107, 122
Pelletreau, William S. 103–5
phoneme pairs **50–2**, 60–4, **61–2**, 129;
categories of 54–8, **55–7**, 68, **94**, 134;
computer analysis of 49–50; in
Moore's manuscript poems 93, **94**, 95,
96; stop/fricative 182*n*1
phonemes: rates of use 36; statistical
analysis of 8
"The Pig and the Rooster: adjective-
noun combinations in 40, 97; date of
composition 32; favorite expressions
in 73–5; medium-high-frequency
words in 89; Moore markers in 130–1;
origins of 12; phoneme pairs in 53,
63; in *Poems* 126; rhymes in 43
Poems (Moore): contents of 1–2; dedi-
cation of 126; inclusion of "Visit" in
9–10, 104, 106, 118, 127; moral tone of
11–13; printer's copy of "Visit" for
173–4; publication of 91; reindeer
names in 16–17, 117, 128
Pope, Alexander 42, 45
Poughkeepsie Journal 10, 25, 156
punctuation 23–4, 74, 100, 106, 117–18,
137, 173

rebuses 45, 68, 71, 179*n*26
reindeer names 4, 15–17, 23–4, 29, 117–
18, 128
repetitive structures 75, 100
Reynolds, Helen W. 109

rhymes 41–3, 47; in Moore's notebook
  poems 98–9; in "Old Santeclaus" 123;
  in reindeer names 16, 20–1; and variant past tenses 25

Sackett, Daniel 16, 178*n*5, 183–4*n*3
Sackett, Sarah 16, 104, 119
"Sages Rebus": attributive adjectives in
  98; rhymes used in 43
"Sages Rebus," trigrams in 46
Saint Nicholas: description in "Visit"
  30, 47, 89; as hero of "Visit" 104–5; in
  History of New-York 27–8; as patron
  of Knickerbockers 17
Salmagundi 29
"Sand" 55, 59, 83, 185*n*5
Santa Claus, modern image of 6
"Scots Wha Hae" 43, 137–8, 154–5
Scott, Sir Walter 18–19, 28
"Sentence pronounced by Judge advo-
  cate Crow" 154
Shakespeare, William: attributions to 3;
  Henry IV, Part 2 25; Livingston's
  knowledge of 45–6
similes 89
Smith, Charlotte Turner 25
Smollett, Tobias 28, 180*n*6
Spearman's rank-order correlation 79
spellings, variant 17–18, 25–6
"Spheres Rebus" 180*n*5
standard deviations, use of term 34–5
statistics, basic concepts of 34–7
Sterne, Lawrence 28–9
Strephon 179*n*29
"strow'd" 13, 177*n*16

t-test 35–6
"that": frequency of use 36–7, **71**, 73; in
  Moore's manuscript poems 94–6, **95**;
  in "Old Santeclaus" 124
"Theresa's Flower" 92, 96, 99
Thomas, Gertrude Fonda 108, 110–11,
  115, 184*n*1
Thomas, Harold Livingston Reeds
  178*n*16
Thomas, Henry Livingston 114–15
Thomas, William Sturges 29, 108–13,
  115, 175*n*2

Thor 29
"To a Young Lady on her Birth-Day"
  90
"To Fanny" 3, 90, 96, 131, 164
"To Little Clem" 3, 90, 96, 131, 164
"To Miss" 151
"To My Little Niece Anne Duyckinck"
  13–14
"To My Little Niece Sally Livingston"
  14, 138, 142
"To Spadille" 43, 63, 146–7
"to the" 75, 99, 131
"To the Memory of Sarah Livingston"
  138
trigrams 44–7, 129
"A Trip to Saratoga" 45, 47, 122
Tristram Shandy 28–9
Troy Colonization Society 119
Troy Sentinel: conveying text of "Visit"
  to 103–5; punctuation in 23; reindeer
  names in 15–18, 20–1; "Visit" as pub-
  lished in 1, 5–7, 173
Tuttle, Norman 16, 24, 103–6, 126

United States National Almanac 16, 117
"Universal Hospital" 159–61

Van Deusen, Mary 108, 184*n*5
"The Vine and the Oak" 11, 144–6,
  177*n*12
"Visit" *see* "The Night Before Christmas"
"A Visit from St. Nicholas," use of title
  4

"War Rebus" 147–8; repetitive structures in 76; syntax in 24–5; trigrams
  in 46
Weir, Robert Walter 9
"West Point" 100
"with the" 75, 99, 131
"Without Distinction" 59, 83, 137, 156,
  185*n*5
"witness letters" 108, 110–11, 115, 176*n*6
word frequencies, analysis of 36–7; *see
  also* high frequency words